NONTRADITIONAL MEDIA in Marketing and Advertising

To my husband, Russ, whose soul
reflects the love of God

NONTRADITIONAL MEDIA in Marketing and Advertising

Robyn Blakeman

University of Tennessee, Knoxville

Los Angeles | London | New Delhi
Singapore | Washington DC

Los Angeles | London | New Delhi
Singapore | Washington DC

FOR INFORMATION:

SAGE Publications, Inc.

2455 Teller Road

Thousand Oaks, California 91320

E-mail: order@sagepub.com

SAGE Publications Ltd.

1 Oliver's Yard

55 City Road

London, EC1Y 1SP

United Kingdom

SAGE Publications India Pvt. Ltd.

B 1/I 1 Mohan Cooperative Industrial Area

Mathura Road, New Delhi 110 044

India

SAGE Publications Asia-Pacific Pte. Ltd.

3 Church Street

#10-04 Samsung Hub

Singapore 049483

Acquisitions Editor: Patricia Quinlin

Editorial Assistant: Katie Guarino

Production Editor: Laureen Gleason

Copy Editor: Janet Ford

Typesetter: Hurix Systems Pvt. Ltd.

Proofreader: Kate Macomber Stern

Indexer: Karen Wiley

Cover Designer: Karine Hovsepian

Marketing Manager: Liz Thornton

Permissions Editor: Adele Hutchinson

Copyright © 2014 by SAGE Publications, Inc.

Figure credits:

3.1 Compliments of Dr. Courtney Childers. Assisted by Price Smith.
4.1 Compliments of Paul Domingo.
4.2 Compliments of Dr. Courtney Childers. Assisted by Caitlin Castainca.
5.1 Compliments of Dr. Courtney Childers.
8.1 Compliments of Dr. Courtney Childers. Assisted by Caitlin Castainca.
10.1 Compliments of Dr. Courtney Childers.

All other figures were photographed or created by the author with the assistance of the people listed above.

Printed in the United States of America.

Library of Congress Cataloging-in-Publication Data

Blakeman, Robyn, 1958-
Nontraditional media in marketing and advertising / Robyn Blakeman, University of Tennessee at Knoxville.
pages cm
Includes bibliographical references and index.
ISBN 978-1-4129-9761-4 (pbk. : alk. paper)
1. Marketing. 2. Advertising. 3. Alternative mass media. I. Title.
HF5415.B455697 2014

658.8'7—dc23   2012031250

This book is printed on acid-free paper.

MIX
Paper from
responsible sources
FSC® C014174

13 14 15 16 17 10 9 8 7 6 5 4 3 2 1

Contents

Acknowledgments

SAGE and the author gratefully acknolwedge the contributions of the following reviewers: H. Stuart Atkins, California State University, Fullerton; Barry Babin, Louisiana Tech University; Gregory G. De Blasio, Northern Kentucky University; Donna Leigh Bliss, University of Georgia; Robert S. Brown, Daniel Webster College; Shari Carpenter Eastern Oregon University; Yun Chu, Robert Morris University; Angie Corbo, Widener University; Kimberly J. Cowden, University of North Dakota; Georgiana Craciun, Slippery Rock University; Linden Dalecki, Pittsburg State University; Darrin C. Duber-Smith, Metropolitan State College of Denver; H. Rika Houston, California State University, Los Angeles; Bruce A. Huhmann, New Mexico State University; Stephen Koernig, DePaul University; Werner H. Kunz, University of Massachusetts Boston; Alexander V. Laskin, Quinnipiac University; Maria Mandel, Mobile Marketing Association North America, and AT&T AdWorks; Sarah Smith-Robbins, Indiana University; Leonard Steinhorn, American University; and Angie Yoo, William Paterson University.

1

Defining Nontraditional Media

In this chapter we will define nontraditional media and look at when it should be employed. Additional topics will include the best time to use traditional media and nontraditional vehicles and their place within the marketing and promotional mix.

So What's in a Name: Do We Call It Nontraditional, Emerging, New, Alternative, or What?

As used in this text, the label *nontraditional media* refers to vehicles that are used as an alternative choice to more traditional mass media vehicles directed at a mass audience such as print (newspaper and magazines) and broadcast (radio and television). These creative and often unusual vehicles deliver ads that are often more effective at reaching the target than traditional vehicles. The goal is to present brand promotion in ways and in places consumers least expect them. Economic factors, fractionalized audiences, and the growing number of media options are just a few of the reasons marketers are looking for innovative ways to reach their *target audience*, or specifically the audience that research has determined most likely to purchase the product or service being advertised. Understanding nontraditional media and its role in delivering a strategic message to the target requires both marketers and advertisers to understand what options are available, how they will be used, and the projected *return on investment* (ROI)—whether the client made more than what was spent on their advertising efforts.

Placing an acceptable identity on any vehicle or medium that does not fall under the traditional label is more a matter of interpretation than of

1

right or wrong. For example, nontraditional or even alternative media can be used to describe any vehicle that is not considered traditional; new media suggests the unlikely possibility the vehicle has never been used before; and emerging media implies the vehicle has had a modicum of success at both delivering the message and reaching the target. But even these labels are not sufficiently comprehensive to define the variations effectively. Because the communication is often interactive, it has also been referred to as user-generated content as many nontraditional options require the target to "opt in" or give their permission to receive the message.

The correct label may depend on the choice of vehicle. For example, the Internet can hardly be described as new or emerging but is an alternative to traditional vehicles. Many still consider nontraditional media as anything associated with computer technology because of its interactive nature. However, the Internet is so vital to all forms of advertising today that it is no longer an alternative to the success of a traditionally launched campaign but is an integral part of promotion. Social media and mobile outlets, on the other hand, are new, emerging, and nontraditional. Shopping bags, cups, and flyers are neither new nor emerging but they are an alternative way to get a visual/verbal message into the hands of the targeted audience. Perhaps the least controversial label is one that groups all vehicles not considered traditional, new, or emerging under the umbrella term of nontraditional, and the most comprehensive definition might be nothing more than the strategic delivery of a message with flair and impeccable timing. No matter what it's called or how it's delivered, it's attractive to consumers because it is often unexpected, unusual, lacks a repetitious message and considers any surface a creative palette.

The goal of these nontraditional vehicles is to advertise without selling. To do this they must use creative visual and verbal messages that grab attention and that are both memorable and educational, in order to prolong the advertised message's life. This is easier said than done; today's consumers are apathetic, often finding advertising messages intrusive, misleading, and lacking credibility. To overcome these feelings, marketers and their advertising agencies must captivate and engage their target audience in such a way as to encourage further research. Whether consumers go online, call a toll-free number, or visit a brick and mortar store, messages delivered electronically or via word of mouth can be a powerful catalyst for initiating additional dialogue between consumers, strengthening the credibility and memorability of its message.

Marketers often choose nontraditional media when traditional mass media vehicles cannot successfully reach the intended target. The number and diversity of these nontraditional media vehicles allow advertising to reach the target where they live, work, or play, with an often creative message. In the book *Strategic uses of alternative media: Just the essentials*, any media vehicle is considered nontraditional

> if it has a large, small, round, flat, stationary or moving, edible or non-edible surface that will hold a message and ensure the targeted consumer will come in contact with it. Often placed in unusual or unconventional places, these highly targeted, creative, and sometimes interactive vehicles are excellent at delivering both a meaningful and memorable ad more effectively than traditional media vehicles. And, unlike most other vehicles, they cannot be clicked out of, turned off, zapped, or deleted. (Blakeman, 2011a, p. 4)

Because of their diversity, no two nontraditional vehicles will reach the target in the same way, so the message is always fresh—which aids in grabbing and holding the attention of an often distracted target audience. The generally colorful displays and unusual delivery or appearance of a nontraditional vehicle have been successful at delivering a message that connects with the coveted 18- to 34-year-old targeted buyers. Although this demographic is the most skeptical of, and resistant to, the advertised message, they are the most likely to generate buzz about a product or service they believe in.

Market research shows that all forms of nontraditional media are growing despite the current economic downturn. Often a highly targetable, creative, interactive, and consumer-focused form of advertising, the use of nontraditional media is a great way to encourage feedback or build or maintain a relationship. Smaller brands find many forms of nontraditional media less expensive than traditional vehicles and a creative way to stand out in brand categories that are often crowded. It is also a great way to grab attention away from big brands with big budgets. The narrow, more defined targets and personalized messages also help keep the costs down by eliminating media waste. Larger brands that are advertising in larger markets can use nontraditional media to reinforce an existing message, or use diverse messages directed at multiple or even multicultural targets to achieve greater reach for less money.

The unique, innovative approach surrounding nontraditional vehicles is all about gaining attention with a creative idea that reduces the target's existing frustration with advertising and its sensational claims. The hard sell no longer works on today's savvy consumers as their lack of trust in the advertised message has led to a more knowledgeable consumer— a consumer who seeks out additional research in order to compare prices, features, and benefits against other brands in the category before making a purchase decision. Today's consumers do find advertising necessary, but they are tired of the overwhelming number of ads that assault their consciousness every day. According to a report by RightNow Technologies, American consumers on average are bombarded with approximately one million advertised messages each year, or just over 2,700 messages of some type a day. Therefore, in order to gain more control, the consumers want marketers to ask for their permission to deliver a specific message; they want the option to give their permission to receive the message; and they want it tailored to their special needs, and even perhaps to their precise location. Since consumers regularly ignore unwanted or intrusive messages, traditional advertising isn't working as effectively as it once did. Due to the multitude of advertising vehicles available in the marketplace, audiences today are so fragmented that it is hard to reach them unless messages resonate with their lifestyle and address their needs and wants.

The choice to use traditional media versus nontraditional vehicles depends on whether the brand appeals to a mass audience or a smaller, more defined niche audience. Products with a mass appeal might include paper towels, shampoo, or cleaning supplies. Those with a smaller, more limited appeal might include lovers of the soft drink Fresca or Apple computers. The appeal for mass-produced products concentrates more on building awareness using media that reaches a wide assortment of demographic groups, while the strategy behind using nontraditional media is all about creatively streamlining and personalizing the message to a smaller target audience.

Most nontraditional vehicles are placed in high traffic areas such as on escalators, elevator doors, at the bottom of stairs, on the back of urinals, the faces and handles of gas pumps, the sides of buildings, and on or in mass transit vehicles, to name just a few. Beyond location, a lot of these vehicles employ an unusual form of execution or delivery such as video projection, the use of smells or sounds, graffiti, temporary street corner showrooms, and street teams. Many of the most interactive nontraditional vehicles such as coffee cups or pizza boxes are used, carried by, or experienced by the target audience, and not only catch the eye of the carrier but anyone else who sees them on the street, at the mall, or at work.

When localized, this form of marketing can both visually and verbally speak to the target in many diverse ways. For example, a family outing to the local swimming pool can be strategically used to reach the target through advertising placed on diving boards, at the bottom of the pool, or on posters, towels, or vending machines. On their way home they may encounter car wraps, street teams if they are walking, billboards, shopping bags, sidewalk advertising, t-shirts, banners, construction barricades, or even skywriting. On the trip, the target may also receive location-based mobile messages, check their e-mail, send a tweet, or check their Facebook page all before they shower and change for a night of television. Add to that, they are exposed to 18 minutes of advertising per each 60 minute television program, all while multitasking on their cell phones or doing a little web surfing.

Strategically, the overall choice of vehicle and placement depends on a number of specifics:

- the product or service offered,
- the size and profile of the target to be reached,
- their individualized media use,
- the overall advertising budget,
- the competition,
- whether or not the message delivered engages individual consumers with interactive options or sends a targeted message with a wider appeal.

Nontraditional vehicles do what traditional vehicles no longer can: they resonate with the target. Because of this, "alternative media is definitely here to stay," said Brian Decker, executive vice president and director of media for the Baltimore advertising agency, Eisner Communications, in an article titled, "Finding alternative sites to TV for advertising messages"(Kridler, 2004). In the same article, Decker is quoted as saying that nontraditional media use is growing because "there is so much competition in the marketplace that you need to look for alternatives to reach out to consumers" (Kridler, 2004). For a short list of nontraditional vehicles, see Chapter 5.

Choosing Traditional Media—The Voice of the Masses or Nontraditional Media—The Voice of the Individual

For most of the twentieth century, thanks to the limited number of available media options, it was easy to ensure the intended target saw the advertised message repeatedly. However, today's consumer can interact with a multitude of different mediums wherever they are and at any time of day. Often the consumer will utilize more than one media vehicle to not only find out more information about a product or service, but to comparison shop. Because of the availability and ease of use that each resource offers, the target can media multitask—the ultimate cause of target fractionalization. The ability to reach the target in the right media, at the right time, with the right message, and provoke the right response requires an enormous amount of research on the type of message and the media vehicles the target is most likely to see and use, whether traditional or nontraditional.

Strategically, campaigns that use a message incorporating both traditional and nontraditional vehicles are not only more successful at building brand awareness and brand image but also at building brand loyalty. A brand-loyal consumer will repeatedly purchase the product or service over competing brands within the category without the need of repetitive or ongoing advertising efforts. It is how the foundation of a long-term relationship and brand equity is built and determines the brand's growth or leadership within a product category. Brand loyalty is neither absolute nor immediate. It requires marketers to concentrate on ways to create a two-way dialogue with the target that ensures their feedback is valuable, that the product repeatedly delivers the desired results, and that their knowledgeable staff of customer service and technical representatives are available 24/7. Additionally, all internal and external employees need to understand the existing advertising message, be aware of any current promotions, and be able to expertly explain any ongoing offers such as guarantees, return policies, and loyalty programs, to name just a few. The consumer's loyalty can also be affected by many intangibles, such as the personal appearance of sales personnel, delivery drivers, the layout of showroom floors, the brand's physical appearance, and even the product and store packaging. All contact points, no matter how big or small, must not only reflect the brand's image but the target's self-image. This ongoing association between the target and the brand is known as *relationship marketing*.

To effectively manage this relationship, marketers need to understand the creative message their target responds to and values about the product or service. This requires a thorough understanding of the target's lifestyle and current needs and wants. Ideally, this means addressing the target by name, incorporating interactive devices into the message, and employing memorable "in your face" language that attracts attention, sets the brand out from competing brands, and helps to retain loyalty.

On the agency side, strategy helps fortify the relationship by using a visual/verbal message that finds a unique way to specifically address the target's lifestyle needs, as well as employing innovative ways to get the product into their hands. For example, the tone of voice used to deliver the visual/verbal message can help project, build, or reinforce the brand's image or persona through the use of humor, testimonials, or via a spokesperson or character representative. Beyond the message, the advertising team also looks at how the brand's relevant features and corresponding benefits can be positioned against competitor's claims and the overall promotional mix to be employed.

The *promotional mix* is a combination of media vehicles used in a campaign that research has shown will both reach the target and accomplish the marketing objectives or goals. Typically, the promotional mix contains public relations, advertising—including print and broadcast, sales promotion, guerrilla marketing events, and a variety of nontraditional media. The advertising team looks at the overall budget and each vehicle's strengths and weaknesses before deciding the best way to leverage the reach or ability to connect with the largest target audience to maximize the ROI.

The promotional mix will also be influenced by the products' *life cycle stage*. There are three stages a typical brand moves through, including new or introductory, mainstream or mature, and reinvention. A new product launch most often uses traditional vehicles and sales promotions to inform and build the brand's image. Mainstream brands are often the ones that employ guerrilla or nontraditional media vehicles as ways to remind the target about the brand and to help achieve top of mind awareness for the brand. Brands that go through a reinvention stage often employ the most diverse promotional mix to announce upgrades, new formulas, and so on. On the flip side, a brand may be reintroduced because of flaws or some type of negative publicity, such as Toyota or British Petroleum (BP) experienced in 2010. As each brand moves through the stages, the marketing and promotional mix is reevaluated and updated as needed.

The next step is to determine the type of *media mix* or the individual vehicles a campaign uses to deliver their visual/verbal message, such as magazines, direct mail, or television. The overall choice of the media mix most often depends on the target, the brand, its life cycle stage, the type of product or service offered (such as commonly used products or smaller more specialized or niche-oriented brands), as well as when each vehicle is seen or employed. As more and more brands see a viable return on their investment, nontraditional vehicles are playing a bigger role in the media mix. Brands using nontraditional media are capitalizing on its popularity and diversity by incorporating nontraditional media into the initial media mix rather than missing contact opportunities by inserting it into the mix later in the campaign.

The choice of media mix is as important as the visual/verbal message. However, it is not the media mix or the visual/verbal message that makes a particular vehicle nontraditional but the strategy employed to deliver the message. Traditionally, the majority of advertising strategies focus on one of the following: 1) the most compelling features and benefits of the product or services, 2) the brand and its role in enhancing the target's lifestyle, or 3) the target's need to be seen as innovative or influential by others when interacting with the brand. Regardless of the vehicle used, it is critical that each visual/verbal message is part of the strategy, on target, and strongly promotes the key consumer benefit or key selling point and accomplishes the stated objectives, as laid out in the marketing plan or advertising agency's creative brief. This is achieved by using an assortment of traditional or brand-centric and/or nontraditional or consumer-centric vehicles. The advertising team, in conjunction with the client, determines which vehicles are selected as the primary sources of delivery and which will be used as the secondary or support vehicles.

Primary media vehicles are those mediums most likely to be seen by the target, or those vehicles that the target is exposed to the most often and where the most advertising dollars are dedicated.

Secondary media are used to support or expound on the messages conveyed in the primary vehicles. Let's take a quick look at the roles each one plays in a campaign.

As a primary vehicle, traditional vehicles are still the best choice for delivering a mass message to a relatively undefined mass audience. Marketers and advertisers often use traditional media as a way to introduce the product or service to the target. Research has shown that traditional vehicles are still the go-to vehicles for capturing attention, launching a new product, reinventing an old product, or as a reminder vehicle. Traditional media is also a great way to build brand awareness, create a brand identity, solicit new users, and increase or build brand equity. As a rule, customers are often introduced to a product or service via traditional advertising. Messages that are correctly targeted should not only inform and entertain but also build interest, increase buzz, and encourage the target to seek out additional information via a more customized or nontraditional vehicle, in order to further educate themselves on the brand's features and benefits. Actions that might be promoted include visiting a website, talking to customer service representatives, requesting a catalog or direct mail piece, or downloading a mobile application, or app.

Today, many campaigns no longer rely on traditional vehicles alone to reach the target because they lack the relationship building capabilities needed to encourage brand loyalty. To counter this and as a way to break down the often passive, nonpersonalized, mass appeal messages delivered by traditional vehicles, nontraditional vehicles are often used as a secondary form of delivery to reinforce the original message. Let's take a look at how a few popular brands have successfully employed both types in their media mix.

The Visual/Verbal Voice of Traditional and Nontraditional Media

Large brands, such as Coke or McDonald's, often use traditional media as the primary vehicles in their media mix and employ nontraditional media as support vehicles. In a supporting role, the nontraditional media is useful for building or maintaining brand awareness, launching a new product, creating curiosity, acting as a reminder vehicle, or reinforcing an existing brand image. Its diverse range of use on display surfaces and its message adaptability make it a great choice for local, national, and international products, companies, or services. Its visual/verbal voice in a campaign largely depends on the target, the overall campaign, the openness to change by the marketer, the media mix, total creative options associated with the key consumer benefit and, of course, the budget.

Domino's is another brand that uses both traditional and nontraditional methods in their risky reinvention campaign titled "Pizza Turnaround." This unusually frank campaign publicly admitted their pizza needed a taste overhaul. To help reinvent not only the taste but also overhaul the image of their pizza, Domino's began by gathering information from consumers compiled from online discussions and focus groups. The new campaign assures the target an improved eating and delivery experience is available and that they are featuring fresher ingredients and using better dough and sauce. In addition to the documentary style television ads, the campaign uses Facebook and Twitter as a way to measure consumers' opinions as well as a way to actively respond to both negative and positive feedback. Using this feedback as a springboard for change, the ongoing word-of-mouth and electronic exchanges were a big part of the campaign's success. In an online National Restaurant Association (NRA) article titled "Domino's CMO to Share 'Pizza Turnaround' Story at NRA Marketing Meeting," Domino's chief marketing officer, Russell Weiner, thought the time was ripe for the campaign, believing that consumers wanted transparency: "after two years of hearing about financial service company failures, government bailouts and high profile swindles, Americans were sick of people lying to them. They wanted people to tell the truth" (Busche, 2011, p. 1). Another brand that successfully uses both traditional and nontraditional media is the beverage company Dr Pepper. To attract attention to its Diet Dr Pepper drink, the soda maker created an interactive Internet campaign called the "Hunt for the Unbelievable." Working with the character first seen in television commercials, a Diet Dr Pepper delivery man finds himself a part of a group of mythical icons, such as Santa Claus and the Easter Bunny.

An online article in the February 7, 2011, *New York Times* by Stuart Elliott titled "Dr, Dr, Give Me Some Clues," explained that in order to understand the idea behind the "Hunt," consumers needed to visit *dietdrpepperhunt.com* where they saw the following: "The members of 'I Exist!' support group have gone missing. Help Diet Dr Pepper Guy find them, and you'll be entered for a chance to win an unbelievably satisfying getaway!" Players were given one minute to locate the characters on the designated web pages. Each time a character was located, the player was entered into a sweepstakes (Elliott, 2011a).

Each of the fictional characters was seen alongside the copy. Moving the mouse across each image told the viewer where each character might be found in the six sections of *Yahoo.com*. For example, the alien could be found in the Yahoo news section and the Easter Bunny was hiding out in games. The leprechaun was lurking in Yahoo music. Santa Claus was undercover on Yahoo TV, the Sasquatch had gone to the movie section, and the Tooth Fairy flew over to the women's section, known as Yahoo Shine. Each section hiding a character had a special page that matched the character's persona. For example, the leprechaun was on a page devoted to the ten best Irish songs.

Diet Dr Pepper also used product placement in an episode of *Cougar Town*. Promotional pieces were run before the episode aired to inform consumers of the soda's special appearance.

When the use of traditional media is not in the budget or is considered too impersonal, marketers should think about nontraditional media vehicles as their primary source of delivery, and as a way to connect with the target on a one-to-one basis. When nontraditional media is used as a primary media source it can deliver a personalized discussion to influence the target to buy and deliver an explanation as to how the product will enhance their lifestyle. These vehicles actively involve the target in the message by 1) asking them to do something, 2) by incorporating in-your-face messages that captivate and build interest, and 3) often employ unusual placement in order to engage the target and promote interaction in some meaningful way.

Traditional media may be used as a secondary source of delivery to announce products or services or when repetition of a desired message is required to remind, position, or reposition the brand in the mind of the consumer. Although creative and often unconventional, many nontraditional vehicles are temporary, single run messages that capture attention and then disappear. However, the "did you see that" comments or additional media coverage surrounding these memorable ads spread the message over a longer period of time than it was actually viewable. The ads never become static because they often come and go so quickly; they add spice to any word-of-mouth and electronic discussions. This is important because the majority of nontraditional vehicles have very little information but are great at: 1) getting the target to a website, 2) encouraging online sales, 3) encouraging the search for additional information (visiting a brick and mortar store, talking to a customer service representative), 4) reaching the skeptical and advertising avoidant 18- to 34-year-old target group, 5) tracking purchasing habits, media usage, and customer feedback, and 6) tracking overall return on investment (ROI).

Nontraditional media use is growing rapidly, but because marketers and advertisers are concerned by the unclear and uncertain measurement factors, it is not yet the dominant influencer in the industry. But the advertising industry is learning, and as a result, nontraditional media is becoming more attractive based on: 1) the abundance of media options that can break large target groups into smaller, more manageable niche groups, 2) a more entertaining message possibility with one or more incentives attached to both reach and increase the time the target spends with a message, 3) the reality that traditional media can no longer reliably reach the target with a repetitive message, and 4) the interactive one-on-one focus of nontraditional advertising messages that are based on and enhance the target's lifestyle.

With that said, you would think that advertising creative teams would push their clients to use nontraditional vehicles more often. The truth is that many smaller marketers are not always that enamored of these nontraditional options, mainly because the reach of the vehicle is often small, many forms are untested, and the nontraditional message is often considered too risky, too promotional, and in many instances even over the top. Many advertisers are also untested in how to strategically insert these vehicles into the media mix to ensure that they accomplish the goal objectives and show a measurable ROI.

When used as a support vehicle and to overcome the lack of accountability, many nontraditional media ads and guerrilla marketing events must find a way to ensure each target contact is measurable in some individual way. This can include a few options such as a quick response code, or QR, that can take the target to a special website via their smartphone; a temporary toll-free number that is specifically attached to the ad; or building a website that requires registration or the input of a promotional or marketing code.

Creatively, nontraditional media is all about reaching the target with a message that surprises and is memorable. This is where an advertising agency can incorporate a bland tweet, coupon, contest, sweepstakes, or scavenger hunt into part of the visual/verbal message. More advanced uses can entice the senses by including alluring smells, tactile elements, tastes, or catchy sounds.

No matter how it is viewed or used, there is no argument that it is an ingenious way to take a traditional message and make it engaging and interactive. Whether used as a primary or secondary vehicle, the visual/verbal message should strategically poke the consumer in the eye with a dazzling idea that stymies their bored indifference long enough to drive home the key selling point. Let's take a look at a few examples.

ABSOLUT vodka teamed up with IKEA on a billboard design featuring ABSOLUT's signature bottle shape and IKEA furniture. The bottle, made to look like wood, was used as the surface for a 3-D IKEA room design. The neck featured a bathroom complete with a sink, toilet, chair, and storage. Moving backwards, the next room design was of a kitchen complete with table, chairs, stove, sink, cabinets, and refrigerator, followed by a living room featuring two couches, rug, chair, and coffee table. The bottom of the bottle is a bedroom with a bed, pillows, and shelving. The copy reads, "ABSOLUT NEW YORK."

IKEA used nontraditional media to promote their fortieth birthday by wrapping their Stockholm store up to look like a cake, covered with vanilla frosting and three rows of succulent strawberries.

BMW found interesting and alternative ways to promote its line of Mini Coopers by hanging the little car from a ski lift, placing it on a billboard, or showing it driving down the side of a skyscraper. One promotion placed the compact mini in a cage with copy that reads, "PLEASE DO NOT FEED, TEASE OR ANNOY THE MINI." Another series uses a building wrap that features a vending machine that showcases six rows of three mini's just waiting to be served up with copy reading "LET'S MOTOR." Another ad places a full-sized mini in a local mall enclosed in a box that looks like one you might find in a toy store. Yet another focuses on its size compared to an SUV by placing the mini on the luggage rack on top with copy reading, "WHAT ARE YOU DOING FOR FUN THIS WEEKEND?"

Nonprofits often use nontraditional media to grab attention and focus consumer eyes on their cause. Casa de Zezinho, an organization that provides food to low income families launched the "Half for Happiness" campaign to bring attention to the issue of malnutrition. This innovative campaign focused on selling only half of a product in grocery stores. For example, if you were hungry for a pizza, in the freezer section you found a cardboard disk holding only half of a pizza. The other side featured copy that read: HOW ABOUT SHARING WITH THOSE IN NEED," followed by a small amount of copy describing how donations are used. The extremely successful campaign raised money and also won a Cannes Lion award in 2011 for the Brazilian agency that created it.

McDonald's used an elegantly curved streetlight as the focal point for its nontraditional vehicle. On the bottom surrounding the streetlight was an orange to-go coffee cup featuring the golden arches and copy reading "FREE COFFEE." At the top of the streetlamp was a coffee pot tipped on its side; the post color (black) and shape was used to simulate the look of coffee being poured into the cup.

Each one of these examples was strategically designed to creatively push the key consumer benefit and accomplish the stated objectives. Even one-shot designs must stay on target and on strategy; those media plans that are not on target or on strategy may be able to *wow* but can also confuse or miss reaching the stated goals altogether.

Visual/Verbal Delivery
Must Be Creative and Memorable

The advertised message is no longer confined to a limited palette of traditional advertising surfaces. Thanks to the unlimited number of unusual surfaces used in nontraditional media, that same advertised message can now effectively reach consumers in new and creative ways that the target audience finds surprising and visually and verbally memorable.

Today, engagement and interactivity must be a part of the visual/verbal message. It must speak to the target in multiple ways with a consistent message. Each message must be a part of a memorable encounter, bigger and more creative than the message itself. Targeted messages, such as the ones used in nontraditional media, will not assault the target with unwanted messages. Some will educate, others will shock, and still others will incite curiosity—all need to inspire some form of action—a search for more information, a visit to a brick and mortar store, or a purchase.

As the name suggests, nontraditional vehicles employ a very creative, unique, and often unconventional strategic approach to increase memorability and encourage further discussion, either online or via word of mouth.

Nontraditional media is effective because its creative and often in-your-face message is hard to ignore. The enormous amount of advertising the target is exposed to every day makes finding the intended target more difficult. This fractionalization has limited the reach and effectiveness of traditional media vehicles. Creatively employing unusual surfaces to attract notice allows nontraditional vehicles to be more personalized, to grab your attention, to create buzz, and to easily mold to fit the target's lifestyle. The popularity of nontraditional media is based on its ability to engage and interact with the targeted audience and to induce them to seek out more information.

The unusual assortment of vehicles available in the promotional mix can often make it difficult to maintain the campaign's visual/verbal voice consistently across all media vehicles employed, so it is important for the creative team to keep both the key consumer benefit and strategy in mind when determining the overall **media mix.**

Each vehicle requires a repetitive visual/verbal appearance. This repetitiveness is made especially difficult since some vehicles will be no more than the logo; others will have a little more to say, while still others will be copy heavy and showcase multiple visuals. Regardless of its length, each visual/verbal message must be tied to the target's lifestyle, speak to them on a one-to-one basis, hammer the message home, and show up in a unique location.

Choosing the right visual/verbal message begins with a well-rounded and creative choice of vehicles that can explain, enhance, and entertain the targeted audience, irrespective of their location. When used as a support vehicle, the visual/verbal look should conform to the overall look and sound used throughout the campaign. Every piece should *scream* the key consumer benefit and feature consistent color, layout style, typeface, logo style, photograph or graphic style, slogan or tagline, and spokesperson or character representative to ensure that the campaign is recognizable, whether it uses 1,500 words in a direct mail piece or nothing more than the logo, tagline, or slogan on a shopping bag.

Each media choice should be balanced in order to ensure continued visibility and message consistency and include an integrated campaign message. For example, if the key consumer benefit's visual/verbal voice employs varied demonstrations or testimonials throughout the campaign, choose nontraditional media vehicles that can easily and creatively deliver that same message visually.

Nontraditional media is here to stay; it is the answer marketers have been looking for to overcome consumers' boredom and cynical attitudes toward advertising. On its own, nontraditional media brings innovation to advertising and marketing by creating memorable encounters and developing campaigns that project a unique identity for old or new brands.

Its very diversity allows marketers and advertisers to reach consumers in ways, places, and at times that traditional advertising cannot—for example while they're pumping gas, riding an escalator, parking their car, buying produce, or walking down the street. Additionally, economic factors, fractionalized audiences, and less effective traditional advertising methods are a few of the reasons marketers are looking for new and innovative ways to reach their target audience.

Memory Box

Target Audience

Return on Investment

Nontraditional Media

Promotional Mix

Life Cycle Stage

Media Mix

Primary Media

Secondary Media

2

Marketing and Advertising Planning for Nontraditional Media

This chapter will look at how nontraditional media is used in both marketing and advertising. Additional discussions will define how a marketing plan is used in advertising to develop a creative brief that will eventually define the brand's visual/verbal voice.

Working Together: How Marketers and Advertisers Define Business and Creative Direction

In this chapter, we first define and outline the differences between advertising and marketing, how they routinely interact with each other, the role of marketing in the advertising process, and how advertisers interpret the business of marketing. Next, we discuss the role research plays in the development of both a marketing plan and creative brief and how each lays the groundwork for the development of a creative idea that sells, resonates with the target, and delivers a consistent and long-lasting message. Understanding how all of the aspects of the business and communication process work together: 1) helps the advertising team understand how the marketing plan lays the foundation for the visual verbal message, 2) lays out for the advertising team what the client wants to accomplish through their advertising efforts, 3) helps the client understand the metamorphic change from marketing plan to creative brief, 4) outlines the creative process for the client, and 5) educates the client on the time, effort, and costs behind last minute changes or imprecise direction.

Being aware of how each team approaches a stated problem is the first step to successfully reaching the intended target audience with a message that triggers their interest and ultimately their reaction. To accomplish this, it is important that students of advertising and marketing, as well as small business owners not only know the ins and outs of their own professions but how each element affects the other. It is simple to reduce any process down to the business and communication or who works for whom, but it's a lot harder to understand how each role or task affects the overall outcome or finished product.

It is not unusual that many people interacting with both professions are confused and uncertain about just exactly what the differences are between marketing and advertising, so let's begin with a few definitions. The American Marketing Association (AMA) defines *marketing* as "the activity, set of institutions, and processes for creating, communication, delivering and exchanging offerings that have value for customers, clients, partners, and society at large."

Advertising, on the other hand, uses a promotional set of vehicles that the sponsoring brand employs to persuade, inform, educate, entertain, and remind in order to build a lasting relationship with the intended target. It almost exclusively uses paid forms of nontraditional and mass media vehicles to clearly and creatively identify the sponsor of an advertised message.

After reading both definitions, it is not surprising people still don't understand the differences between advertising and marketing. Don E. Schultz in his book "*Essentials of Advertising Strategy*, clarifies the differences even more when he says, "marketing is all those factors which go into the sale of a product or service such as price, distribution, wholesale and retail support, plus advertising and promotion" (Schultz, 1996). "Advertising," Schultz goes on to say, "consists of only two basic parts, the creative product or message and the medium or method used to get the message to the audience" (Schultz, 1996).

Despite their definitions, advertising and marketing are two professions that have a long history of successfully blending business with creativity. Advertising is probably the best known aspect of marketing, but the reality is that advertising is only one aspect of the marketing process. At its core, marketing is all about: 1) the conceptualizing of a product or service based on research gathered, 2) the development of the product or service, 3) using advertising to promote the product or service, and 4) sales. It is the goal of advertising to use research to develop a creative and brand-unique visual/verbal message, and to use one or more media vehicles to successfully promote the brand product or service.

Marketing Is the Product or Service

A marketer is the company who produces a specific product or offers a specific service to the public. The individual who works as the liaison between the brand or the specific product or service and the advertising agency can be known by many titles but the most common are brand manager, marketing manager, and business or communications manager. This individual is responsible for creating a marketing plan or the brand's business plan of action for the forthcoming year.

Depending on the requirements and the overall size of the company producing the brand, it is the brand representative's job to act as a bridge between the company's upper management, any inside and/or outside advertising agencies, and other involved departments in the company, such as development, customer service, and distribution.

These diverse and combined company and agency efforts then educate everyone on what the brand can do, what the target wants, what competitors are doing, and so on. Input and cooperation between departments and outside agencies helps develop a consistent visual/verbal message throughout all internal and external communication channels and helps to build a strong loyal consumer base.

Although advertising first ignites awareness and may encourage trial, consumer loyalty has very little to do with advertising and a lot to do with product quality, and level of customer service. It cannot overcome inconsistent or poorly made products or rude or incompetent customer or technical service representatives. Creating and maintaining strong relationships is essential for a successful marketing plan. Many businesses consider *customer relationship management* (CRM) as an important part of their day-to-day business practice. Relationship marketing makes it easier for marketing and advertising efforts to focus on those individuals most likely to purchase the designated product or service, to design products or services that address that specific target's needs and wants, and to reach those selected individuals with a customized message.

It is not the job of the marketing department to write copy or stage a photo shoot. However, it is the role of company marketing: to approve all creative before it goes public in any form; ensure all visual/verbal messages are cohesive; strategically accomplish the marketing and communication objectives; and focus on a specific feature and benefit, or a combination of features and benefits, that strongly promote the product or service offered.

It is important that the brand manager be very clear to all involved parties about what needs to be accomplished. It is equally important that the advertising team keep the brand manager informed about any changes or problems that may arise while the visual/verbal message is in development. If all elements are not constantly updated, indecision and second-guessing become a part of the final approval process, ultimately resulting in often expensive and time-consuming changes.

Changes are inevitable, even if the client was actively involved during the campaign's development. Most changes are inconsequential, while others may require major design alterations, especially if the client changes or dislikes the final visual/verbal look of the campaign. Deadlines for publication and production dates do not change based on client changes, so it is important for the brand manager to understand that any drastic changes made late in the design schedule must be made within the existing timeframe.

Advertising, the Visual/Verbal Voice of a Product or Service

When a brand needs to reach a large number of consumers belonging to no particular market segment, advertising is the best way to deliver the message. It's the brand's visual and/or verbal voice that reflects the times in which we live and catalogs our history of consumption, attitudes, beliefs, and social norms. Advertising not only sets trends and reflects social and cultural influences, but also it can induce change. For example, by using science to prove certain foods can lower cholesterol, it can influence what people buy and how they eat. Additionally, advertising must constantly reflect what is happening locally, nationally, and internationally, as well as being economically and politically relevant to the target.

Advertising is only one piece of the marketing puzzle. Its job is to visually and verbally bring the brand to life, by publicizing its attributes and tying those attributes to the target's lifestyle so that the brand becomes important and significant to them. Advertising is also responsible for developing a promotional and media mix that strategically reaches the target wherever they are located. This is both a time consuming and expensive process, but when done right, advertising can propel a product or service into the limelight. The ability to talk to the target in a language they understand, about a problem they have, is the essence of advertising.

To ensure the success of a brand, the advertising must:

- Creatively and accurately promote a company's product or service,
- Increase sales,
- Actively develop and maintain both the brand's identity and image,
- Launch new products or services,
- Announce updates or improvements to existing products,

- Make a product stand out among the competition, and
- Encourage buzz.

Good advertising is more than a creative visual/verbal message; it's about knowing who the target is and knowing what they want. Messages that help the target accomplish something—satisfy a need or want, or solve a problem—are more successful than any single brilliant idea that doesn't achieve anything.

In its simplest form, advertising is the art and science of reaching the correct target with the correct message, at the right time and place. And to do that effectively requires having a media vehicle and a creative idea that the audience is not expecting in order to ensure that they see and respond to the message. When advertising is successful at accomplishing all of the steps defined above, then it should be viewed as an investment. However, if even one of these steps misses the mark, it becomes an expense.

Although advertising's form and delivery methods have multiplied and changed over time, "Many a small thing has been made large by the right kind of advertising," said Mark Twain, and never has that been truer than in today's multimedia, target-fractionalized world (Twain, 1889).

The Working Relationship Between Advertising and Marketing

The main objective of both advertising and marketing is to build awareness for a product or service, to build consumer loyalty and brand equity, and to increase sales.

To do this effectively, the brand manager (client) works with the account management or account executive (advertising) to coordinate what the company wants to achieve over the next six months to a year and to produce a creative campaign designed to achieve those goals. It takes a team of advertising professionals to bring an advertising campaign to fruition. Typically, there are three very distinct components to an advertising team: account management, creative group, and media group. The account manager is the liaison between the agency and the client. He or she develops the creative brief, advises team members on what needs to be accomplished, and presents final creative direction to the client. Along with the client, the account manager may attend brainstorming sessions, approve changes to strategy, media, copy, and layout. Typically, the two may also attend production meetings, photo and television shoots, and approve ads.

The advertising creative team is composed of at least one copywriter and one art director. Each is responsible for developing a consistent visual/verbal message that is on-target, on-strategy, and memorable. The advertising media team includes at a minimum one media buyer and one media planner. Their job is to plan for and buy the media vehicles that reach the target, at the right time and place.

The remaining team members might include, for example, specialists in public relations, digital, guerrilla or direct marketing, and sales promotion, depending on the promotional mix employed and the direction of the overall campaign. Aside from using these outside agency groups, many large corporations have their own in-house agencies that design and write copy for only their company brand(s). Additional projects that require advanced skills have to be delegated to freelancers or to the advertising agency of record.

In the past, it was not unusual for the partnership between a marketer and their agency of record to last decades; the agencies often knew the company brand almost as intimately as the client, which resulted in many memorable agency campaigns. However, today's relationship between a marketer and agency is no longer an intimate one; it is less secure and more temporary, with the average working relationship usually lasting only four to five years.

One of the reasons for a more strained client/agency relationship is the fractionalization of media options, or the movement from a limited assortment of traditional or mass media vehicles to the inclusion of a multitude of diverse nontraditionl options. In order to ensure the best results and to capitalize on the multiplicity of choices, many marketers have become more comfortable employing multiple agencies that specialize in traditional, nontraditional, direct marketing, sales promotion, and digital options, to name a few. Because communication between these different agencies is often minimal, it is critical that the brand manager ensure everyone involved in the campaign is on the same page with the content, timing, delivery, and business goals of the message.

An online *Advertising Age* article titled, "Why the Client-Agency Bond Just Isn't What It Used to Be," quotes Bill Duggan, executive vice president for the Association of National Advertisers: "There are always peaks and valleys in relationships. Before, clients were more willing to ride out the valleys because they knew that the peak was around the corner. Unfortunately, brands don't value agencies as much as they once did" (Parek, 2011, para. 8). However, this trend may be changing, according to a recent research poll appearing in the August 8, 2011, online MediaDailyNews, by Steve McClellan, entitled "CMOs Using Less Agencies, More Collaboration." The poll was commissioned by the digital communications firm The Horn Group and conducted by Kelton Research and shows that marketers are looking at reducing the number of agency collaborations for simplification and better management and supervision, while acknowledging the difficulty of finding a fully functional all-purpose agency. Additionally, many marketing executives reported that multiple agencies do not always work well together, even though over half of those surveyed acknowledged that most of the problems originated within the company and not with the agencies.

Telling the Brand's Business Story

The brand manager, research, and the marketing plan all help the advertising team understand the product or service, the target audience, and the overall objectives that any communication efforts are to address. Once this information is conveyed, it is the advertising team that first converts the marketing plan into a creative brief and then into a visual/verbal message that educates, entertains, and sells.

Let's begin by looking at how marketers determine how to integrate a systematic approach to developing products and services that fit and enhance the target's lifestyle, address their individual needs, and assimilate the entire marketing effort. Each step helps develop the final visual/verbal message, beginning with research and ending with a detailed marketing plan that the advertising team uses to develop a creative brief.

The Role of Research in Marketing and Advertising

Before any product can be developed, sold, or integrated with a creative message, both marketers and advertisers must determine who will ultimately purchase the product and what kind of trigger(s) can activate a purchase. What is happening in the marketplace that might negatively or positively affect product development? What are competitors doing? How does their brand compare to your brand? What does the intended target think of the brand and/or any additional brands your company might currently offer? What needs to be said, shown, or demonstrated? Where will the target most likely see the message?

The questions asked and research gathered depend on the product or service offered, its life cycle stage, economic conditions, and what competitors are offering and saying in their advertising efforts.

Research for both the marketing and advertising teams is conducted in basically the same manner. The major difference is in the desired information extracted from the research. Marketers focus on the marketplace and how it affects the brand, target audience, and their competitors. Research helps to build competitor and target profiles, establish target behaviors, suggest the appropriate type of advertising and promotions, as well as assist in determining pricing and distribution issues. Advertising research, to identify just a few objectives, focuses on the brand's role in the lifestyle of the target, determines what the competition currently does or does not say in their advertising efforts, and assesses what the competition currently delivers within the brand category and the brand's position in the target's mind compared to the competition. In their pursuit of answers and opinions, marketers and advertisers rely on quantitative, qualitative, observational research, and focus groups. Let's take a quick look at each one.

Quantitative Research

Deductive research, also known as **quantitative** or **primary research**, is original or new data that is gathered by either the marketing or advertising team. This type of research uses a large sample of respondents in an attempt to find the answer(s) to a specific set of questions.

Quantitative data is very specific about its objectives. Usually, it employs the use of controlled response surveys where there are a finite number of responses from which participants can choose their answers. There are two types of surveys: formal and informal. Formal surveys are most often employed when the survey taker wants to know how the respondents feel about something or requires responses to be ranked in some kind of categorical order. This type of survey typically uses closed-ended questions where participants choose from a predetermined set of responses, such as strongly agree, agree, disagree, and strongly disagree. Informal surveys are used when there is no definitive answer solicited or you want the respondent to give an opinion in their own words. These surveys often yield a great amount of quotable material, which can be used in later testimonials.

Qualitative Research

Qualitative research, also known as *inductive* or *secondary research,* uses existing data and/or small groups of respondents to gather information that will not be analyzed using statistical techniques. This type of research assists in pinpointing any past trends or significant changes, or trends that are currently occurring in the marketplace, and to identify any emerging opportunities or threats to the brand. Rather than using predetermined responses, it allows participants to freely give their opinions to questions asked. Qualitative techniques may also employ the use of surveys, one-on-one interviews, or focus groups. The use of observational techniques also falls under this qualitative research umbrella (e.g., where shopping, television, or Internet habits are surveyed to determine brand perception or target audience usage).

Focus Group

Although the client supplies the majority of research, agencies often need to isolate the target's opinion on any number of topics such as their knowledge about a brand and competing brands, as well as receiving feedback on copy, layout, packaging, and so on.

A *focus group* is usually made up of 10 or 12 members of the researched target audience, who are asked to interact with the brand or its advertised message in a controlled environment. Participants are asked to openly discuss a series of topics or respond to a set of questions that are prepared in advance. The session(s) may be conducted by the agency's creative team or by an experienced moderator, usually in an environment where both the client and advertising team can watch the proceedings through a two-way mirror. To ensure honesty, it is important respondents are secure in their anonymity. Anyone participating in the focus group who is interested in the results should receive a copy on completion of the research. Opinion-generated research is a great way to collect and decipher demographics, psychographics, and business data in order to improve both the product and advertising visual/verbal messages.

Each type of research method is designed to define a problem or to understand the participants' knowledge, attitudes, and beliefs about the product or service. Research reveals that when honest reasons are given for the research gathering, the less intrusive the research seems to potential respondents.

Business and Communication Plans

Marketers and advertising agencies work with a clearly defined plan. Marketers lay out their sales objectives in a marketing plan. Advertising agencies use a creative brief to plan their communication objectives in order for the marketing plan to be successful. Business plans make certain that everyone is on the same page and that directions are clearly communicated to all involved parties.

The Marketing Plan

Very basically, a *marketing plan* is a company's business plan of action. It is often a hefty sales-related document that varies in scope depending on the size of the company. Its purpose is to detail what the brand wants to accomplish, usually over the next fiscal year. Each plan is implemented based on a detailed analysis of the target to be reached, competitive brands, the marketing objectives or goals the company wants to achieve, what strategy or tactics will be implemented to achieve the objectives, as well as budget issues and evaluation tactics.

The look and scope of a marketing plan varies by brand and/or company, so finding a traditional format or outline is difficult. However, a typical marketing plan might include the following: 1) executive summary or mission statement, 2) target market overview, 3) competitive review, 4) product and/or business review, 5) situation analysis using SWOT/SLOT (Strengths, Weaknesses/Limitations, Opportunities, and Threats), 6) marketing plan objectives, 7) marketing strategy, 8) performance analysis and implementation schedule, and 9) evaluation methods. Let's take a very brief look at each one.

1. **The Executive Summary or Mission Statement.** Although placed first in the written order, the mission statement is often written last, after all research has been gathered, analyzed, and detailed. It presents a brief summary addressing each of the sections found within the plan.

2. **Target Market Overview.** The target market or target audience is the group that marketers aspire to reach through their advertising efforts. This section involves identifying and profiling potential primary and secondary buyer groups in order to understand: who they are; why they buy; what characteristics define them as potential buyers of a product or users of a service; how the product or service fits into their lifestyle; and the profile of their buying patterns.

Marketers will use the research gathered to analyze and accurately describe the target most likely to buy their product or use their service. In order for advertising efforts to talk to the target in relatable and understandable language, analysis breaks the target down into four different market segments, including demographics, psychographics, geographics, and behavioralistics.

Demographics deals with characteristics such as age, gender, income, marital status, level of education, and number of children in the household, to name just a few. This type of information helps marketers and advertisers alike speculate about how this group makes purchase decisions. For example, a young married couple with two children is more likely to buy a minivan or SUV than a sports car. These statistics also define the type and size of the message delivered. For example, for consumers age 48 to 65 years of age, ad copy might use a slightly larger type size and include more detailed copy in comparison to an ad targeted to the young married couple above.

Psychographic data focuses on the target's lifestyle, attitudes, activities, and interests, and how this information affects the target's views on product repurchase. This data determines if they are loyal to a particular brand or open to new products or trends, how the product or service affects their lifestyle, if it fulfills a rational need such as food, or an emotional want such as jewelry or expensive electronic gadgetry. As the advertised message becomes more individualized and interactive, advertisers and marketers are increasingly finding that psychographics is a very powerful resource. For example, research consistently corroborates that using a target's age alone shows no direct correlation between purchases and media viewing habits.

Understanding a target's lifestyle often defines where they reside geographically. *Geographics* are used to determine where the target lives regionally, with additional breakdowns by state, city, and even zip code. Where a person lives also reveals a lot about how they live. For example, people living in northern climates will rely less on air conditioning and more on heating options than those living in Florida or the Deep South. Where a person lives increases the ability to isolate cultural influences that can affect purchasing decisions, such as finding more Hispanic groceries or restaurants in larger multicultural cities throughout the United States. Geographic profiles can also be used to gauge the type of media vehicles and events that the target is exposed to on a regular basis.

Behavioristics or behavioristic segmentation is basically a combination of all target data that help to determine the reasons why a person buys and how they purchase. Do they buy on a whim or are they more prone to research before buying? Are they brand loyal? Do they spend time browsing in brick and mortar stores or do they do most of their buying online or through catalogs?

These basic segmentation profiles can be used in any combination to influence creative direction and to select the most appropriate media vehicle(s) to deliver the marketing message. The target may also be segmented by usage patterns, economics, marketplace opportunities, or any other relevant segment based on the brand's overall business objectives. Segmentation can also be based on purchase behavior—for example, whether the target makes self-purchases (primary) or purchases on behalf of another (secondary).

The *primary market* refers to the users/consumers currently using the product or service or those who are likely to use the product in the future. The *secondary market* encompasses those users/consumers most likely to purchase the product on behalf of the primary audience or those who influence the purchases of the primary audiences. For example, commercials for the Apple iPhone may advertise its cool features to high school kids, but the price generally requires a parent or grandparent's purchase before the primary target can own it. To reach this secondary audience, it requires a different creative message, strategy, and media mix than the advertising directed at the primary audience.

3. **Competitive Review.** Once the target has been identified, research is used to analyze how the competition positions itself within the market category, identifying any shared or unique product features that may or may not be associated with other brands, and classifying current advertising, packaging, media use, and so on. A breakdown of competing attributes assists both marketing and advertising to determine ways that the product or service can set itself apart in some memorable way from the competition.

This section in the plan thoroughly outlines who the brand's closest competitors are, or those who offer a similar product with similar attributes. It is also a good idea to look at products that may not actually be similar to the product but offer a variation. For example, if you sell coffee you are also competing with other types of coffee: decaf, flavored coffees, instant coffees, and coffee beans.

4. **Product and/or Business Review.** This section lays out the details of the brand, such as use, price, features, positioning in the brand category and in the target's mind, current advertising and promotions, and packaging and distribution channels.

5. **SWOT/SLOT Analysis.** This section looks at the strengths and weaknesses of a product, service, or company, and any external threats and opportunities presented. Each is closely examined in order to determine a market strategy. The analysis helps the marketing representative predict the direction of the marketing activities, the current status of the brand or company, and future projections. The selected direction often depends on several factors; therefore, it is necessary to review other factors within the marketplace that might affect the marketing efforts and strategy—for instance, the current social and political atmosphere, any technological advancements, or competing brands. Advertisers look closely at the SWOT analysis to help determine the ideal strategic direction for the visual/verbal message.

6. **Marketing Objectives.** This section, usually written in terms of sales goals, describes what the brand or company wants to accomplish within a certain time frame, typically for one year. This is where the executive summary or mission statement is fleshed out into achievable actions or objectives, and eventually into results or goals to be reached.

Under this heading you find both sales and marketing objectives. Sales objectives outline goals to be achieved such as profit margins, advertising, distribution channels, and targeted markets, as well as the ways that sales initiatives will be achieved. Marketing objectives are measurable, time sensitive goals that look at what a brand or company is attempting to achieve with its marketing activities. Marketing objectives also determine the expectations for each target segment based on the advertising message (this includes existing and new customers).

After the target has been selected, the marketing objectives outlined, the current and desired positioning for the company, product, or service determined, then the next step is to determine the best way to strategically implement the marketing strategy.

> 7. **Marketing Strategy.** This section outlines the tactics to use in the marketing mix to accomplish the stated objectives.

The marketing mix is the specific type and number of vehicles that a company uses to control, orchestrate, and accomplish its business objectives. The four Ps of product, price, promotion, and place (or distribution) make up what is known as the *marketing mix*. All elements of the mix must work together in order to successfully facilitate a relationship between the buyer—the targeted audience—and the product, company or service—the seller. Very basically, the marketing mix entails all the steps a company employs in order to efficiently drive a brand into the marketplace while executing the marketing strategy. The marketing mix needs to deliver a quality driven product or service that reinforces the company's position and successfully continues to build consumer loyalty and brand equity, as well as accomplishing the stated marketing and financial objectives. Because advertising today is so consumer-focused, many marketers have added a fifth P—people—to the marketing mix.

- **Product.** Product or services' tangible attributes—for example, features, packaging
- **Price.** Price paid for any product or service affects how it is marketed
- **Promotion.** Deals with any method of advertising or promotion
- **Place or Distribution.** Refers to where a product or service can be obtained
- **People and/or Personnel.** Includes anyone—outside target or inside personnel—who uses or comes in contact with the product or service as well as the competence level of customer contact points

A well-researched, well-developed marketing plan ensures each of the five P's has been thoroughly addressed in the overall plan.

Basic marketing strategies employ two fundamental types of marketing principles, "push" and "pull." Marketers decide to use either a push or pull strategy as a way to encourage purchase or the use of a product or service. Each strategy type reaches different consumers. For example, a *pull* strategy is most commonly used for promoting consumer products and targets those consumers most likely to buy the product or use the service. The targeted message is often delivered using advertising, sales promotion, and direct response to "pull" the target in or nearer to the brand. A *push* strategy, on the other hand, focuses its messages on members of the distribution channel such as retailers and wholesalers. It is their job to "push" the message to the consumers.

It's the controllable combination of all the "P" elements that make up the whole of the marketing pie. The level of control depends on the internal environment of the originating brand and external perception. Each decision surrounding the five P's should be consumer-focused in order to establish a value-driven position in the target's mind as compared to the competition.

8. **Performance Analysis and Implementation.** This section is a type of media plan that outlines what specific vehicles will be used in promotional efforts. This will become more finely tuned when dealing with the brand's advertising agency. It consists of three specific areas: Budget, performance analysis, and implementation schedule. The budget section outlines the cost to carry out the projected marketing plan as well as outlining the expenditures necessary to accomplish the plan's objectives. The implementation schedule is the marketing plan of action; it contains a timeline of when specific tasks will be performed, the responsible parties for the tasks, and the overall financial implications. The performance analysis outlines the expected results and financial impact of the plan.

9. **Evaluation.** This section very simply looks at what is working and what is not. What should be continued and what should be tweaked or completely discarded (see Fig 2.1 at the end of the chapter for a sample marketing plan).

From an advertising perspective, before the visual/verbal solution can be found and before developing the creative brief, the account management team meets with the client to review the marketing plan in order to thoroughly understand the client's strategies and objectives for their advertising or communication efforts.

Advertising, the Marketing Plan, and the Development of the Creative Brief

Once the advertising team understands what the client wants to accomplish, the account executive assigned to the account uses the marketing plan as a template to develop a *creative brief*. The brief is the first step in the communication process. The creative and media teams, along with any nontraditional media suppliers, use the brief as a springboard to determine what communication activities need to be accomplished. It is the creative brief that outlines how advertising efforts are to achieve the business directives laid out in the marketing plan.

This small one or two page internal agency document keeps all team members on-target and on-strategy throughout the development stage. Although there is no set length for this brief, it has a large mission: It redefines the primary and secondary target audience; sets communication goals; outlines individual brand features and their benefits or relevance to the target; determines a key consumer benefit, also known as a big idea or unique selling proposition, that is emphasized throughout the campaign; highlights the competition and basic brand positioning; determines a tone of voice; and, finally, outlines tactics. It is the document that summarizes all the information the advertising team needs to define the visual/verbal message. Think of it as a roadmap that helps the advertising team to find the best concept or idea, and to guide the target with a message directed to initiate their response.

The creative brief is built from solid research; it does not generalize or speculate, nor does it determine the look or sound of the creative element. Its job is to ensure that everyone working on the campaign, including the client, understands all objectives that need to be met.

Elements Contained Within the Creative Brief

Similar to a marketing plan, the content and format of a creative brief varies by agency but usually contains a mixture of the following: 1) target profile, 2) communication objective(s), 3) product features and benefits, 4) competitive outline, 5) product positioning, 6) key consumer benefit, 7) creative strategy, 8) tone, 9) support statement, and 10) tagline or slogan and logo.

1. **Target Profile.** The creative brief takes a less detailed look at the target than the marketing plan. However, the same four categories that applied to the marketing plan are just as import: demographics, psychographics, geographics and behavioralistics. The advertising team uses the information they have about the target to determine the overall message, and the media team uses the data to determine media placement.

Research on the target informs both the client and the agency about how the target buys, their level of brand loyalty, their purchase reasons, and the best media mix required to reach them, as well as helping solidify the best visual/verbal message to inspire the target to action.

Larry Percy discusses in his book *Strategies for Implementing Integrated Marketing Communication* (IMC) that to further increase sales the target audience can be divided into one or more of the following four groups: a) New brand category users. The message should encourage trial based on specific features and benefits, b) Brand loyal users. Message should encourage expanding current use, c) Brand switchers. Message should feature reasons why target should switch permanently rather than wait for a promotion, d) Consumers loyal to other brands. Message should compare and contrast features against a competitor's brand (Percy, 1997).

2. **Communication Objectives.** Communication objectives are the attainable goals advertising efforts need to accomplish. Highly structured campaigns focus on one to three objectives. Most objectives focus on what consumers should think or feel about a brand or what advertising efforts should motivate the target to do. To effectively achieve such a goal advertisers need to know the extent of the target's knowledge about a brand. This sometimes requires a quick look at the brand's life cycle in order to determine the brand or product stage and whether to assess, review, update, highlight, or reinvent based on the stage.

Communication objectives look at the size of the target audience to be reached, how often they need to be exposed to the message for recall and action, and the type of interaction required.

3. **Product Features and Benefits.** This is a short list of product features such as size, colors, uses that are unique or inherent to the product and their relevance or benefit to the target. Although features are important, it's benefits that catch and hold the target's attention and ultimately sell a product.

4. **Competitive Outline.** This section briefly outlines the brands that are in direct competition with the client's brand. It is important to know what competitors are saying and showing in their advertising as well as in their package or product design, in order to ensure that the client's brand is not following what others are doing but setting the standard in the brand category.

5. **Product Positioning.** Positioning looks at how the target perceives competitors' products as compared to the client's brand. It is not unusual for this section to include focus group or other feedback gathered by advertising researchers, such as survey collection, or observational sessions, to name just a few. This section uses information gathered to carve out and create a unique brand position in the target's mind. Most brands are not unique to any one product or service category, so it is important to find a new use or to focus advertising efforts on a feature to make it unique to the brand—this feature might be inherent in all category brands, but the competitors are not using this element in their advertising. This type of approach forces competitors into a "me too" category. It takes more than one advertisement to build

up a distinctive position; this individuality develops a unique persona and fortifies a distinctive brand identity as opposed to the sameness presented by competitors within the brand category.

6. **Key Consumer Benefit.** The key consumer benefit (KCB) is the one feature/benefit combination that is either unique to the brand—known as a *unique selling proposition* (USP)—or can be positioned as unique through creative advertising efforts, known as a *big idea*. The KCB is that one feature/benefit combination that research has shown is important to the target. Because of this, it drives the campaign's visual/verbal message. It is featured in headlines, demonstrated in visuals, and defined in copy as well as is the centerpiece in promotional events. This key selling point may or may not have been identified in the marketing plan but was later identified as important during subsequent advertising research, so it is important the client buy into the reasoning behind the focus on this particular feature/benefit combination. Because of its relevance to the target, it must speak directly to their interests and reflect their lifestyle in such a way that it encourages the desired action outlined in the communication objectives.

Ways to determine the KCB:

- List one or two features and benefits unique to the product or service.
- Does the product or service fulfill a rational or emotional need for the target?
- What can the product or service do that competitors are either not pushing in their advertising or that the competitive product or service physically cannot do?
- How can you strategically deliver these differences and still accomplish the communication objectives?
- Know the reasons why your target would use your product or service or switch from their current brand.

Brands lacking a unique selling proposition should avoid using vehicles employed by the competition. Duplication can affect memorability, retard growth, and greatly affect ROI. Brands with a truly unique feature, stronger image, or with a larger share of equity in the category, which are focusing efforts on the same or a similar target as the competition will stand out when placed within the same vehicles. Mass-produced brands in categories with a large amount of product parity often require more advertising to compete in a brand category, and thus require a bigger budget in order to stand out, gain, and retain market share.

7. **Creative Strategy.** Strategy refers to the tactics that will be used to accomplish the communication goals. It tells the creative team the best way to talk to the target, exploit the key consumer benefit, position the brand in order to effectively stand out from competing brands, and how to assure that the brand is top of mind when repurchasing. Most strategies focus on either the brand or the consumer and determine whether an emotional or rational appeal will be employed.

Strategies also are influenced by the brand's life cycle stage. A brand-based strategy builds up or focuses on an existing brand personality for the purpose of building or reinforcing a relationship with the target. A consumer-based strategy will focus on the brand's benefits to the targeted audience.

8. **Tone.** The tone section of the brief defines the personality and overall tone of voice the advertising efforts employ. The choice of tone depends on the key consumer benefit and the determined target audience. Once the direction of the creative effort is determined, it is important to decided how the information is to be delivered. There are basically two types of tones used in advertising, emotional and rational. The difference between an emotional and rational approach depends on the content delivery. For example, an emotional tone can use sex to sell the product or service or employ testimonials that use humor, whimsy, threats, or even reprimands, to name a few. A rational tone, as expected, uses facts, employs a technical or scientific approach, or can be authoritative or instructional, to name just a few. Whatever the tone applied, it must be the unifying element between the target, key consumer benefit, and the strategy.

9. **Support Statement.** Often the brief also promotes a support statement or another important feature/benefit combination that is used to support the key consumer benefit.

10. **Slogan or Tagline and Logo.** Most logos are accompanied by either a slogan or tagline. Wherever used, these three to five word statements can usually be located either above or below the logo. A *slogan* can be used indefinitely and is most often tied to company philosophy or overall mission statement. A *tagline*, on the other hand, is temporary and is usually tied to a current campaign. A *logo* is a product, service, or corporate symbol. It appears everywhere the brand or company is seen. It can be a single line of text, a simple graphic, or a combination of the two (see Fig 2.2 at the end of the chapter for a sample creative brief).

It is important that the creative team adhere as closely as possible to the creative brief in order to accomplish both the marketing and communication goals. However, based on research there can be times when the brief needs to be overhauled in order to reflect new attitudes, image, use, and so on.

Nothing happens to a product, a service, or any advertising message until both marketing and advertising have a solid direction shaped by the assembled research. Research is the first step each team must undertake before the brand manager can develop a marketing plan or the account manager can develop a creative brief. Working together, they define the target, their needs, wants, and lifestyle, what competitors are or are not doing to respond to these needs, what media vehicles can reach the target where they work, play, or live, and send an active message that initiates a reaction from the target.

A thorough understanding about the target, marketplace, brand, economic and cultural or social trends ultimately helps the creative team develop a creative direction and helps marketers with increased sales, and ultimately builds brand equity.

Chapter 2 Exercises

1. Break up into groups of four or more. Divide one half of the group into the marketing team and the other half into the advertising team.

2. Using a new or existing marketing plan for a national brand, develop a creative brief for that product or service.

3. Members of the advertising team must present, defend, and sell the direction laid out in the brief and explain how the directives presented in the marketing plan would be accomplished. Additionally, both teams must discuss how and why the business/creative direction is different from the competition's.

4. Create or use a second marketing plan for a small business. Then create another brief, but this time, reverse the advertising and marketing roles.

Memory Box

Marketing

Advertising

Marketing Mix

Unique Selling Proposition/Big Idea

Qualitative Research

Quantitative Research

Marketing Plan

Demographics

Psychographics

Geographics

Behavioristics

Primary Market

Secondary Audience

Creative Brief

1. Executive Summary

2. Market Overview
   a. market segmentation
   b. target audience profile
   c. primary audience breakdown
   d. secondary audience breakdown

3. Competitive Review

4. Product and Business Review

5. SWOT Analysis

6. Marketing Objectives
   a. sales objectives
   b. marketing objectives

7. Marketing Strategy
   a. product
   b. price
   c. promotion
   d. place or distribution

8. Performance Analysis and Implementation
   a. media plan
   b. budget
   c. implementation schedule for media plan
   d. performance analysis
   e. people

9. Evaluation

Figure 2.1   Sample Marketing Plan

1. Target Profile

2. Communication Objective(s)

3. Product Features and Benefits

4. Competitive Outline

5. Product Positioning

6. Key Consumer Benefit

7. Creative Strategy

8. Tone

9. Support Statement

10. Tagline or Slogan and Logo

Figure 2.2   Sample Creative Brief

3

Guerrilla Marketing

Guerrilla marketing engages and often interacts with the target audience through innovative advertising and promotional public events, online, and even in some unusual guises and locations. This chapter defines how marketers should view guerilla marketing as a valuable outlet for reaching their intended target, describes how this type of marketing works, and outlines some of the possible pitfalls of using guerrilla marketing without thorough planning and research.

Guerrilla Marketing Personalizes the Brand

George Bernard Shaw once wrote, "The reasonable man adapts himself to the world: the unreasonable one persists in trying to adapt the world to himself. Therefore, all progress depends on the unreasonable man" (Shaw, 1903). Guerrilla marketing techniques accomplish the unreasonable; they entice consumers to stop, and to interact with the advertising.

Jay Conrad Levinson popularized the term *guerrilla marketing* in his 1984 book, *Guerilla Marketing*. The term may be defined as tactics that surprise in an unexpected way for less cost than traditional advertising tactics. Levinson conceived guerrilla marketing as a creative and inexpensive way for small business owners to compete against larger competitors offering immediate consumer feedback (Levinson, 2001). Guerrilla marketing, also known as *ambient* or *experiential* marketing, is a grassroots form of promotion that is successful because of its nontraditional use of space and often unorthodox staging of events, successfully maximizing exposure using minimal resources. The events involved in this type of marketing are often so unusual that they can capture an enormous audience. Successful events are often interactive and surprising, and always engaging, before revealing their true purpose—advertising.

The overall goal of guerrilla marketing is to capture attention using promotional tactics that are meant to entertain the target rather than deliver a hard sell advertising message. The more extraordinary the experience or atypical the location or surface, the larger the impression on the target. Because it is more difficult to isolate the consumer and overcome their apathy toward the advertised message, nontraditional media and guerrilla marketing must find a unique and memorable way to supersede any mistrust on the part of the target and surprise and entertain them with something totally unexpected. Engaging the target in a stunt or event, such as the type used in guerrilla marketing, is a great way to isolate a product or service from the competitors' brands by giving the target a chance to experience or interact with the messaged brand. The sheer uniqueness and innovative promotional tactics of most guerilla marketing are memorable, often extending the messages beyond the event, via electronic marketing and word of mouth.

Alexander Reidl, a former marketing director for Volvo Middle East, in a *guerrillaonline.com* article titled "Guerrilla Marketing Principles," divided guerrilla marketing into six diverse *must have* characteristics in order for a selected event to succeed, including: 1) be completely unexpected, 2) be drastic, 3) be humorous, 4) be able to deliver the message in one shot, 5) be low cost, and 6) promote goodwill.

With consumers overwhelmed by thousands of advertised messages a day, it's no wonder that traditional advertising does not reach as many consumers as it once did. Skeptical of any advertised message, consumers shut out the hard sell message, but if the message is presented in a new way and is entertaining, it can still be memorable.

Often using very diverse techniques, these strategic messages can reach consumers in strange ways: using venues such as graveyards; with unusual events such as staging a demonstration on an airline, or creating memorable happenings that cause buzz; and in unique product placements. One of the earliest recorded guerilla marketing events used elephants. P. T. Barnum was hired by New York City to prove the strength of the newly opened Brooklyn Bridge by walking a herd of elephants (each weighed about a ton) across the bridge. The Goodyear blimp, now almost 90 years old, was the first blimp used in a guerrilla marketing campaign and still travels across the country promoting events. Another on going guerrilla marketing icon is the Oscar Meyer Weinermobile.

Consider some of these attention-grabbing techniques:

1. Selling mobile phones in an area with no coverage.

2. Bringing attention to the issue of homelessness in Paris by giving away hundreds of tents to Parisians living on the streets of that beautiful city. Dubbed

"tent city," the event drew the solicited attention, forcing city officials to take action to help alleviate the problem.

3. Placing orange-clad brand representatives on public transportation in specific cities is how ING promoted its new "Orange" service. Each "ambassador handed" out leaflets outlining the new service. To further promote the events, transit signs were placed in subway cars and on the sides of buses featuring the orange-clad spokespersons.

4. Eukanuba in South Africa, to promote its dog food, trained several dogs to carry a bag of the delicious morsels between preset locations in a local mall.

5. Taco Bell created a guerrilla marketing campaign in the mid 1990s using newspaper ads to inform the public that they had purchased the Liberty Bell, which caused an uproar. The promotion caused a lot of clamor on its own, but when Taco Bell then announced that they were renaming it the Taco Bell Liberty Bell, all heck broke loose. Taco Bell basked in all the attention before explaining it was nothing more than promotional hype.

6. Spotlighting attention on shelter cats, Meow Mix cat food created a reality show featuring cats that ran on Animal Planet. Using webcams placed in ten shelters across the country, viewers were invited into the "Meow Mix House" to watch the cats playing, sleeping, grooming, and just generally being cats. Every week, viewers were informed which cat had been "voted out" or put up for adoption. Viewers who adopted cats also received a year's supply of Meow Mix cat food.

Street Marketing

Street marketing refers to specialized marketing techniques used in public places to promote a product or service in a personalized, yet often unconventional way. Traditional advertising and other forms of supportive nontraditional media promotions precede most street marketing. It is memorable due to the often emotional, one-to-one contact created between the target and the brand by the street teams.

A big part of guerrilla marketing, a *street team* is composed of a group of individuals who move among pedestrians to promote a product or service. It is an inexpensive way to get the brand into the target's hand and to personally deliver a message. Teams are usually hired to hand out samples, demonstrate, or promote a brand at local events, bars, or coffee shops, to name just a few venues. During the events, the team becomes the face of the brand. These grassroots teams can also be found canvassing neighborhoods, shopping malls, college campuses, parks, and street fairs—anywhere the targeted audience gathers. It is important that team members look, dress, and act in a way that matches the psychographics of the targeted audience.

The use of guerrilla tactics does not work for all brands; it is most often used by brands that want to reach a younger target audience or for those brands within crowded brand categories. Unfortunately, it is easy to over-step the personal intrusion guardrail and to antagonize consumers. Many simulated events can make it difficult for consumers to tell the difference between great advertising and subterfuge, or what's known as "astroturf-ing" or the creation of artificial buzz. It is important that both marketers and advertisers think through their tactics in order to avoid possibly alien-ating their target audience.

The old adage that any publicity is good publicity does not always transfer itself to brand advertising. An unsuccessful guerrilla marketing campaign can affect brand image. Before any guerrilla launch, it is critical that the creative team research not only the tolerance level of government officials but understand where consumers draw the line between entertain-ment and offensive and/or destructive actions.

Guerrilla marketers know that any campaign not only needs to surprise consumers but must find a way to get those same consumers to participate in the event. For example, the "FCG" event for Nautica handed out cou-pons on the streets of several southern cities to consumers labeled "fashion shipwrecks."

No matter the surface or type of event, guerrilla marketing works because it's always creative and engaging, sometimes covert and contro-versial, and often interactive. Combine all these elements together and you are certain to get a memorable and popular conversational topic—the main reason to advertise. For guerrilla marketing to reach the target in a memorable way, in addition to Reidl's six elements, it must have four more: 1) impact, 2) exposure, 3) media reach, and 4) creativity and innovation.

It's important to remember that guerrilla marketing is used to support messages advertised elsewhere. Its job is not to encourage an immediate sale but to encourage ongoing word-of-mouth discussions, the most believable and inexpensive form of advertising.

Brandweek.com authors David Kiley and Roberta Klara, in an October 31, 2010, article titled "Guerrilla marketing 2010," reported: "'The best engagements that I see,' observed David Meerman Scott, author of *The New Rules of Marketing and PR*, 'are when the audience is involved and participating while they are being entertained'" (Scott, 2006 as cited in Kiley & Klara, 2010, para. 6). Its use and importance can be traced to economic downturns, fractionalized target audiences, increased media options, and the continued ineffectiveness of some tra-ditional media vehicles. Let's take a look at some very creative examples of guerilla marketing.

Identifying a Medium's Strengths and Weaknesses Reinforces and Highlights the Visual/Verbal Message

Before deciding where guerrilla marketing fits in a campaign, it is important that both marketers and the advertising teams understand how an event can positively enhance or negatively affect a campaign's message. Let's take a quick look at both the capabilities and limitations of guerrilla marketing.

Strengths

- **Cost.** Because many events can be inexpensive, it is a great way for small businesses to compete against larger competitors.
- **Memorable.** Because events are unexpected and often interactive, they are remembered longer than any single advertisement.
- **Word of Mouth.** Many guerrilla marketing events are worth sharing with friends and family and are often picked up by the media, extending the message experience beyond the event.

Weaknesses

- **Return on Investment.** Guerrilla marketing events are not measureable.
- **Public Relations.** Events that are intrusive or break city or state laws can cause negative publicity for a brand.
- **Time Investment.** Many larger, more spectacular events are not only costly to produce but require a great deal of time to pull off successfully.

Taking the Brand's Message to the Streets

IKEA used a guerrilla marketing campaign titled "A Little Fabric Makes A Big Difference" to draw attention to their brand. The eye-catching event put curtains up in buses, and put slipcovers on transit benches, bus shelters, parking meters, and bicycle seats, all sporting the same tagline.

Volkswagen, to hammer home their promotion of "driven by fun" for the Polo GTI, wanted to prove that they were the king of fun, installing a big slide over a flight of stairs that encouraged everyone to have fun in the "fast lane."

Some of the most talked about guerrilla marketing stunts take ordinary items and put them in unexpected locations or situations. For example, IKEA dressed up the streets of New York by placing a colorful rug, table, two chairs, and two very unusual lamps on a very busy pedestrian route to modernize the "décor."

Guerrilla marketing in foreign markets is often a little more shocking than that found in the United States, which Marisa Lingerie proved when it took peeping to a new level. Behind a pink construction barricade, this very interactive event placed their logo and an arrow that directed passersby to a peephole where they could watch a lingerie clad female construction crew.

Polo Ralph Lauren attracted attention in their tailored men's store when they hired waiters dressed to the nines to deliver champagne to their guests at a cocktail reception before the start of the main event. To keep guests engrossed, they were asked to step outside into the cold night air and prepare for a multi-sensory experience that mixed a little bit of fashion and fragrance with video and music. The company could have used live models as a living history of the brand or created a catalog, but that would not have been as memorable. Instead, *RalphLauren.com* projected a short video onto the building that featured virtual models on a virtual catwalk along with an in-your-face display of running polo horses, and mega-sized ties projecting down the side of the building. As a finale, a mist of the Big Pony fragrance collection was gently spewed over those gathered below. Polo chose to use imagination and technology to tell an interactive and memorable story about the brand, avoiding the "been there, done that" staging of a typical fashion show.

Trident chewing gum company chose Times Square and New York taxis as an attention-getting vehicle. This single day promotion allowed riders who hailed a cab from a predetermined stand to pay their fares with gum. All riders needed to do was to present a gum pack they already had or one of the available free samples to get a free lift to anywhere within the city limits.

Trident chose this type of promotion because it strategically meshed with their integrated marketing communication (IMC) campaign's verbal message of "so good you'll want to get paid in gum." Those willing to wait for a cab were kept busy with games, meeting and posing for photographs with celebrities, and picking up a few coupons.

Fiat used guerrilla marketing to launch its arrival in the United States after an absence of twenty-five years. They decided to use a grassroots approach rather than mass media to get the word out to leery Americans. Lacking a positive reputation, Fiat wanted to get Americans up close and personal with the new Fiat 500 by using Times Square to hold an event where they served espresso and gelato, showcasing the car, garnering attention with music, and hosting rounds of bocce ball. After dark, consumers were entertained by classic movies shown on the Jumbotron television. At other U.S. stops, Fiat gave out car parts to consumers attending a music festival so they could use them to make music, and at an art show they asked artists to use the cars as a canvas for their artwork. The creative stops and venues all helped to showcase the Fiat 500 as the perfect outlet for those who belong to a creative class of car buying consumers.

The Heavenly Mountain Resort in Lake Tahoe, Nevada, knew that the best way to promote its new ski passes was not through the use of traditional media. Instead, they chose to develop a guerrilla marketing event that featured a truck filled with snow cones manned by two local comedians to spread their message. What do snow cones have to do with skiing, you may wonder? According to a 2010 online *New York Times* article by Tanzina Vega titled "Marketers Discover Trucks Can Deliver More Than Food," Heavenly decided they "were going to give you a little bit of the mountain" (Vega, 2010b).

Each truck was outfitted with iPads and large television screens that showed skiing and snowboarding videos in order to promote the resort's $379 ski season passes available on the campaign's Facebook page. The snow cones offered up a taste of the forthcoming ski season.

HSBC bank also chose guerilla marketing with the decision to sponsor a local New York festival and used food trucks to promote its involvement. Six trucks representing six different restaurants were wrapped up for the HSBC ad campaign. To make the encounter extra tasty, each restaurant featured a special dish created for the event. Existing HSBC customers could walk up to any of the food vending trucks, show their bank cards, and receive a free drink or free scoop of ice cream, with napkins featuring the bank's logo.

Another successful guerilla event was when Heinz used branded trucks equipped with a complete kitchen to promote its new Heinz Dip & Squeeze Ketchup. The wrap on each truck promoted the "Heinz Ketchup Road Trip" and also advertised their Twitter and Facebook information. To ensure that everyone got a chance to try the new product, every visitor received a free serving of regular Ore-Ida fries or sweet potato fries and a packet of the Dip & Squeeze Ketchup.

The campaign also gave away t-shirts to consumers who participated in one of the campaign's social media options. Free t-shirts were also given out to anyone who proved that they had "checked in" to the "Ketchup Road Trip" on Foursquare or who posted their preference for dipping or squeezing on Facebook or Twitter.

To promote *The Walking Dead* cable show, AMC and Fox International Channels planned to stage "zombie attacks" in over 25 large cities. Each attack was to include hundreds of extras wearing zombie make-up, roaming landmarks such as the Brooklyn Bridge in New York and Big Ben in London. The coordinated walks will begin at sunrise in Taipei and Hong Kong, moving across the globe over the ensuing 24 hours. The walk is to terminate at the *The Walking Dead* premiere in Los Angeles, California.

To capture the attention of fashion conscious consumers in a stylish way, Target rented an entire hotel and decorated 155 exterior rooms with LEDs. When the curtains were pulled back, viewers saw 66 dancers under gyrating LED lights showcased in the windows, wearing DayGlo skeleton costumes and dancing to music.

Crowds got to watch the event from risers. The guerrilla marketing event was successful, driving people to the Target website in droves as well as attracting additional media attention.

Getting the public to visit local museums is not always easy. Using their very limited budget, the Chicago Museum of Science and Industry decided that creating a social, crowdsourced (*crowdsourcing* is the act of taking a job traditionally performed by a designated agent [usually an employee] and outsourcing it to an undefined, generally large group of people in the form of an open call), guerrilla campaign was the least expensive way to advance its new age awareness message.

The campaign promised participants the opportunity to spend a "Month at the Museum." Not visiting but actually living there, in a specially created room, the offer also included meals for the month. The museum's chief marketing officer (CMO) Rob Gallas explained in a 2010 online Brandweek article, "we were thinking of this person as an ambassador, a mirror that will reflect all of the energy and things that go on here" (Kiley & Klara, 2010, p. 3). Because entrants had to prepare an essay and video, museum officials expected a relatively small pool of respondents. Instead, the guerrilla marketing event attracted more than 1,500 applications from an international pool. Word of mouth brought the attention of local media as well as ABC's Good Morning America, and the event has been talked about in hundreds of blogs and succeeded in nearly doubling the Chicago museum's Facebook fan base.

The winner got $10,000 and was asked to use social media outlets such as Facebook, Twitter, YouTube, and/or Flickr to talk about their experience as a "human exhibit."

The winner was chosen through online balloting. By using guerrilla marketing and social media networks, the museum effectively put a younger, hipper face on not only the museum, but their events and exhibits.

Coca-Cola Company decided to use a guerrilla marketing event to get college students' attention with a promotion they called "Happiness Machine," which revolved around a particular cafeteria vending machine. While students were away for the holidays, Coke's guerrilla marketing agency was at work rigging up a very special vending machine. This vending machine not only contained cold drinks, but the people and props needed to pull off the event. To record the event, small video cameras were set up around the machine's location to record student reactions.

The first users of the machine received their beverages without experiencing anything strange when they initially dropped their change into the machine. Eventually, however, the cost of a Coke bought thirsty users bouquets of flowers, balloons, a large submarine sandwich, and a hot and ready-to-eat pepperoni pizza. The video footage recorded the various student reactions such as nervous laughter, screams, bewildered stares, as well as the inevitable crowd response, which all ended up on YouTube. The return on investment (ROI) that this vending machine stunt achieved was to receive over two million Internet hits for Coca-Cola, but it also was used to create a 30-second television commercial.

Another event that was created for McDonald's restaurants received a lot of buzz or interest but not a lot of revenue. It was a digital outdoor board seen in Stockholm that doubled as a videogame. The interactive idea featured menu items that bounced across the board. All gamers had to do was use their Smartphone to capture a menu item. Participants who brought the photo into the restaurant got that item for free.

Guerrilla marketing can even help make an unpalatable brand palatable, by turning it into an event and then inviting a few friends over to participate in the experience. That's what cemeteries across the nation are doing to encourage partygoers to remember them when the time comes. If you're invited to one of these "grave parties," you might find events that include concerts, barbecues, dance performances, and maybe a clown or two.

A cemetery in California draws crowds to films that are projected onto mausoleum walls. Another holds poetry workshops, bird walks, and art shows. One cemetery in Michigan invites disabled children to fish in the pond located on the grounds. Still another in Nebraska holds a Shakespeare festival and rents out its chapel for weddings. A Colorado graveyard hosts Memorial Day events with skydivers and fireworks.

The "social gatherings" are resurrecting the days when cemeteries were often a place to gather. In the past, the cemetery was one of the few green spaces in many cities and towns; it was a great place for family picnics, near a loved one's final resting place.

Another interesting event, promoting an upcoming superhero-based television show, *The Cape*, had advertisers commandeering several historical statues throughout New York City and draping them in capes. Working with the Department of Parks and Recreation, black capes will drape the shoulders of George Washington, William Shakespeare, and Eleanor Roosevelt. To explain the promotion, temporary plaques will tie the historical figures into the series. Other than the plaques, the capes will have no logos or other identifying marks. The promotion instead uses social media and a sweepstakes to get the word out. All it cost the producers of the show was the price of a small honorarium to the Parks and Recreation Department, and with very little work, a very inexpensive way to gain a lot of impressions.

The BlackBerry Smartphone hired attractive actresses to openly carry their brand into a bar and flirt with the male patrons. The goal was to grab attention to the woman and then the phone. After the actress had the rapt attention of a male, she handed over the phone, asking him to enter his phone number and telling him that she would call him, which of course she never did. This type of guerrilla event, known as *stealth marketing,* is used to attract attention in the hopes that participants in the covert promotion would spread a positive message about the product (either electronically or via word of mouth) to friends, who would share it with their friends and so on.

To promote AIDS awareness, sponsors are turning to hairdressers and social media to promote their campaign. With the "Reduce your risk" and "Get tested" promotion, over 500,000 hairdressers will receive kits with brochures and decals about the fight against HIV and AIDS. Materials will also steer interested consumers to the campaign's website.

In an article titled "Pass the Hairspray, Fight Aids," Christine Schuster, Senior Vice President of Worldwide Education for the Redken and PureOlogy Lines at L'Oreal in New York, says, "the relationship a man or a woman has with a hairdresser can be an intimate, personal relationship, one in which advice is freely imparted—and frequently followed" (Elliot, 2010b, p. 3).

To promote further awareness of the campaign, 500 hairdressers from salons nationwide will be placed inside video booths throughout Manhattan to help interested pedestrians create their own short videos about HIV prevention. The campaign will also show celebrity videos on the NASDAQ Reuters Building in Time Square.

Memorable Messages Created by the Target or Through Cross-Promotional Efforts

Red Bull is one of the few brands to buck the traditional media onslaught of new product launches. The company relies on word of mouth and the only place you will see their advertisements is on television, featuring its simplistic line drawn characters.

Grassroots Marketing is the term for brands built by word-of-mouth advertising, such as the marketing used by Red Bull; this type of marketing is on the rise. The aversion to in-your-face messages is increasing because the 20-something market is skeptical of traditional advertising messages, as well as messages delivered by celebrity spokespersons. Each contact with the target must offer a definable and useful key consumer benefit, or they will tune out. Red Bull enhances its simple grassroots message by using student brand managers or brand ambassadors whose endorsement ultimately gives the brand an aura of credibility.

Red Bull has also had a great deal of success with what they call "consumer educators." These are the people who pull up in the Red Bull vans at local establishments and events to hand out free samples to anyone who needs a boost of energy.

Cross-promotion entails a type of guerilla marketing where similar products are promoted together, which is a great way to bring attention to two or more brands at the same time. For example, if a local store is selling cookbooks, why not promote on-site produce that is featured in the recipes in the cookbooks. Nowhere is it written that fruits and vegetables are only sold at the grocery store or local farmers market. Why not feature them in an actual cooking store or near the cookbook aisle at the local bookstore?

What is required to achieve a successful cross-promotional opportunity?

1. Know your local businesses.

2. Stop by and visit with other business owners. If short on time, consider joining the local Rotary Club to get to know the individual business community better. For example, if you sell pet supplies, consider shared business interests in the area—think about offering coupons for carpet cleaning, or kennels, or pet sitters, in tandem with promoting your own supplies.

3. Keep the first try simple and easy. This allows for the necessary, and inevitable, trial and error stage of any new program.

4. If you're not certain what businesses might be effective cross-promotional partners, ask your target audience who they think would be a good match.

This chapter has detailed a number of successful and very divergent guerilla marketing programs. Now, let's take a look at some examples of guerrilla marketing that were not so successful.

Guerrilla Marketing Events That Crash and Burn Lack Foresight

Marketers have to decide just how much latitude they allow their agency with any planned guerrilla marketing event. Depending on the event, promotions are often risky undertakings that walk a fine line between entertainment, and legal, and sometimes ethical disasters. Promotions that failed have been known to have incurred fines for the sponsoring companies or even had individuals sentenced to jail time. The resulting negative publicity is usually protracted and any attention-grabbing headlines are often difficult to label as good or bad. Large corporations with ever-changing brand offerings and ongoing advertising and charity involvement can easily absorb any negative publicity; however, smaller businesses should diligently plan to avoid troublesome projects as negative publicity is much harder to deflect.

A planned event does not guarantee success if efforts do not include the cooperation of state and local government officials. Similar to any form of communication, when something goes wrong, it can oftentimes go very wrong—such as in Boston, Massachusetts, during the promotion for the movie, *Aqua Teen Hunger Force*. Without getting clearance from city officials or the local police, little black boxes that projected characters from the film were placed around Boston. Once discovered, uninformed officials believed them to be possible bombs, prompting officials to shut down the entire city. Once the guerrilla campaign was exposed, the sponsoring television network, TNT, was forced to repay the city for expenses incurred.

After the Boston bomb scare, one would assume that Hollywood would be more careful with its guerrilla promotions. However, yet another bomb scare was attached to a guerrilla promotion for the 2006 release of the film, *Mission Impossible II*. The campaign focused on the placement of small music players inside of 4,500 freestanding newspaper boxes. When opened, newspaper shoppers would hear the well-known *Mission Impossible* theme music. The promotion backfired because consumers could see the music player and mistook it for a possible bomb, prompting them to call police.

Events such as these emphasize the need for prelaunch promotions and focus group testing to assist marketing and advertisers alike with anticipating the public's reaction to a planned event.

Stealth marketing techniques, also known as **undercover marketing** or ambush marketing, are often misleading since the targeted consumer does not immediately realize that they are the recipient of a marketing message. Some of the more recent examples have occurred online when companies post their own biased reviews of a brand without openly informing readers of their affiliation with the product or service being discussed.

In his book *The Tipping Point*, author Malcom Gladwell calls stealth marketing a type of con game:

> Well, there's an element, obviously, of deception involved that I don't think is the case in conventional advertising. Conventional advertising is about trying to charm us or trying to persuade us. But it's not usually trying to trick us. And it's the trickery part, I think, that makes this different. (Gladwell, 2002)

Let's look at some other guerilla marketing examples that engendered negative consumer and local community responses.

Oftentimes, when guerrilla marketing uses a more in-your-face, or in this case, an up-your-nose form of advertising tactic, it can be so new and unexpected that a company can encounter unforeseen problems from consumers, such as in the "Got Milk" campaign. Consumers complained about the odor surrounding advertisements placed in bus shelters around San Francisco. The ads promoted the combined use of cookies and milk and went one step too far when the campaign added the smell of chocolate chip cookies into the marketing posters used in the bus shelters. Commuters complained that the smell gave them headaches, made them hungry, or aggravated allergies.

Dr Pepper also ran into some trouble in the United Kingdom with a campaign they were running online. As a way to update the brand, the parent company, Coca-Cola, decided that participants could manipulate a Facebook users' status updates and post embarrassing messages at random.

Participants were able to do this by using Dr Pepper's takeover widget to make posts and to win a chance at a weekly prize. The contest tagline was "What's the worst that could happen?" Well, in this case when you ask a silly question, you get a disaster. When a mother in Glasgow spotted foul messages posted on her teenage daughter's Facebook page, the worst happened—an irate parent.

Coke immediately stopped the campaign, apologized, and promptly fired their agency. The original idea was dull at best; on the other hand, the result was a great deal of buzz. The goal, of course, for both Coke and the Aqua Teen promotion was to create publicity and buzz.

In Leeds, United Kingdom, in 2003, to promote its Smirnoff Ice brand, Smirnoff vodka used stencils to display their message on an underpass without first gaining permission from local government officials. The oversight led to the displays being labeled as vandalism by authorities, who quickly levied the vodka producer with a cleaning fine. Smirnoff apologized for the oversight and agreed to pay for clean up, once the campaign had ended.

In 2002, New York based computer game company Acclaim Entertainment decided to use a guerrilla marketing campaign to promote the release of their new race car inspired game, "Burnout 2." On its release, Acclaim surprised everyone, including local law enforcement, by announcing that they would pay for any speeding fines consumers received on the release date. Great for consumers, but the Department of Transportation and the public at large declared the promotion would only encourage the young "targeted" audience to speed. Acclaim's position in the furor was that the promotion was a great way "to ease the financial pain" for any drivers who were stopped and ticketed.

Again in 2002, the cell phone provider Vodafone also received some negative publicity when they hired two guys to streak across the field at an international rugby game. Each runner was clothed only in the Vodafone logo that was strategically painted on his back. Like the Acclaim example above, both companies received a lot of publicity beyond the legal ramifications, which served to give the stunts a longer life-span and encouraged a barrage of word-of-mouth coverage. By drawing the attention of local officials and invoking criticism from consumers, each attempt went too far.

Taking Guerrilla Marketing Online

Guerrilla marketing used to be confined only to street stunts that engaged the consumer in some interesting and entertaining way. But today, in order to extend the life of the event, almost all guerrilla marketing tactics include some form of social media.

Most campaigns start out with the traditional street event; videos of the event are then posted on YouTube. Those with just enough kitsch and perhaps some divine intervention buzz hope it goes viral, as it did for Coke with its rigged up "Happiness Machine." Some guerrilla events ask consumers to participate by posting their reactions and contributions online, which is what Panasonic did when it strategically placed a 9-foot-tall pigeon and other oversized and unusual sculptures throughout London and other major cities. The plan was to intentionally create buzz around the launch of its new Lumix DMC-ZX1 camera, featuring an optical zoom lens capable of blowing any image up to eight times its normal size. Getting park visitors to talk about the enormous images didn't take long. To keep the momentum going, Panasonic included a contest that invited consumers to use the camera's zoom lens to distort other commonly used items and then post them on a specially designed Facebook page. The winning photographer would receive a trip to the Vancouver Winter Olympics. The weird, the unexpected, the unusual, or the use of everyday items in unexpected ways are all great buzz-building devices.

Some brands only reach out to a web audience to create attention. For example, one flamboyant or over-the-top campaign by a German airline, Euro Carrier Germanwings, sent a public relations sabotage group aboard a rival airline to spend their time in the air holding up cardboard signs and complaining aloud about the legroom and surcharges. Each sign featured copy bubbles, with the last one reading, "Next time, let's just fly Germanwings." Because only a small number of passengers would experience the event, the whole thing was filmed and placed on YouTube to increase the number of people experiencing the event and talking about being inconvenienced by the airlines.

Figure 3.1

Heineken used people's natural enthusiasm and also trash in their guerrilla marketing event titled, "Walk-In-Fridge." The Amsterdam-based campaign released a web video that compared what excited women versus men. With no dialogue, the video showed women gathered at a friend's housewarming party jumping up and down with excitement as they experienced the owner's walk-in closet. In another room, the same scenario is played out, only this time it's all about men and beer. The excited group of men is also jumping up and down with excitement at the owner's walk-in fridge. The coveted appliance is lined with shelves of ice-cold Heineken beer.

Reaping a large ROI of 4.4 million web views, Heineken wasn't finished. All over Amsterdam, guerrilla marketing events were catching people's attention. For example, one event placed boxes out on the curb labeled "Walk-In-Fridge." Along with the trash, witnesses saw young men trying to get the enormous fridge through their small and narrow doorways. Many times a street event is the first step in a guerrilla marketing campaign. Then the second step is the anticipated and hoped-for buzz, and third is the resulting video of the event being posted or landing on the social networks. For this guerrilla campaign, the order was reversed. The idea was bizarre enough to get consumers wondering if these giant refrigerators actually existed.

To keep curiosity high TBWA, Heineken's agency of record, built a real walk-in refrigerator and sent it around to local events. Visitors to events were asked to replicate the video and place it on YouTube.

Sadly, many marketers are abandoning the very entertaining and engaging events that have built a reputation for guerrilla marketing and are relying instead on allowing the consumer to carry the message via the many digital options now available, avoiding the overall cost and possible legal ramifications of an event.

A Pop-Up Form of Guerrilla Marketing

Another form of guerrilla marketing are *pop ups* or temporary retail stores that promote a product or service or are used as a way to sell seasonal products, such as Christmas decorations or Halloween costumes. Demands for these types of products are either short-lived or created through interaction. For example, in 2002 Target used a barge that they docked in a New York City harbor to sell holiday related merchandise. In 2010, fashion designer Cynthia Rowley took her designs to Atlanta consumers in a converted DHL truck. Using it as a shop front, she fitted the bland truck with hardwood floors, fabric covered walls, and added light fixtures and fitting rooms. In a May 18, 2011, article by Nedra Rhone, "Local pop-up shops gain popularity," a spokeswomen for the designer said, "The intention was to provide customers a retail vehicle in locations where Cynthia Rowley does not currently have a brick and mortar boutique." She goes on to say, "the shop on wheels is a new way to think about retail and for Cynthia Rowley to offer her customers the ultimate in service—the store literally comes to them" (Rhone, 2011, p. 1).

TV Guide Network also commandeered a truck to promote a new series, *Nail Files*, about a nail salon, by creating a mobile spa. They offered free manicures to people who passed by, while they showed clips of the upcoming series.

Marketing giants such as Procter & Gamble and Levi's use temporary stores as a way for the target to get up close and personal with their brand, or as a way to extend or support an existing campaign message.

Procter & Gamble used a pop-up store, not to sell a product, but to build brand loyalty by giving away free CoverGirl makeovers and a wash and blow-dry featuring Head & Shoulders products. Christian Charapata, a Procter & Gamble pop-up store manager, in a November 11, 2010, online article titled "The Staying Power of Pop-Up Stores" punctuated their importance by saying, "The woman getting her hair colored will remember this the rest of her life" (Townsend, 2010, p. 1).

To create lasting memories, Levi's opened a "workshop" (pop-up store) that focuses on the bygone art of traditional photography techniques; the store is a direct by-product of their "Go Forth" advertising campaign that focuses on craftsmanship and the down and dirty activities of community members working in their Levi's pants to rebuild a "Rust Belt town." Those stopping by the vacant Soho art gallery location can rent vintage cameras and sign up to attend free photography classes. Ideally, Levi hopes participants will post on Facebook, extending the campaign by talking, texting, and tweeting about their experience.

Pop-up stores like those used by Procter & Gamble and Levi's are a great way to communicate with their target and to build awareness about their brands in interactive and memorable ways. This evolution in pop-up stores not only engages visitors in an activity but uses them to introduce and give away free items.

To stimulate sales and get feedback on its snack brands, Lays, Sunchips, and Tostitos, the packaged goods manufacturer, Frito-Lay is placing their pop-up kitchen on top of the Hard Rock Café in New York's Times Square. The objective of the promotion is to dispel any thoughts consumers may have about their snacks being "unhealthy junk food." The promotion plans to use chefs to educate consumers on how each snack is made, to allow the chefs to give immediate feedback on taste and flavors, and to allow the chefs a chance at suggesting alternative uses for the aforementioned products. These types of events give marketers a type of impromptu focus group where they can gather ideas, improve the brand, as well as use the feedback in future promotional efforts. The ambitious campaign also includes mobile interactive barcodes or quick response (QR) codes placed on in-store displays, and print ads that feature recipes and video clips about the ingredients used in Frito-Lay products. The only action that is required by the consumer is to scan the barcode with their smartphone to immediately view the information.

Other taste-testing events using pop-up "lounges" are now being seen in airlines. To encourage passengers to buy in-flight meals, airlines are bringing taste tests to the streets. Australian airlines used street teams on street corners in Washington, D.C., to pour samples of its "Jet Fuel" coffee to passing pedestrians. They are also highlighting the taste of their airline food by using chefs from their catering company to distribute a type of sweet Bundt cake, known as *guglhupf*, to New Yorkers with a sweet tooth. Other planned promotions include handing out chocolate and schnitzel. Air France turned a truck into a kitchen and equipped it with chefs from their catering company. The varied culinary delights distributed included crepes with ham, chicken, and mushrooms, a French version of shepherd's pie, and various macaroons and *petit fours* desserts. In an August 4, 2011, online *New York Times* article by Mickey Meece titled "Ground-Level Tasting of the Best Food in the Sky," Raymond Kollu, the founder of *airlinetrends .com*, reports that "[a]s people are bombarded with marketing messages, real life interaction with products and brands has become increasingly valuable for airlines to get their message across" (Meece, 2011, p. 2).

According to the same article, other airlines such as Delta have stationed their Sky360 lounges at sporting events and film and food festivals. Southwest Airlines refers to its pop-up locations as "porches," which often include porch swings and rocking chairs, where interested pedestrians can sit a while and try a few delicacies prepared by Wichcraft catering chef Tom Colicchio.

Before pop-up stores took to the streets, they commonly utilized unoccupied space in local malls that featured temporary signage and shelving. Today, signage is professionally done and features colorful, well-designed displays that look more stable than temporary. The most common forms of temporary storefronts encountered by consumers are the kiosks they see in their local malls. These are usually stocked with the brand products and manned by a single retailer, who asks passersby if they would like to try their hair extensions, body oil, or the latest toy. In the past, brands such as Toys 'R' Us and Borders Books, to name just a few, cashed in on the growing popularity of the pop-up, slowly overcoming its negative image.

These temporary storefronts work because there is little overhead and they can effectively reach a designated target audience when they are in a mall, presumably in a buying mood and environment. This type of pop-up is also a great way to encourage trial, build awareness, or reintroduce a reinvented brand. The one-to-one contact with the target personalizes any promotion as well as encouraging feedback.

Guerrilla Marketing Soars Above the Crowds

Airborne Advertising. Guerrilla marketing events do not need to be firmly planted on the ground when there is so much unused air space available for promotion. To take advantage of that blank canvas, LivingSocial, an online deal-of-the-day company abandoned the Internet to stand out in the skyline by using aerial advertising to spell out "Dollar Lunch Day."

This low cost promotional vehicle, also known as *skywriting*, uses exhaust from a plane (in the case of LivingSocial's advertising, they used 5 planes) to create white puffy letters. These mega-sized messages are difficult to ignore as there is no page to turn or remote to click. Lasting anywhere from five minutes to an hour, on a clear day these messages can be seen up to 30 miles away. Letters are around a mile tall, and depending on the length of the message, can be almost 15 miles in length.

Other brands that have used aerial advertising include Sony Pictures, which used banners towed by small aircraft to promote the premier of their film *The Smurfs*. During the 2011 Grammy Awards, the Tequila Avion brand used aerial banners for its brand launch with the slogan, "Taste Elevated," as well as skywriting that could be seen by Grammy watchers.

To be readable, banners need to be around 50 feet tall and 100 feet long. Since most aerial advertising appears above beaches, products that celebrate summer tend to be the most advertised. However, Oregon-based Rouge Federal Credit Union decided to tow a banner that read "Cruisin 4 Great Rates" over a four-day antique car show. Their first foray into the sky was so successful, the resulting business raised nine times what was initially spent on the ad campaign.

Other aerial advertising uses hot air balloons. These colorful vehicles offer a message featuring 360-degree coverage. Airship or blimp advertising has been around for almost a hundred years, with the Goodyear Tires and Met Life ships as the most recognizable examples. Many of these air balloons now can scroll digital messages or video as well as showcase traditional logos. Aerial advertising is a great way to reach large numbers of people, it's inexpensive, and usually generates an enormous amount of social chatter.

In its role as a support vehicle, guerrilla marketing is a great way to showcase a key consumer benefit, or remind, launch, relaunch, or reinforce existing advertising efforts. Logos and other recognizable images can reach the consumer when projected onto a surface, placed in the sky, and displayed on the sides of buildings. Corporate images can now be projected in so many ways that a company can display their message as a handout, or an item you can sit on, carry around, or drink out of, to name just a few. Spectacular promotions can create jaw-dropping and awe-inspiring memories, and treasure hunts and product drops can create engaging interactive events.

Chapter 3 Exercises

1. Working in the same or new groups and using the creative brief from Chapter 2 that was developed for a national brand, determine what type—or whether—any type of guerilla marketing can be employed in the campaign.

2. What visual/verbal direction will accomplish the directives laid out in both the marketing plan and creative brief?

3. Groups deciding against using any type of guerrilla marketing must defend their position based on information found in both documents.

4. The group's decision-making process and final creative choice must be presented to the class or to the marketing team.

5. Repeat the process with the creative brief for the small local business selected in Chapter 2.

Memory Box

Guerrilla Marketing

Street Marketing

Street Team

Grassroots

Cross-Promotion

Stealth Marketing

Pop-Up Stores

Aerial Advertising

Covert Marketing

Ambient Marketing

Experiential Marketing

4

The Alternative Use of
Traditional Media Vehicles

This chapter explores how traditional media does not have to reach the target in a traditional way. Marketers and advertisers are finding new, engaging, and interactive ways to use both print and broadcast vehicles.

Traditional Media Vehicles
Are No Longer Traditional

The reports surrounding the demise of traditional media are more speculation than fact. No matter how all-encompassing the digital age becomes, no consumer can spend all their time online. It's not a matter of choosing between social, nontraditional, or traditional vehicles but choosing the right vehicles to reach the target, successfully promote the brand, and still incorporate social components into the visual/verbal message. Traditional media helps advertisers both to lay the foundation for the message they want the target to hear, and also control the content. So, when consumers do go online they are sharing information with friends and family, not only about the brand but repeating advertised facts they found relevant.

A traditional message can automatically become social when a creative campaign (e.g., the Old Spice campaign, the Apple versus PC guy promotion, or almost any Super Bowl commercial of the last several decades) gets the target talking freely about the brand, giving it more exposure and credibility. A consumer who repeatedly sings or hums a brand's jingle or uses its tagline in everyday conversation inadvertently becomes the brand's mouthpiece, helping to keep the brand message top of mind. Rena Bernstein, in a 2010 online article, "Integrate social media with traditional advertising for higher returns," wrote,

> Balancing the free-form messaging of social media with the control, consistency and mass reach of traditional media can offer the best of both worlds. Today the focus needs to be on building an opt-in audience in order to create community, foster loyalty and generate conversations. (Bernstein, 2010, p.1)

One of the best examples of a brand successfully using social media conversations to promote a brand was Trident Chewing Gum. After receiving permission, Trident prominently featured unsolicited tweets posted by consumers about their newest gum, Trident Layers, in a full page *USA Today* advertisement. Using consumers' own words or testimonials gives the message more credibility since they were not sought out through traditional research efforts but were posted freely by avid, unbiased fans.

Research Confirms the Relevancy of Traditional Media to Consumers

Numerous studies over the last several years have consistently found that all forms of traditional media are still relevant to both advertisers and consumers, with many ads leaving a more positive impression than those encountered when using digital venues. A study conducted by Yankelovich in association with Sequent Partners, "When Advertising Works," appeared in a June 18, 2008, online *New York Times* article by Stuart Elliot titled "Traditional Media Not Dead Yet for Marketing, Study Says." The study confirmed the relevance of traditional media, finding that 56% of survey respondents believed that ads seen on traditional media left a more positive impression after viewing. Only 31% reported the same feelings after viewing ads on digital devices (Elliot, 2008).

Researchers believed the results reflected the mood consumers were in when using the different media. Those using traditional vehicles were more relaxed and responsive to the messages. On the other hand, when using digital media devices consumers were busier and often had to wade through annoying pop-ups and links to find an answer or solve a problem. Other results found traditional media, especially television ads, were more memorable to consumers and thus more likely to increase the chance of sharing the content via word of mouth.

Additional research presented in an August 1, 2011 online *Advertising Age* article by Stephen Kraus and Bob Shullman called "Among Affluent

Americans, Print Media Is Tops," points out that even the difficult to reach 18- to 34-year-old consumer, the heaviest user group of digital media, turn for information to traditional vehicles more often than digital. Results showed that

- 88% read magazines in print, followed by 35% who read them online.
- Newspapers showed the greatest amount of experimentation, with 70% reading newspapers in print form versus 54% who read them online.
- 94% view video content on television, followed by 35% who view on computers.
- 93% read websites on computers, followed by 38% who read website content on smartphones.

Knowing When to Use Traditional Media

Beyond their significance to the target, the choice to use traditional vehicles in any campaign depends on the marketing and communication goals to be accomplished, the brand's life cycle stage, and whether the product or service advertised is a rational or emotional purchase. Additional concerns include target media use and determining the best media platform to showcase the visual/verbal message. Before employing traditional media or any combination of vehicles, agencies and clients alike need to understand the specific message, the location of the target, and the brand's current perception. If the goal is to build brand awareness and image for a new or reinvented brand, consider using television. Radio is a great publicity vehicle that can generate interest and get the brand in the target's hand via on-site promotional events. Newspapers are great retail sales vehicles that research shows consumers still turn to for coupons and information on sales, and magazines are a great place to inform, find interactive advertising, and further enhance a company's image.

The new age of print and TV ads can now ask consumers to: 1) interact with the message by scanning an ad with their cell phones, 2) go to a website, 3) open and/or fold an ad, 4) hold it up to the light to view the message, 5) use an enclosed pair of 3D glasses to view the ad, and 6) go one step further and encourage readers to eat the pages of the ad, to name just a few. Because all consumers experience traditional vehicles similarly it is easier to ensure the quality than with the use of digital vehicles. Digital vehicles, such as mobile and the Internet are dependent on the age of the consumer's equipment and the speed of the Internet connection to determine how the message reaches the target and their ability to interact with it.

A brand's life cycle stage determines what needs to be said and where it will be seen or heard. New brands may employ traditional vehicles to build both brand awareness and brand image. Brands in their maintenance stage may also employ traditional vehicles as reminder options. Reinvented brands find that the ability to frequently repeat a message helps to educate and inform. Nontraditional or new age vehicles may be used to distribute coupons, induce trial, enhance awareness to a niche audience, get the brand into the target's hands, or announce or direct the target to something first introduced through traditional outlets.

Brands that fall under a *rational purchase* or those used on a day-to-day basis by the majority of the population such as food, cleaning products, and toiletries should consider employing traditional media. The additional use of nontraditional media vehicles can add to the effectiveness of traditional media by offering free samples or employing the use of demonstrations that feature, to name just a few, sound, smell, or taste tests to prove a point. *Emotional purchases* such as jewelry, expensive cars, or digital equipment are purchases that do not sustain life, but they may enhance it. This type of purchase can often benefit from the additional exposure and image enhancement traditional media can bring. As a support vehicle, nontraditional media can deliver a more personalized form of advertising to a smaller niche audience. This one-on-one interaction lends itself to more alternative options in order to tailor the message directly to the target's lifestyle and needs.

Knowing what vehicles will capture and hold the target's attention is also critical. Developing the correct media mix requires special care and research since placement is based on the target audience watching a specific program, listening to a specific kind of music, or picking up and reading a specific magazine or newspaper. Because of this, media often eats up a large portion of a brand's overall advertising budget. Ultimately the choice of vehicle(s), placement, and how often the message is seen depends on these resources. Because of this, it is important the media team choose the right combination and number of vehicles to reach the largest percentage of the target audience.

Successfully mixing traditional and nontraditional media vehicles together also requires a thorough understanding of the visual/verbal message and how it can be innovatively delivered to the target. Most campaigns today use a diverse number of traditional and nontraditional media vehicles. However, depending on the brand, target, budget, and the product or service, other campaigns may not use traditional vehicles at all, and instead will employ only one type of vehicle or concentrate all resources on nontraditional media vehicles.

There are many products and services on the market that do not need the mass exposure traditional media delivers, either because their market is small or because of budget restrictions. Smaller businesses, in particular, may not be able to afford traditional media vehicles and should look toward alternative media options such as public relations, the Internet, mobile, social, or more visual options such as point of purchase displays, sponsorships, transit advertising, or any number of other nontraditional options. Before deciding on the appropriate media mix, it is important to know what attributes each vehicle does or does not bring to a campaign. Let's take a look at the pros and cons surrounding the use of traditional media.

Identifying a Medium's Strengths and Weaknesses Reinforces and Highlights the Visual/Verbal Message

Before deciding where traditional media fits in a campaign, it is important that both marketers and the advertising teams understand how each vehicle can positively enhance or negatively affect a campaign's message. Let's examine both its capabilities and limitations.

Traditional Media Strengths

1. Reach. It reaches a large mass audience—great for generic products used by a large percentage of the population, such as deodorant or shampoo.

2. Targetability. It has the ability to target by section, hobby, music, or programming. Advertising can be attached to programming or appear in print articles that the target is sure to watch or read.

3. Creative. It is great at building and maintaining awareness and image. Because these vehicles can saturate the airwaves with entertaining commercials, and inundate the pages of magazines, they are a great way to gain attention.

4. Accepted. It is better received than advertising that appears in electronic vehicles. Research has shown consumers still like to see commercials or ads and use them to further their research efforts.

Traditional Media Weaknesses

1. Mass Media. It uses a generic message and cannot target specific individuals.

2. Cost. It is often more expensive than nontraditional vehicles and can be very expensive to advertise in the majority of traditional vehicles.

3. Media Saturation. Fragmentation makes it difficult to reach the intended target audience. The target is no longer getting their advertising from only a small number of vehicles.

4. Message Life. Most vehicles have a short life span. If you miss the paper today or the broadcast, you have to wait to see the message again.

Traditional vehicles are currently experiencing an evolutionary period and this is remaking how the consumers experience and interact with advertising. Research continues to bear out the relevancy of traditional vehicles to the consumer. By incorporating more types of digital devices into the message, such as a web address or *quick response* (QR) code, a company can strengthen the target's level of engagement with the ad by becoming more interactive. Traditional media use is no longer a passive activity. Its new role is to involve the target in the message, and in many cases make it easier for the target to purchase from their recliner or desk chair, twenty-four hours a day, seven days a week. The creative team's overall knowledge of the inherent traits in each of the varied vehicles helps them to match media choice to the target's needs, wants, lifestyle, values, and beliefs.

Let's take a look at the changing faces of traditional media.

Newspaper Goes Digital

It's no surprise to anyone that newspapers around the country are struggling to attract both readers and advertisers mainly due to its slow response to adapt to technology and demographic changes.

The recession and a dwindling readership over the last several years are causing newspapers around the country to cut costs in order to increase revenue. Steps include layoffs, raising prices, and reducing the overall size of its pages, to name just a few. In many cities, in an attempt to retain advertisers, newspapers are allowing advertising for the first time ever below the fold, or on the bottom half of their front covers.

In an attempt to resuscitate revenue and compete with twenty-four hour news shows, newspapers have moved their pages online. Most online editions are currently free to the public with profits generated from advertising and search engine optimization (SEO). However, to economically survive, many others, both large and small, have found it necessary to make the move toward charging for online subscriptions.

With the often large number of special interest sections that newspapers offer (e.g., business, lifestyle, sports, travel, etc.), it is important that they feature ads matching the editorial style of the section, similar to what special interest magazines have done for decades. However, this becomes difficult in sections covering hard news that might be discussing the latest local robbery or murder. In this case, using research that builds on the reader's past preferences not only helps determine exposure to future stories but advertising placement. For example, if someone online recently clicked on the real estate section, or a restaurant ad, future ads and story content could address these interests by offering links to more information or coupons. Personalization of content helps hold the target's attention, keeping them engaged for a longer period of time. Search engines can also control the types of headlines each searcher encounters. If someone searches for U.S. economic indicators for their hometown, a search engine could link them to a story. While catching up on the latest news they could also see links to other similar news stories as well as additional options such as sports, business, or lifestyle stories in tandem with a few restaurant ads.

Each click highlights additional options and by assessing repeated use can successfully lay out a map of the reader's interests. Successful retail sites, such as Amazon, serve as great examples of how to customize and use past purchase patterns to encourage purchases. Profitable newspapers will not only continue to rely on advertising to generate revenue but also SEO. By placing more emphasis on search engine results, the content viewed can be customized and advertising can be personalized and targeted to ensure not only a nonintrusive delivery but a correct match to the target's interests.

Beyond online options, newspapers are employing various types of nontraditional media to generate interest. For example, to attract attention and become more interactive, *The Sacramento Bee* redesigned its newsstands to not only dispense newspapers, but talk. Every time a newspaper is purchased, the dispenser delivers a 15-second prerecorded message. The promotional "news talk" can cover anything from the day's top headlines, a message from the editor, and of course, advertising.

Ford Motor Company incorporated an interactive device in both the *New York Times* newspaper and in mobile ads to promote its Edge Crossover model that included a 2-D, QR code sent directly to the target's cell phones, giving readers additional access to the paper's articles on technology and fashion. Every time readers used the code to link to the articles, Ford had banner ads that appeared at the top of each mobile page. Those without a camera phone could text a specific code for each article appearing on the mobile site.

Interactive devices and online access give newspapers a much needed 21st-century facelift, and according to research, at the same time, it has not lost its relevancy to consumers. In an April 13, 2011, *Media Daily News* online article titled "Newspaper Ads Still Guide Shopping," Erik Sass cites the latest poll for the Newspaper Association of America, indicating that newspaper advertising is still the place consumers go for sales and coupons.

The Newspaper Association of America study (NAA-Magid) titled "How America Shops and Spends 2011," also reported that

52 percent of adults surveyed identified newspaper as the most important medium informing their purchase decision. Seventy-nine percent recalled taking some kind of action in response to newspaper advertising in the preceding month." Results also showed a diverse range of use, including "clipping a

coupon (54%); buying a product (46%); and visiting a website to get more information. (37%). (NAA-Magid as cited in Sass, 2011, paras. 3, 4)

Previous results also acknowledged that newspaper advertising was successful at encouraging consumers to try new products, switch brands, or purchase a more expensive brand.

Finally, newspaper is still a relatively inexpensive way for small businesses to reach their target with a coupon offer or special sale to quickly generate revenue and build goodwill by interacting with those who respond to the message. Because of the short message life, newspaper ads have a sense of urgency other traditional vehicles lack. Coupon devices and sales are often valid for only a short time so consumers must act quickly to cash in on the best deals.

Of all the traditional vehicles, newspaper's fate is the most in doubt. No one is entirely certain what the future holds. An aging baby boomer generation, the heaviest readers of newspaper, and an ever-shrinking acceptance rate by the younger demographic continue to retard growth and limit options.

Magazines Engage Readers With Interactive Options

Magazine ads reflect image, define trends, and popularize fads. Its colorful imagery and often copy-heavy pages educate and entice loyal readers who elect to receive their favorite publication either through subscriptions or by picking them up at local newsstands. A feature exclusive to magazines is their long life span. Because magazines are so personalized, content is read and held onto or passed along to others with the same or similar interests. Like all traditional vehicles, magazines can be broken down into special interest categories, making them a highly targetable medium.

Advertising should not only reflect the brand's image but visually and verbally tie it to the target's self image, lifestyle, and interests as well as try to mirror the target's social and personal values. In order to successfully match visual/verbal content to overall lifestyle, it is important that the advertising match the editorial style of the magazine in which it appears. For example, do it yourself (DIY) enthusiasts see ads for paint and tools, while avid gardeners see advertising for fertilizer and lawn mowers. These built-in interests of the target can be further expanded by showcasing the brand in the advertising in new or unusual ways: through imaginative photographs, illustrations, or graphics, lengthy fact-based or thought-provoking copy, or by including some type of interactive device that not only engages but encourages trial or further research. Even creative and unique headlines can capture and hold the attention of today's time-starved consumer, such as the headlines seen in *Bon Appetit* magazine that encouraged readers to "Bite Me."

Whether or not to use magazines often depends on budget and time restrictions. Budget issues such as pricey photo shoots, the hiring of spokespersons or development of character representatives, model searches, and printing costs, make it an expensive member of the overall media mix. Lengthy print/production schedules, often as much as 60 to 90 days in advance of the magazine's publication date make it difficult for ads to adapt to social, political, or economic trends in a timely manner. For example, ads that are tied to movie or car launches are traditionally planned a year or more in advance of publication so marketers must often keep innovations under wraps to adapt to publication and production schedules. As a rule, magazines are a great choice if dealing with a niche audience, selling a generic or rational product to a mass audience, or promoting a brand that fulfills an emotional need or want.

Creatively, the often simple but elegant visual approach of magazines sets a mood, a style, and an attitude that allows the product to visually speak and/or demonstrate use or style. The diverse visual/verbal options magazines offer gives the design team a colorful pallet in which to accomplish the stated objectives and strategically promote the key consumer benefit. It is a great vehicle for launching new or repositioned products or those that have a truly unique selling proposition. They are a great choice for consumer-based, emotionally charged strategies that focus on image, lifestyle, and brand identity.

Depending on the product to be sold or the service offered, the tone of "voice" that the advertising adopts for a magazine helps to creatively shape the visual/verbal message. For example, informational ads can demonstrate use and engage; how-to ads solve problems through demonstrations. Testimonials are great relationship builders, and tones such as humor, sex, or fantasy help flesh out the product's personality in a way that not only captures the target's attention but also encourages further discussion.

Word-of-mouth discussions can also be ignited by including some type of interactive device such as free samples, varied types of folds, order forms, pop-ups, and QR codes. Condé Nast magazines, for example, want to entice readers to use their smartphones to photograph the barcodes that are strategically placed throughout their magazines. Each code offers the reader something of value such as additional content, clues to a contest or sweepstakes, information about giveaways, and any coupons or other discounts sponsored by either the magazines or advertisers.

Figure 4.1

The inability of magazines to create a dialog with the target suggests that it should be mixed with nontraditional vehicles that are better at initiating, building, and maintaining relationships. Whether using a rational or emotional appeal, magazines are a great choice to announce, launch, or remind the target about a new, existing, or reinvented product or service. Because the majority of products advertised are expensive, the target will often use additional media vehicles to research a desired product or service before making an informed buying decision. Consumer magazines that cater to a smaller niche audience might consider mixing magazine advertising with the Internet, e-mail messages, mobile texting, or direct mail, to name just a few. If the product is more rational and mainstream, a suitable media mix might consist of national television, newspaper, out-of-home (outdoor or transit), samples, or sales promotion. Successfully mixing diverse vehicles together requires a strong visual/verbal message that can be adapted to various vehicles without sacrificing message quality. Honda Motors, to creatively promote their new CR-Z model, used an inventive way to attract attention and interactively engage the target in a memorable way by using a media mix that included both traditional and alternative vehicles as well as interactive devices.

To capture the attention of those difficult to reach 18- to 34-year-olds, Honda harnessed the imaginative power of 3-D technology to promote the launch of their new CR-Z on their website and in their cinema and print ads. Taking 3-D to an even bigger level, they also incorporated it into a billboard featured in New York's Times Square. To ensure pedestrians could view the ad, Honda used street teams to hand out the special glasses needed to immediately experience the projected message. Other billboards and displays will feature the new CR-Z, and an on-site Sony racing simulator is planned where pedestrians can interact with the car while playing Sony's "Grand Turismo 5" video game.

Ads featured in magazines also use 3-D technology. Each issue comes with cobranded 3-D glasses and features a 3-D phantaglyph or elevated images that appear to levitate on the page. According to Honda, in a September 9, 2010, *Marketing Daily* online article, "Honda campaign shows how opposites attract," phantaglyph technology "makes images more dimensional and realistic-looking. Instead of floating off the page, the CR-Z looks like it is sitting on the page" (Greenburg, 2010, para. 6).

Additionally for the campaign, Honda is also planning to do a CR-Z takeover of such sites as *Sports Illustrated* and the *Washington Post*, develop a game for Facebook called "Car Town," as well as produce an interactive digital brochure and downloadable mobile app.

Allowing the target to experience an ad not only increases memorability but extends its life span longer than ever before as consumers share their experiences both virally and through on-going word-of-mouth discussions. Let's take a look at a few very creative examples from the new and innovative age of magazine advertising.

Magazine Advertising Goes Interactive

For most automobile brands it's difficult to show car safety in a magazine ad; the best they can do is talk about it and describe it. But Peugeot knew that was no longer enough. They understood they had to show how safe the Peugeot 408 actually was and they chose to do it with an airbag and not one, not two, but a three page magazine ad. Placed on the right side of the magazine, the first ad features a black-and-white visual showing a front view of the car with copy enclosed in a circle that reads: "Hit this ad hard to find out why the Peugeot 408 provides a lot more safety." A hefty blow to the page activates the inflatable airbag on the following page spread. As it fills up with air the page automatically turns almost all the way over by itself. Once opened the little airbag sits securely on the steering wheel of the vehicle. The two page spread features a black-and-white visual of the inside of the car. Copy on the passenger side reads: "6 airbags with 8 protection points to absorb any impact." As an additional safety measure, magazines were shipped in individual boxes to keep the airbags from going off prematurely during delivery.

The free press advocacy group, Reporters Without Borders ran several 4-color magazine ads that featured a large visual of well-known dictators and a quick response code (QR) to bring attention to media censorship in Iran, Russia, and Libya. All readers had to do was scan the code with their cell phones and then place the phone over the dictators mouth to activate the ad. In the phone's viewfinder a real mouth would show that speaks to the viewer. Predictably, it is not the dictator's voice we hear but that of a journalist.

Another creative ad on the promotion of green energy backed up its message by actually using solar power to illustrate their copy. This new age magazine ad initially showcased a black-and-white sketch of a meadow that used informative copy to tell the reader what actions to take: "Look at the page facing the sunlight." For those who followed the instructions carefully and held the sketch up to the sun, it exploded into a full-color ad. The top three-quarters of the page showcases a blue sky, with the additional line of copy that reads: "And see how you can benefit from it." The bottom quarter shows a meadow with a fence in the background and big red poppies in the foreground. In the lower right corner is copy that reads, "Shikun & Binui Solaria produces green energy using natural sunlight, to help preserve our planet," followed by the company logo and the tagline, "Because the future is around us."

Carlsberg beer shows its target how to use the ad as a bottle opener. The black-and-white ad features small sketches and little copy. The background is all white with black copy that reads, "Probably the best ad in the world." Five small sketches show the reader how to fold the ad into a bottle opener. The only color is the green logo located on the bottom right of the ad.

No one could ever accuse Volkswagen of creating mundane advertising. Their newest message for VW South Africa offers a magazine ad you can actually eat. To showcase the Golf R's road-eating acceleration, the copy informs us to "Eat the Road. Seriously, Eat It." This is about as enticing as it gets in a magazine. The double spread ad uses three-quarters of the page to show a close up of the road and three white dashes like those you would encounter when driving. The lower quarter shows the car, logo, and tag. To ensure you know what you're eating, the ingredients are listed on the side of the page as "glutinous rice flour, water, salt, propylene glycol, FD&C colour, glycerin."

A double page 4-color ad for Wonder Bra caught everybody's attention with a close-up visual of a model wearing the bra. Attached to the ad was a string that holds the cups together. Readers can pull this string to see the bras push up capabilities in action. As the string is pulled it actually pushes the pages and the model's breasts closer together. Sometimes a single visual, with props, is worth a thousand words.

How about test driving a print ad? A Norwegian print ad for Volkswagen used a double page ad, featuring a visual of a long, curving road that passes through a housing area. Volkswagen wanted to show not only how innovative their cars were but their advertising as well, by featuring the first test drive through a print ad. Volkswagen believes innovations must be experienced so they created an app that allowed readers to do just that, with a little help from their cell phones and a magazine ad. Readers are asked to first download an app in order to take a test drive. Next, all they have to do is hold their phones over the road and drive. Enthusiasts who want to do more than read about a feature could actually experience three of the car's features, including cruise control, lane assist, and adaptive lights. In lane-assist mode, drivers could feel the phone vibrate if they got too close to the side of the road. In the adaptive lights mode, readers could experience how the car's lights adapted to the curve of the road, and in the adaptive cruise control system, readers could experience how the vehicle automatically maintained a safe distance between itself and the car in front.

To bring attention to deforestation, Greenpeace used a three-page ad to get its point across. The single page ad was a half-inch shorter than the other pages in the magazine. The page featured a visual of a tree. Because of the short page the viewer could see the bottom of the trunk peeking through from the next page. When the reader turned the page both pages of the spread were all white. The right hand page featured the logo in the upper right corner and the only visual no longer showed a tree but only the stump we glimpsed before turning the page.

In order to show the thinness of the new Macbook Pro, Apple Inc. used a spread that when turned on its side looked like an open laptop computer. That is "ultra thin."

Arcor Bubble Gum advertised in a Brazilian magazine that also used a spread showing a close-up of a man's face. When the spread was opened, a big pink 3-D crepe paper circle or bubble popped open over the man's mouth.

Lastly, many magazines are bringing sight, sound, and motion to advertising on computer tablets by creating their own iPad applications. Apps like the one created by *The New Yorker,* for example, allow magazines to take engagement one step further by incorporating a tablet's unique appurtenances to both content and advertising. Consider the following:

1. Read aloud to the user and content can be seen in action through video options, photo galleries, and links to websites.

2. Assist reader/viewers with content; clear instructions keep the consumer from missing anything.

3. Create new material; this is not a place for a TV commercial.

4. Tell a story. Visuals are more memorable than even the best copy. Show how a product works, new uses for an old product, accessories, and so on. Making the product or service useful makes it a must-have.

5. Make it relevant. Give more specifics about colors, sizes and pricing; do not offer just a link without enticements.

In an effort to retain readers and maintain relevancy, magazines are finding ways to excite consumers with technology. Accordingly, just as in the case of newspapers, research by Deloitte has found that 70% of all Americans prefer reading a printed version of their favorite magazine, even though they can find an online version.

So Why Use Radio Advertising?

Radio has been referred to as the theater of the mind because its verbal-only format requires the listener to visualize what the copy is saying or imagine using the product or service. The portability of radio makes it a great medium to reach a target while they are on hold on the telephone, driving, shopping, or even while waiting to see the dentist. Consumer inattentiveness requires that the message be simple and to the point, well written, informative, and with relatable scenarios tailored to the target. The more personalized the message, the easier it is for the target to envision the brand in their lives or as the solution to their current problem.

Brands that can be identified by their jingles, spokespersons, character representatives, or their interactive storylines are especially memorable as the target replays them in their heads or hums them in the shower, thus extending the brand's message beyond the 30-second spot. Identifiers such as unusual sounds or voices that help define what the product does or help exemplify the brand's image are also memorable. Spots that include some type of interactive and/or engaging activity can also help capture and hold the target's attention such as contests, sweepstakes, or local events, creating ongoing storylines, producing coupons accessible through the website or mobile phone, or participating in remote broadcasts. Each promotional activity increases awareness and works to get the brand into the target's hands.

Small business owners will find radio a relatively inexpensive vehicle with enormous reach that can be customized to ignite or renew interest in a current campaign and include local celebrities, special events, and sales. It is one of the few mediums that allow marketers to tap into a community's values and reflect its local flavor and overall tone of voice. Its variety makes it a great sales, promotional, and entertainment venue.

Similar to magazines, radio is highly targetable due to the diverse types of radio formats (e.g., news, talk, hip-hop, rock, jazz, or country-western), making it easier to reach the target with a customized message. Additionally, messages featuring a strong key consumer benefit can be easily adapted to reflect, reinforce, or enhance messages used in other media as well as cost-efficiently increase exposure and the frequency of the ads.

Successful targeting also details the length the radio spot needs to be to get the message out, the time of day the message is delivered and the actual words of the message. The typical radio spot is 30- to 60-seconds long. If you have a brand that is well-known to the target, consider using a 30-second spot. If introducing a new or reinvented brand, a 60-second spot allows enough time to inform listeners about the features and benefits and how and where to obtain the brand or service. It is important today that all messages, regardless of the length, focus not only on educating the target but informing, building awareness, and creating some type of desired action.

Radio's reach is greatest during the morning and afternoon drive times, so take advantage of this semi-captive audience to remind the intended target to drop off their dry cleaning before work, and while commuting, get them thinking about dinner. Tasty copy that can get their stomachs growling accompanied by enticing sound effects can effectively alter the driver's route home.

Distracted, bored consumers will not tune into a radio spot if it does not strategically deliver the key consumer benefit within the first three seconds. It is important that copy be engaging and creative in order to set the visual stage for capturing the target's attention. It is equally important that each message reflect the target's personal taste and style, making it easier to match the copy to the their lifestyle. One great way to engage imagination is to incorporate the brand into intriguing slice-of-life vignettes, turning each commercial into a minidramatization that keeps listeners tuning in. These soap-opera type messages create ongoing storylines reminiscent of old fashioned radio programming. Bury clues to a contest, sweepstakes, or scavenger hunt in the copy and you have a great way to hold a listener's attention and to build anticipation for the next storyline. Whether using drama or a comedic format, writing must be visual, interesting, and creative. It is also a great way to give character representatives or spokespersons a voice and personality that can be reflected consistently throughout the storylines.

Another approach allows the local radio personalities to do the talking for the brand. Their easy unrehearsed delivery can project the brand in a more realistic and engaging light and help to personalize the brand. For example, Sears used local radio personalities to extend their "Wake-Up Call" campaign that was currently running on television. Local DJ's from around the country were tapped to participate in the Wake-Up Call experience by phoning preselected listeners and awarding them a prize or gift certificate courtesy of Sears.

Beyond the advertised message another way to bring attention to a brand is to sponsor the news, weather, sports, or traffic reports. To keep listeners from changing the channel this is a great time to announce one-time or limited sales or special events that the brand is holding. Brands that sponsor events not only receive free on-air mentions but a great deal of positive public relations. Not all events are created equally, so be sure the event is heavily attended and popular with the target audience.

As a support vehicle, radio is a great way to reinforce a message heard or seen elsewhere or to introduce a brand to potential new users. Marketers looking to reach a particular target will find radio a great launching point for their event. For example, The Crowne Plaza Hotels and Resorts announced a promotion directed at couples who wanted to get married on 11/11/11. The campaign used a diverse media mix that included radio, social media, and sales promotions to introduce a contest asking couples across the country to write their personal love story. To increase their chances to win, the entrants were encouraged to get their friends and family to vote for them online. The hotel chain kicked off the promotion on radio with the hotel's spokesman appearing on numerous morning news and popular drive-time hours across the country.

Marketers include radio in their media mix because it's relatively inexpensive, can effectively reach a large chunk of their target. An ad can keep messages timely and be produced and aired quickly—often within twenty-four hours, or less if read directly by a disc jockey (DJ).

Just as with other traditional vehicles, radio is changing how they do business. Like print, radio is being hit hard not only by the economy but digital music devices like satellite radio, iPods, and MP3 players; to ensure a satisfactory return on investment marketers are looking for some type of *return on engagement* (ROE). Relatively new to radio advertising, ROE is all about developing a message that asks the target to do something (active) rather than just sitting back and listening (passive). The goal is to encourage the target to interact with a product or service through some type of additional research, make a visit to a brick and mortar store, witness a demonstration, or make a purchase. The more interactive opportunities there are between the target and the brand, the better the chance to generate positive word of mouth.

Other changes include the use of radio to drive the target to the brand's website. A growing number of stations regularly place their programming on the Internet in order to reach a greater number of local and national listeners. This increases the number of people who hear the advertised message and makes it easy for them to respond to the message with a single click.

It is important to point out that radio is not the medium that will close the sale or carry a campaign, but it is still relevant to marketers according to Chris Schembri, AT&T's vice president of media services. In a March 18, 2009, *Advertising Age* online article called "Opportunities for Selling More Radio Ads Still Out There," Schembri says, "Radio will always have a place within our media mix, but the challenge will be to keep it innovative enough for us to socialize the value of radio within our media mix." Mr. Schembri went on to say, "What I'm really looking forward to are seeing some really good ideas from the radio groups to connect technology with our brands" (Hampp, 2009, p. 1).

Television and Radio Jingles

You can't talk about broadcast vehicles without discussing jingles and how they are used by marketers to promote their products or services. The first decade of the new millennium saw a decrease in the number of jingles used to praise a brand's virtues. Instead, brands were using pop music from the 60s, 70s, and 80s. Still other brands used music from up-and-coming bands to correlate the brand to an image or situation. Today, the use of the song jingle is back, helping to tie brand advantages and performance to a catchy, easy to remember tune.

All a good jingle has to do is sing the brand's praises, repeat or spell out the brand's name, and be catchy. If you've ever caught yourself singing a brand's representative song, such as the original *Free Credit Report.com* jingle, you understand the marketing significance of a catchy tune. Alka Seltzer's long running jingle perfectly explained the sounds of the product and Oscar Meyer wants you to spell its name whenever you think of the luncheon meat, baloney. Original music can define a brand for decades to come; it's real, it's honest, it's interactive, and it's usually very simple to remember. A good catchy jingle has equity.

Television Involves Viewers in the Message

Commercials bore us; usually when a commercial is playing we take a bathroom break, take out the trash, or get a sandwich—anything but waste our time just sitting and absorbing. Our dismissive attitude may have something to do with the fact that we are seeing more and more commercials today than ever before. According to a 2009 *Advertising Age* online article "'Chris Isaak Hour' Makes Debut with New Ad Format," Brian Steinberg tells us, "the amount of airtime devoted by broadcast networks to either commercials or promotions for network shows has risen as high as 15 minutes per hour, and to 16 minutes or more at some cable networks, according to 2007 report from Mindshare, a WPP media-buying concern (Steinberg, 2009, para. 8).

Regardless of the level of bombardment, TV is still considered by consumers as relevant and enticing and the first place they go for news on advertising. Research by Deloitte has found that not only do almost three-quarters of Americans surveyed still watch television, they don't care what device they watch it on. Over 85% said that TV advertising is the most persuasive medium when it comes to making purchasing decisions. The report also showed that nearly three-quarters of American TV watchers are multitasking (i.e., surfing the web, talking on the phone, texting, or instant messaging), while watching their favorite programs. This television attention deficit disorder has led to the term *media convergence*. Here's how this phenomenon works: while watching American Idol, viewers are also texting and/or exchanging comments on Facebook and Twitter about contestants, songs, judges' comments, and so on. Marketers are now taking media convergence into account when they decide to mix mass media vehicles with varying digital technology in order to ensure that the target is getting a synergistic visual/verbal message everywhere they encounter the brand. TV is no longer the last word on the advertised message. It is now the opening shot over the target's bow that then sends them to websites and social media sites for more information. Copy or dialogue may ask them to download a mobile app or use their smartphone to photograph a QR code, all in the name of furthering their knowledge about the brand, or introducing some type of promotion.

Even though television advertising is great for initiating interest, creating awareness, and building or maintaining image, revenue is down. Many consumers are turning to other options to view programming and to keep them entertained, such as DVDs, online games, Hulu, YouTube, and social networking sites. This fractionalization of the target's attention has caused small business owners to cut back on their TV budgets and look to spread the wealth among more, and less expensive options, especially social media and mobile. At the same time, major marketers are increasing their budgets.

Although programming may be losing viewers, television is still considered by marketers as a powerful and wide-reaching vehicle.

Insiders predict that in five years, network television will look completely different than it does today. Primetime hours (8:00–11:00 pm EST) will most likely be shorter and feature programming that is targeted to a more specific audience. Advertising will not only run between breaks but within programming, while the most radical change predicted includes the idea of the networks opening up programming slots to outsiders or even to local programming. Some suggest that eventually network programming will parallel cable programming that is highly targeted to specific groups (e.g., Lifetime to women and Spike to men).

Marketers and their agencies continue to search for the best way to keep consumers entertained while they are watching commercials. One of the most noticeable experiments is to alter the length of commercials in an attempt to find the magic number of seconds that will hold the viewer's attention. Short, 10- to 15-second spots have not been successful, so anticipate longer, more informative ads to be on the rise. Another test puts a new twist on product placement by creating tie-ins with the movie or show currently being watched by the target. To hold consumer's attention a little longer many commercials are mimicking the storylines of the programs selected for ad placement. For example, Target placed ads in the season finale of *Lost* that referred to life on the island. General Motors integrated its brand into the show *Damages*, and Honda used actors from the show *Chuck* to literally drive their brand during commercial breaks. Porsche Cars of North America will use their spots, during the History Channel's *Brad Meltzer's Decoded*, to not only chauffeur cast members from one historical place to another, but will match the program's theme by tracing the historical origins of the Porsche crest. Finally, another automaker has also tapped program content to promote their brand. Toyota featured the Corolla as the hero of their spot when zombies went in for the kill during a commercial break shown during AMC's *The Walking Dead,* by showing up just in time to rescue a couple from becoming dinner. According to a December 20, 2010 online *New York Times* article, "The myth of fast-forwarding past the ads," Brian Stelter comments, "the scene stopped some people from fast-forwarding through the commercial break—and perhaps that was the point" (Stelter, 2010, para. 2).

From its humble beginnings, television has always been popular because it's a great place to tell a good story and reach a mass audience. That's why heavily watched events like the Super Bowl cost marketers $3 million for a 30-second spot. Innovative commercials that capture a multitasking target's attention and prompt them to virally share or talk about the spot around the water cooler are worth their weight in gold to marketers.

Since the inception of TV, how a marketer promotes a brand on television has changed dramatically. But what hasn't changed much over the years is how the message is delivered to individual households—until now, with the arrival of interactive television. Its debut will introduce an even greater way to bring personalized, targeted, database-driven messages to consumers.

According to the Museum of Broadcast Communications, interactive television (iTV)

> represents the convergence of interactive technology and television which allows the exchange of information between the sender and the receiver. Potentially, it offers increased control over programming content by enabling the viewer to immediately respond to the programming—and even alter it. By offering such control, interactive television has the potential to redefine what producers of television and viewers mean by "television" and to redefine communication processes in society. (Constantakis-Valdez, 2009, para. 1)

To increase broadcast interactivity for viewers, several networks are testing new options that can make shows and special events more interactive by using Yahoo Connected. For example, if Showtime is featuring a boxing match, viewers could, in theory, bring up statistics on the boxers, or place a few bets with other viewers. Other shows might offer biographies on the actors or offer a Q&A session. Commercials might allow viewers to pull up statistics, uses, recipes, and so on from their remote controls. Yahoo Connected is built around specially created apps, unlike Google TV, which promises access to the entire Internet via the user's television screen. All interaction takes place via the user's remote control, no touch screen, mouse or keyboard needed.

According to a January 5, 2011 online Adweek article, "Yahoo zeros in on Google's turf with 'connected TV' play," author Mike Shields tells us, "connected TV is more about enhancing TV than displacing it" (Shields, 2011, p. 2).

Available now, other interactive options include the use of *quick response codes* or QR codes. The QR codes allow visitors to quickly and wirelessly connect to websites and view photos or videos from the sponsoring advertiser. The increasingly popular little black-and-white barcodes are no longer exclusive to magazines, posters, and billboards. Using the same technique, all a smartphone user has to do is scan the barcode without ever leaving their seats. Codes embedded in commercials will immediately take viewers to information about a product shown and offer a discount as an added bonus. Brands such as Bluefly (an online clothing company), for example, have created 45-second commercials for Bravo's *The Real*

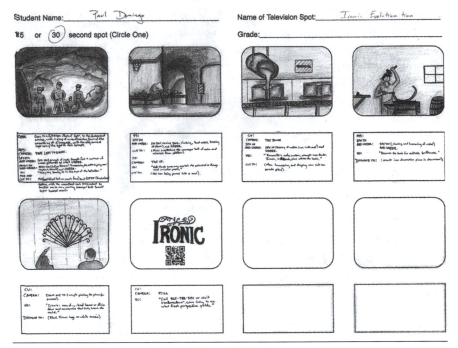

Figure 4.2

Housewives of New York City. Viewers scanning the code will see short interviews with designers and celebrities. Each "closet confession" can last up to five minutes, and earn each viewer $30 off any purchase of $150 or more at *bluefly.com*.

"'We see this as a great way to expand our audience in a measurable way,'" said Bradford Matson, Bluefly's chief marketing officer, quoted in an 2010 *New York Times* online article titled "Bar Codes Add Detail on Items in TV Ads." Mr. Matson goes on to say, "'This is new for us, but we expect our page views to double.'" Bravo's audience "'is very engaged in fashion and pop culture'" (Olson, 2010c, paras. 5, 6).

The use of QR television codes is still in its infancy. Besides Bluefly, only the Weather Channel and HBO have given it a try. The Weather Channel used their code to encourage viewers to keep up with their local weather. HBO used the code in select cities to promote the third season of its vampire series, *True Blood.* To keep the code in character, instead of the traditional black-and-white coloring, the 30-second commercial used a black and red code that sported a drop of blood.

Touted as a way to extend the commercial, television barcodes often offer those who participate a sneak peak or an insider's view of something to do with the brand or show. For example, in Bluefly's commercial visitors could open the closet doors of fashion designers and models.

In the future, as interactive television becomes more commonplace, viewers will be able to click on the product featured in the program via their remote control device or keyboard. They can then decide if they want to immediately purchase, continue their search, or request additional information.

Traditional Forms of Product Placement

With so many commercials running during a single program, marketers are trying to find ways to stand out from the clutter. One way to do this is by placing their brand into a character's hand or portraying the characters actually using the brand. The big difference between this form of product placement and actually tying the message to the program's plot or using characters in commercial breaks is the brand is used more as a prop. For example, to promote its refreshing taste, Snapple is using product placement on the TV show "The Amazing Race," as well as promoting the show on the product's label. Taking the promotion one step further, the two brands cosponsored a contest on Snapple's Facebook site.

The contest is called Snap-a-Snapple and presents fans with varied situations where they can photograph a bottle of the new flavor, Papaya Mango Tea. The first contestant to post for any given challenge will be featured in a "winner's gallery" and be entered for a chance to win $5,000. For anyone else who wants to try the new flavor, Snapple is offering a $1 coupon on its Facebook page.

So what has fueled the growth of product placement? Specifically, 1) traditional advertising methods are less successful at reaching the target audience, 2) crowded commercial breaks, and 3) the emergence of reality television.

The thin line between an intrusive message and an entertaining one is a difficult line to walk. Viewers will tolerate seamless insertion into regular programming; however, a glaring commercial break hurts both the brand's image and program ratings. To be successful, the message must not interrupt a scene but be seamlessly integrated into the action or dialogue. The ability to effortlessly integrate products into entertainment vehicles is becoming a great way for marketers to expand their reach by incorporating nontraditional media into their traditional media mix.

With that said, online programming takes product placement one step further, giving more control to the sponsoring brands. Kmart for example, wants to see more than just its logo in online programs they sponsor. These new branded opportunities allow marketers to have a say in both storylines and scripts. In Kmart's case, characters are required to appear dressed in Kmart fashions. Other brands to dip their toes into this form of sponsorship include Intel, General Motors, and Anheuser-Busch InBev.

Spokespersons or Character Representatives

When picking a visual/verbal mouthpiece for a product or service it is important to choose wisely. The spokesperson's image, good or bad, will reflect on the brand's overall image. Consumers may love them, but marketers know there is always a risk that a celebrity scandal could reflect poorly on a brand. Tarnished stars are often an unwelcome type of publicity for a brand. When Michael Phelps, a spokesperson for several products such as Nike, Speedo, Visa, Subway, and Kellogg's, was photographed smoking marijuana, he damaged more than his own image; this was also the case in Coca-Cola's relationship with Michael Vick, and Gillette and Nike's relationship with Tiger Woods. While some brands stick by their spokespersons in a scandal, others do not.

It is becoming more and more common for companies to have "disgrace insurance" or morality clauses in their contracts, in order to recoup losses in the event that their celebrity endorser become *persona non grata*. Sometimes the negative publicity that surrounds a spokesperson can boost a brand's bottom line. Other times, the apologies may reflect positively on the celebrity but not necessarily on the brand.

Studies tracking the effects of celebrity endorsers have shown that for some brands, sales have risen as much as 20%. In a September 22, 2010, online article for *Advertising Age*, titled "Celebrity endorsements still push product," author Dean Crutchfield tells us,

> There is the issue of overexposure to consider. We receive more than 3,000 commercial images a day and our subconscious absorbs more than 150 images and roughly 30 reach our conscious mind. Therefore, practice has it that if you use a celebrity-endorsement strategy, you dramatically accelerate the potential for your brand to reach the conscious mind of the consumer, especially given research for Weber Shandwick that finds peer endorsement trumps advertising. (Crutchfield, 2010, para. 4)

He goes on to say,

> On the upside, celebrity endorsement has the power to instigate and inspire, enlighten and enrage, entertain and edify the consumer. Its inherent benefits are

that it can be leveraged across multiple channel experiences (and potentially services), cuts through advertising clutter, creates a brand narrative and allows for channel-specific optimization. It's an expensive but easy option for companies, but it should be treated like a marriage with added creative comforts that make the partnership invaluable. (para. 6)

To increase a celebrity's value to both the brand and the target, the celebrity should use the brand, appear to use the brand, or have the brand in some way reflect their image, and the target not only needs to find the brand relevant to their life, but additionally relate to the celebrity endorser.

On the flipside, new research reports show that celebrity ties are largely ineffective, barely moving the bottom line, if at all. Celebrities, in some reports, are taking a backseat as influencers. Trust in advertising today requires a message spread across multiple media vehicles that is delivered by experts, or delivered by friends and family, making the message significantly more believable than if endorsed by a "paid" celebrity. Research also confirms that good ads prevail without the celebrity boost, and ads without a celebrity endorser regularly outperform ads featuring one.

The ads that were rated the worst by consumers usually had a weak message that compounded the consumer's confusion or dislike of the endorser. Bad creative cannot be saved by anyone, nor can a celebrity serve as an effective patch for a poorly constructed ad.

What attributes should be considered when choosing a spokesperson? Consider the following:

1. Be certain that the spokesperson matches and/or can relate to the target audience.

2. Be aware of the costs. Spokespersons can be expensive—celebrities and sports figures do not work for free. Local celebrities are often easier for consumers to relate to and are frequently considered more believable.

3. Require a detailed contract so the spokesperson knows all the elements and actions demanded.

4. Make the relationship believable. Ensure the celebrity either uses the brand or appears likely to use the product or service.

5. Maximize exposure by using the spokesperson in any medium where the target is sure to see or hear them.

It is important to note that brands that are well known are the best outlets for celebrity use. This is because brands (e.g., Coca-Cola, which often uses celebrity endorsers) are not selling features and benefits but image. Brands bank on the fact that the spokesperson's popularity will draw consumers to the brand.

Character Representatives are Easy to Work With

The choice of spokesperson or character representative is always a tricky one. Who will your target like or hate? Will they represent the brand realistically? Is their image and personality questionable? Whether a character representative tests well with the target or does not, the fact is that few character representatives negatively affect the brand, and all are creative. Some have been around so long that they often need a little tweaking, such as Mr. Peanut or Chester Cheetah. Mr. Peanut, the character representative for Planters Nuts, recently received an complete update, taking on an attitude, moving from a static illustration to a computer animated figure, and speaking for the first time, thanks to the voice of actor Robert Downey Jr.

The character representative for Cheetos, Chester Cheetah, originally was aimed at children, but that changed when research showed that the snack food was a favorite among adults. Frito-Lay updated his cartoon look, giving him a cultured voice and a more sophisticated, but still mischievous personality that is able to recite, "It's not easy being cheesy," with class.

Like most character representatives, these days going athletic and buffing up is part of the updated image. Following in the footsteps of Ronald McDonald and Tony the Tiger, the Michelin Man, in order to authoritatively push the slogan, "The right tire changes everything," has grown to reflect the strength and durability of the tire.

Who are the top spokespersons or character representatives according to a survey by F-poll Market Research: 1) Snoopy: The Met Life Representative, 2) The Old Spice guy, 3) The talking M&Ms, 4) Allstate's Mayhem Guy, and 5) the Dos Equis Most Interesting Man in the World guy. Characters that don't poll well do not necessarily hurt a brand, such as the Geico Cavemen and the plastic looking Burger King.

Brands who own their own character representatives can sell or market the image, such as creating a Mr. Peanut dispenser, for example. Because Planters owns the image they could decide to give him a voice. Met Life Insurance, on the other hand, does not own the licensing rights to Snoopy so don't anticipate hearing him speak.

Here are some of the most recognized character representatives of the past decade.

1. Travelocity, Roaming Gnome

2. Geico Cavemen

3. Old Spice, The Man Your Man Could Smell Like

4. Apple Mac and PC

5. Capital One, Visigoths

6. Burger King, The King

7. E-Trade, Talking Baby

8. Charmin, The Charmin Bears

9. Mucinex, Mucus Monsters

10. Dos Equis, Most Interesting Man in the World

11. Aflac Duck

12. Verizon Wireless, Can You Hear Me Now, Guy

13. Geico Gecko

14. Flo from Progressive Insurance

The advantage to using any character representative is that they never age, never get involved in contract disputes, or have a personal public relations meltdown that can reflect negatively on the brand. Peter Murane, CEO of BrandJuice, in a March 14, 2011, online *Forbes* article by Jeff Bercovici, "America's Most Loved Spokescharacters," tells us, "It allows you to deliver the brand message you want without any of the downside that comes with [real] people" (Bercovici, 2011, para. 7). Don't give up on traditional vehicles; they can still sell and surprise. Mark Twain once said, "The reports of my death are greatly exaggerated," as are the rumors surrounding the demise of traditional media. Traditional vehicles are alive and well—and changing with the times. Some are struggling to find their place in the digital world while others are leaving their roots behind and developing in very creative ways.

Chapter 4 Exercises

1. Working in the same or new groups, use the creative brief that was developed for the national brand from Chapter 2. Determine what type of traditional vehicles can be employed in the campaign, if any.

2. What visual/verbal direction will accomplish the directives laid out in both the marketing plan and creative brief?

3. Groups deciding against using any type of traditional vehicle must defend their position based on information found in both documents.

4. Make a presentation to the class or to the marketing team.

5. Do the same thing for the small local business determined in Chapter 2.

Memory Box

Traditional Media

Print

Broadcast

Rational Purchase

Emotional Purchase

Return on Engagement

Product Placement

Spokespersons

Character Representatives

Quick Response (QR) Code

5

Nontraditional Media

This chapter lists the different types of nontraditional media and discusses how they can be used to give a brand a unique identity distinct from those of competing brands. Emphasis is placed on how the innovative use of these unique vehicles does not have to be expensive.

Nontraditional Media Can Reach the Target Alone or In Conjunction With Traditional Vehicles

There is no longer anywhere a consumer can go without being exposed to some form of advertising, whether an ad is in the restroom, on gas pumps or toll-gates, on or near an escalator, or even on the bald guy's head standing in front of you in the checkout line. PQ Media, one of the top research distributors of media econometrics, labels these diverse forms of media as alternative or nontraditional and defines it as "media buying strategies that attempt to bypass the clutter of traditional advertising and marketing in an effort to reach target audiences, primarily through new media...but also by using alternative means through traditional media" (PQ Media, 2006, p. 3).

Strategically, the majority of media mixes today use a combination of both traditional and nontraditional media vehicles to reach the target. *Traditional media* uses vehicles directed at a mass audience such as print (newspaper and magazines) and broadcast (radio and television). However, traditional media alone can no longer be relied on to deliver the advertised message to the target. Lacking the relationship-building capabilities needed to connect with the target on a one-to-one basis, traditional vehicles need to employ alternative ways to break the larger message down in order to reach a more targeted niche audience. Mass messages aimed at mass audiences cannot effectively address the target's two most important questions: 1) Why should I buy? 2) What's in it for me? To do that, marketers and their agencies must focus instead on using rapport building nontraditional alternatives to fill in the relationship gap. When traditional vehicles are used as a primary source of delivery, nontraditional vehicles work great as support vehicles helping to break down the nonpersonalized mass appeal message into more individualized discussions about the product or service. When nontraditional media is used as a primary media source, it is important the message have several versions or ideas and is distinctive enough to encourage further discussion among the target audience.

Although many traditional vehicles are becoming more interactive, they have for some time now incorporated or referenced some form of nontraditional media device, including a web address, initiating a contest or sweepstakes, encouraging the target to tweet or visit a Facebook page, incorporating product placement into movies or television programming, or using the pages of a magazine to deliver a product sample, to name just a few.

Because of its ability to spotlight a product or service, nontraditional media is alluring to marketers and advertisers, giving a unique identity different from other competitors in the brand category. Creative use of promotions and ads that can tantalize, and/or shock, leave a memorable impression that the target will hopefully share with others, increasing the reach of the brand's initial message. When combined with traditional media, the message can be personalized or designed to create opportunities for dialogue between the product or service and the target.

Today's savvy, advertising-avoidant consumer considers one-way messages not only impersonal but also *passé*. The inclusion of any vehicle that invokes a two-way conversation between the target and the brand is an open invitation for feedback and the foundation for a long-lasting, brand-loyal relationship. Nontraditional media works because 1) it is difficult for consumers to ignore an interactive message, one that is considered interesting rather than annoying, 2) consumers often enjoy being a part of the brand's message, 3) advertising that is interactive doesn't seem like a blatant form of advertising, and 4) interactive messages encourage buzz and excitement.

However, creating buzz is no longer enough, as authors Beard and McCrindle tell us in the e-book *Seriously Cool-Marketing & Communicating with Diverse Generations*:

> While marketers for many decades recognized the value of word-of-mouth communication, where consumers spread good reports about products and services they enjoy, [nontraditional advertising practices go] a step beyond this.

Effective [alternative] marketing is authentic, not preachy, and seamless[ly] embedded into the lives of consumers. The key is to market *with* them—not *at* them. (Beard & McCrindle, 2010, p. 30)

Marketers who are open to the use of nontraditional media are those looking for something innovative, something that not only attracts their target but that also encourages the consumer to research, visit a brick and mortar store, or just share their experiences virally or through word of mouth. Reaching the target where they are with a message that they will respond to is one of the many aspects that makes nontraditional media so attractive to both advertisers and marketers. Its personalized approach and ability to get the product into the hands of consumers helps build a relationship between the buyer and seller, encourages interaction on updates, service, and new product launches, as well as helping to quickly address or avoid any adverse comments or publicity before they become a public relations issue.

Most forms of nontraditional advertising are relatively inexpensive, requiring more creative ingenuity, time, and energy than anything else. The idea that nontraditional messages can literally appear anywhere and at any time allows this form of advertising the best chance to be innovative without becoming routine or expected. Its very exceptionality not only makes the encounter a part of the promotional experience but also a part of the brand's image, making it a great way to attract consumer attention.

Nontraditional media has continued to increase because 1) traditional media does not have the power to attract and hold a viewer's attention by itself, in the same way it once did, 2) it is versatile, 3) it can be very creative and engaging, 4) it is often less expensive than traditional vehicles, 5) it is highly targetable, and 6) many options allow for personalization. These attributes are what had PQ Media, in a March 27, 2008, online article by Helen Leggatt, "Use of alternative media to rise," predicting that by 2012, marketers will spend one out of every four dollars on alternative media (Leggatt, 2008).

Because of their often in-your-face visual/verbal messages, most nontraditional vehicles are placed in high traffic areas that are seen by, or are a part of, the target's everyday activities. Advertisers use these visible locations or surfaces to reach them in an unusual way but also as a curiosity device to attract attention and encourage further participation or input into the promotion. For example, *Hotels.com* is hoping their target can help them develop a new animated figure that will prominently represent the service in future promotional efforts.

The campaign, known as "Clay Yourself," asks consumers to create a digitally animated figure of themselves rendered in clay. Once submitted, a weekly winner, based on viewer votes, will win $200 vouchers from *Hotels. com*. The final winner will not only get to see their clay figure in a commercial but will also receive a three-day, two-night Los Angeles getaway that includes a sneak peek at the production of the ad.

Despite the difficulties of measurement, marketers are more open to including nontraditional media in the media mix because the public is still surprised by its very creative visual/verbal voice. There are far too many forms of nontraditional media available to creative teams to list here, but suffice it to say that there are hundreds, perhaps even thousands, of vehicles that can be called on to deliver a brand's message. The following "short list" from the book *Strategic Uses of Alternative Media* will kick-start both your business and creative senses into action (Blakeman, 2011a, pp. 6–8).

Airborne Advertising

Aerial advertising

Bubble clouds

Body Advertising

Hand stamp advertising

Temporary tattoos

Direct Marketing

Card deck mailings (Poly packs)

Catalog bind-ins/blow-ins

Co-op mailings

Direct mail

Door-to-door advertising

E-direct marketing

E-mails

Endorsements

Interactive TV

Sponsorships

Issue advertising

Newsletters

Payroll/credit card stuffers

Ride alongs

Telemarketing

Tradeshows

Electronic Media

Augmented reality

Banners

Blogs

Buzz advertising (Word-of-mouth/viral)

Social media

DVR advertising

Downloadable videos

E-zines

iPods

Online classifieds

Online video advertising

Podcasts

RSS (Really simple syndication)

Satellite radio

Search advertising

Viral marketing

Webisodes

Websites

Furniture/Machines

ATM machine advertising

Chairs/benches

Exercise equipment

Gas pump tops

Gus pump nozzles

Grocery/golf carts

Scaffolding

Gaming

Advergaming

Videogame/online gaming

Guerrilla Marketing

Bilingual street teams

Postering campaigns (Splash/blanket)

Wild posting

Rip-away wild posters

Snipe media wild postings

Static-cling wild postings

Urban street postings

Mobile

Location-based advertising

Mobile couponing

Mobile video

Texting

Out-of-Home

3-D out-of-home (Extreme out-of-home)

Billboards

Digital out-of-home

Wallscapes

Live mobile billboards

Mobile billboards

Mobile video cubes

Moving walkways

Parking garage advertising (Entrance/exit gates)

Parking meters

Street art (Sidewalks/streets)

Video projection advertising

Print

3-D catalogs

Flyers (Traditional/suction cups)

Freestanding inserts

Sales Promotion

Automated shelf and aisle advertising

Card deck mailings

Coupons

Package inserts (PIP)

Point of purchase displays (POP)

Product placement

Sampling programs (Product/brand sampling)

Event–based sampling

Flash mob brand sampling

Fill concept brand sampling

Point-of-use product sampling

Nightlife product sampling

Covert product sampling

In-venue brand sampling

Van/truck product sampling

Intercept brand sampling

Supermarket Shelf Talkers

Sweepstakes/contests

Take-a-ways

Specialty

Bathroom advertising

Body billboards

Branded vinyl stickers

Business card backs

CDs

Chopstick advertising

Cinema advertising

Coffee cup sleeves

Doggie bag advertising

Escalator handrail and steps

Fruits and vegetables

Green graffiti

Manhole covers

Milk cartons

Movie promotions

Parking garage ticket backs

Pop-up brand experiences

Shopping bags

Sidewalk chalkings

Sidewalk decals

Snappable ads

Sports marketing

Stickers (All types)

Tissue-packs

Toilet seats

Toilet stalls

Vacant storefront windows

Valet parking tickets/parking permits

Word-of-Mouth marketing

Transit

Airport advertising

Buses (Inside and out)

Bus shelters

Bus/train/subway terminals

Bus wraps

Pedicabs

Police cars

Taxi cabs (Inside/outside)

Ticket jackets (Airline, rail, bus)

Trucks

Vehicle wraps

Since no surface is immune to carrying a promotional message, it is easier to customize it based on where the target is and what they are doing. Best of all, since the environment in which the message appears is not controllable by the consumer it cannot be deleted, turned off, or removed by a simple click. Its very uniqueness and often interactive features hold the target's attention longer, limiting the impulse to multitask while engaged with the message. The idea is to put a creative experience in front of the target rather than a hard-sell brand-focused message.

The inclusion of some type of thought provoking element is essential to stopping attention and creating memorable encounters. Whether done with visual images or colorful copy, the diversity of this medium ensures that it never speaks to the target in the same way twice. Some approaches are funny, others shocking, and still others defy classification—they are just downright creative.

Identifying a Medium's Strengths and Weaknesses Reinforces and Highlights the Visual/Verbal Message

Before deciding where nontraditional media fits in a campaign, it is important that both marketers and the advertising teams understand how each vehicle can positively enhance or negatively affect a campaign's message. Let's take a quick look at both its capabilities and limitations.

Nontraditional Media Strengths

1. **Consumer-Focused.** Messages can be personalized, making it a great way to encourage feedback and build or maintain a relationship.

2. **Creative.** Messages are often in-your-face, unusual, colorful, interactive, and engaging. Because of this, it is a great way to spread the message beyond the initial encounter through viral sharing or word of mouth.

3. **Targetable.** Many vehicles are permission-based or require the target to "opt-in" to receive them. Additionally, the diversity of vehicles makes it easier to place them where the target is sure to see them.

4. **Less Media Waste.** Because they are more targetable, there is less waste spent on media that the target does not see or interact with.

5. **Interactive.** Many vehicles are designed to capture and hold attention through some type of interaction with the brand, making them more memorable.

6. **Budget.** Many alternative options can be employed on a small budget.

Nontraditional Media Weaknesses

1. **Reach.** Unless dealing with small niche markets, the use of nontraditional media vehicles alone cannot effectively reach the target. Successful ROI (return on investment) usually requires the use of traditional vehicles to initially get the word out and attract attention.

2. **ROI.** Difficult to determine and measure whether the target saw the message, interacted with the message, or responded to it.

3. **Budget.** Some alternative options can be very expensive as well as time consuming. The more spectacular or specialized vehicles require additional planning and budgetary allowances.

4. **Buzz.** Information spread virally or by word of mouth is good but lacks the repetition or frequency needed to keep the message alive for the long term.

The choice to use nontraditional media depends on the brand, the target, and the overall marketing budget. It is important to remember that unique or innovative products will grab the consumer's attention without the use of outrageous stunts or novel creative approaches. These tactics work best for products with little or no differentiation from other brands in the product category. Groundbreaking creative ideas can take "me too" brands or reinvented brands to the front of their product category. Messages using an *avant-garde* approach in an interesting way not only attract the target's attention but also produce a memorable experience. This way the target will choose to share with others via word of mouth or virally via e-mail, text, or social media sites, thereby successfully extending the life of the message.

The strategy behind using nontraditional media is all about creatively streamlining and personalizing the message. How nontraditional media can be weaved into a campaign requires taking a thorough look at both the marketing plan and creative brief. If the strategy is to build awareness, remind, reinvent a brand's image, or *wow*, nontraditional vehicles have enough media choices to astound. Erasing the prejudicial and apathetic views that consumers have about advertising takes planning and a creative approach that engages through innovation. Nothing stops attention or is more memorable than an ingenious approach to promoting a brand's mundane features and benefits. Turning mundane into extraordinary often requires both the marketing and advertising teams to reimagine the brand. Marketers are often leery of nontraditional media because ROI cannot always be measured in the same way as traditional vehicles. Oftentimes, being able to envision its sheer creativity helps them to understand its power to grab attention in ways traditional media is never able to do. Let's take a look at a few creative and innovative ads that have successfully employed nontraditional vehicles.

Many Great Alternative Ideas Often Cost More Creatively Than Monetarily

Nestlé Global is using television in a nontraditional way to advertise its line of dog food with a commercial targeted to dogs. The extremely targeted commercial uses a high-pitched whistle only a dog can hear. According to an October 4, 2011 online *Washington Post* article titled, "TV commercial is meant for dogs," Nestle's Anna Rabanus tells us, "We wanted to create a TV commercial that our four-legged friends can enjoy . . . but also allow the owner and dog to experience it together."

A Chinese restaurant helped the History Channel advertise its documentary "Lost Book of Nostradamus" by placing the promotion in their fortune cookies.

To remind consumers to dunk, Oreo's placed a bigger than life Oreo into a very large glass of milk in the lobby of a building. This very visual appetite stimulant required only the logo to complete the message.

To raise money, UNICEF placed vending machines on the street that showcased a bottle of dirty water to educate pedestrians about unsafe drinking water in third world countries. Although you could not buy one of the imaginatively offered flavors like Typhoid and Cholera, you could donate to the cause by feeding money into the vending machine.

To alert homeowners to the rising crime rate and advertise their free home security check, Schussel & Schloss used street teams to place a direct mailer that looked very much like a real crowbar into doorframes of local homeowners.

One inventive insurance company placed very large branded air-filled pillows on the corners of local parking garages where cars are most commonly damaged.

An online seller of suits in Holland advertised their site by placing a sign listing their website on a poster held by a man standing along a busy highway clad only in boxer shorts and a T-shirt.

A charity that works to feed the homeless used a flat-topped steel outdoor trashcan to deliver their message. The trash filled hole on the top took on the look of a plate when advertisers added stickers of a knife, fork, and napkin on either side, simulating a place setting. Copy read: "For The Homeless, Everyday Is a Struggle. Donate today and help us feed the homeless." Additional information included a website and the logo.

A karate school placed a wallscape at ground level that featured a man in a karate pose, looking down. His face is scrunched up as he appears to release a grunt before his downward projected fist appears to hit the sidewalk, where, coincidentally, there is a crack to emphasize the results.

The Turkish department store, YKM, to bring attention to its brand used shopping bags featuring an athletic looking woman in one version and a man in another who appear to be jumping rope. The handles play the role of the rope popping out from each raised arm. When held, the rope appears over their heads; when down, it's at their feet.

Big box retailers like Lowe's and Home Depot are placing QR barcodes on a variety of merchandise throughout their stores. Any consumer who can't find a sales assistant to answer their questions no longer has to wait or search for one. The barcodes, when scanned by their smartphone, deliver helpful and immediate information.

The aquarium in one city is not only using traditional media to promote their "Share the Love" campaign, but nontraditional vehicles such as social media and interactive options as well. The campaign uses a branded truck that travels to neighboring cities showcasing an interactive video screen dubbed the "virtual aquarium dive adventure." There is also a mobile application that consumers can download, featuring an interactive game. Moreover, ads were featured on the sides of trucks, and also on bicycles that traveled back and forth within the city limits. Additional promotions included sponsoring the *Kiss Cam* at the local major league ball park, and oversized displays featuring the aquarium's fish placed in the lobby of a local Hyatt in order to encourage tourists visiting the area to take time out to stop by the aquarium. One of the most in-your-face displays used photos of penguins placed on either side of the elevator doors so that when they closed, it looked as if the penguins stopped for a little smooch.

To update its image and reinstate an aura of prestige, the French clothier Lacoste usually relies on a professional athlete or celebrity to wear its clothing. To widen their reach and bring more attention to the brand, the company decided to dress up the very visible employees (i.e., the wait staff, bus boys, and valets) at an upscale restaurant in the Hamptons as well as employees of several fine Manhattan hotels. All apparel, of course sported the Lacoste logo to invite conversation about the brand and promotion. Additionally, they employed the use of branded trucks to deliver food and hand out Lacoste's red crocodile mascot to pedestrians on busy city streets. Other promotional events included street teams handing out coupons, and a seventeen-foot-tall Lacoste shirt marking the entrance to the store.

Another different, effective, and nontraditional way to raise awareness about skin cancer was used as people at one beach discovered an ownerless orange towel with a white police outline of a body on it.

KFC Corporation used the backsides of young female college students to advertise its new Double Down Sandwich. The promotion throughout the country required young women to wear sweat pants with "Double Down" printed on the back and hand out gift certificates on campuses. The goal: encourage its male target to try the sandwich without a bun.

Why use an outdoor board to capture the target as they move from place to place when you can put the message a mere six feet in front of their face on a tollbooth gate? That's exactly what a small seasonal New York based business recently did when they used the entire four feet of the tollgate to advertise their website address. Each commuter had approximately three to five seconds to view the unusually placed ad before driving past. "This is so 'in your face' advertising we couldn't pass it up," said co-owner Nancy Jubie, in an October 26, 2011, online *Advertising Age* article by Rich Thomaselli, titled "Hey Advertisers: New York Has a Bridge to Sell You" (Thomaselli, 2011).

This small handful of creative approaches underlines the importance of having an idea that informs, titillates, and/or astounds. The more creative and unusual the visual and/or verbal message, the more attention the product, service, cause, or event will receive. The goal is to not only get the target to act, but to stop and take pictures with their phone and send them on to friends and family or post them to their Facebook page, successfully extending the life of the message.

Tying the Visual/Verbal Message to the Media Mix and Campaign Direction

A product or service's overall visual/verbal direction is developed based on information found in the creative brief. The brief helps the creative team determine what needs to be said and shown to strategically highlight the brand's key consumer benefit. In order to be effective, creative direction must capture the target's attention and tie the brand's image to the target's self image and current lifestyle. Brands that can successfully weave these combined images into the visual and/or verbal message will isolate the brand from the competition, create interest, and encourage the target's further action.

Image also helps determine the tone of voice the visual/verbal message projects, such as whether it uses humor, scientific facts, fantasy, testimonials, or demonstrations. This image choice not only sets the stage for what will be repeatedly said and shown but assists in creating a cohesive message that is recognizable regardless of the medium used.

Elements that help to maintain a cohesive look across diverse types of vehicles might include layout or headline style, color or color combinations, typeface and style, repetitive use of visual images and styles such as photographs, illustrations or graphics, or the use of a spokesperson or character representative. Any campaign using actors or spokespersons must ensure each choice matches the look, age, dress, professional background, and lifestyle of the selected target audience in order to ensure believability and solidify image.

Additionally, a product or service's logo, tagline, or slogan is one of the most unifying visual/verbal devices available to a brand; consumers recognize it and, in turn, associate and respond to the brand and its reputation.

Slogans and/or taglines that are visually written should expressively tell the brand's story. Nike's "Just do it" slogan conjures up varied visuals in the target's mind depending on their level of activity. Wendy's classic and now reintroduced "Where's the beef" slogan is not only visual but thought provoking. M&M's "Melts in Your Mouth, Not in Your Hand" tagline addresses issues many of us have with chocolate, but also alludes to its ease of use and rich taste.

What cohesive elements are employed depends on the key consumer benefit advanced, the target to be reached, the media mix employed, and whether or not the campaign's overall strategy can be simply delivered or requires a more complex series of messages in order to tell the brand's story.

Determining how to strategically use the key consumer benefit on any nontraditional vehicle is difficult. Many options, such as stickers placed on fruits and vegetables use only the logo, slogan, or tagline, while others (e.g., shopping bags, coffee sleeves, or parking meters) may involve using a graphic, illustration, or photograph accompanied by the logo and tag or slogan. Vehicles such as transit shelters, mobiles, posters, elevators, payroll or credit card stuffers can combine a visual with a small amount of copy. Still others—for example, direct mail and website messages—can use multiple visuals supported by lengthy copy. More complicated messages can use sight, sound, and motion to tell a lengthier brand story such as with infomercials or cinema advertising.

A strong key consumer benefit must be adaptable to all surfaces, whether small or large, both strategically and visually and/or verbally, so as to reach the target in multiple ways. In order to project a key consumer benefit that concentrates on a brand's heavenly aroma, for example, small compact surfaces might use a visual that mimics the look of someone taking a deep aroma-filled breath. The tagline or slogan might give the target an idea of what the aroma is like such as, "it reminds me of apple cider," or "a clean breeze after a summer storm." This type of visual/verbal message has little to say and show, but represents the brand's key consumer benefit by invoking both the target's imagination and senses. A more intense assault on their senses might use a creative direction employing nontraditional vehicles that can also release the brand's smell in subways or transit shelters, for example. Other options might include setting up a pop-up store where the product can not only be smelled by passing pedestrians, but eaten or used. Outside, street teams could be employed to hand out samples in front of the temporary store or near retail stores that sell the product.

Creative adaptability allows nontraditional vehicles to appear anywhere the target is located with an unusual and captivating message capable of igniting interest in the advertised communication. It is a creative, inexpensive, and

Figure 5.1

consumer-focused way to create awareness, build or maintain a brand's identity, or inform and remind the target about a product or service in order to build or maintain an ongoing relationship with the target.

After being continuously exposed to conventional forms of advertising, today's consumer finds most messages easy to dismiss. The very uniqueness of a promotion using nontraditional vehicles as a secondary or primary source of delivery helps to build a brand's identity through recall. As more ways are found to measure its effectiveness, nontraditional media will continue its slow but steady rise in the marketing mix, looking for an ever-increasing piece of the marketing budget.

Chapter 5 Exercises

1. Working in the same or new groups, use the brief that was developed for the national brand from Chapter 2. Determine how nontraditional media can be employed in the campaign or be combined with traditional and/or guerrilla marketing.

2. What visual/verbal direction will accomplish the directives laid out in both the marketing plan and creative brief? How will you tie the visual/verbal message together to create a cohesive look across vehicles?

3. Groups must use some type of nontraditional media. The goal from here on out is to look to competitors to see what they are doing and do it differently with nontraditional media alone or in combination with other traditional vehicles. Each team must defend their position based on information found in both documents. Tie creative decisions back to the creative brief and marketing plan.

4. Consider whether or not you will delete any mediums based on what you now know about nontraditional vehicles. If you do not delete and continue to use the same vehicles, how can you tie nontraditional media into the existing direction? Be able to back up your decisions either way. Tie creative decisions back to the creative brief and marketing plan.

5. Present your conclusions to the class or to the marketing team.

6. Follow the same exercises for the small local business using the selected brief from Chapter 2.

Memory Box

Nontraditional Media

Traditional Media

Media Mix

6

Electronic Media

This chapter dissects the assorted forms of digital media and looks at how this form of media can be used to increase engagements between buyer and seller. Discussions include what type of digital vehicle is best employed to reach the target with a visual/verbal message that they are interested in and that addresses their individual needs and wants.

Digital Marketing Encourages Engagement

Digital or Internet marketing creates opportunities for marketers to interact with a vast number of consumers on a one-to-one basis and gives consumers quick access to product information, promotions, and customer or technical service initiatives. The numerous and diverse types of marketing technology and techniques allow for personalized content built around consumer interests, necessities, and desires, making it a very interactive and personal form of communication.

It is the distinctive interactive qualities of the Internet and social media outlets that often lead people to incorrectly consider them the only forms of nontraditional delivery. In fact, as we have seen, they are only two of a very large and diverse group of delivery options available to marketers and their agencies. What digital media has done is influence the way consumers interact with both the brand and advertising. It can be argued that the Internet, specifically, is so vital to reaching the target with an informed message encouraging feedback that it is no longer a nontraditional component within a traditionally launched campaign but an integral part of its overall success and visual/verbal voice. Its growth as a "mass medium" is due to the enormous number of consumers who have access to the Internet of all ages, locations, and socioeconomic backgrounds, though with a lower proportion among the old, rural, and poor.

To effectively reach this diverse target, it is important that all Internet sites educate, encourage discussion, and assist with building or maintaining a relationship with the target. It is also important that visitors find multiple channels of communication that can promote interaction and feedback through simple activities: scrolling or clicking on a link; participating in a blog or webinar; interacting with customer service representatives through toll-free numbers; sending an instant message; watching and/or listening to streaming audio and video clips; printing a coupon; or making a purchase. To encourage feedback many brands also incorporate live chats, polls, or questionnaires. Discussions can focus on anything from new product performance, additional services, and contests and sweepstakes announcements, to the effectiveness of current advertising efforts.

Brands that openly solicit consumer input and then react to that input are a relatively new marketing concept. Before the advent of the Internet, consumers purchased goods and services from local merchants. The resulting lack of competition required the buyer to assume the responsibility before buying for assessing the quality of any product sold. The lack of regulation led to the phrase *caveat emptor,* translated as "buyer beware." Thanks to the Internet, buyers now have a greater choice of products from which to choose. In a modern marketplace, quality products and excellent customer service options are what every brand strives to deliver. Consumers who find these traits lacking in brands are putting marketers on notice to *caveat venditor* (or *vendor*)—"seller beware." The target has numerous, almost identical brands from which to choose, so to maintain a relationship, the product or service had better live up to their advertised claims.

Consumers using the Internet to pursue additional information to validate product or service claims can find two basic types of websites: informational or destination. Very basically, informational or e-commerce sites sell merchandise directly to businesses or consumers and destination sites offer the target some type of entertainment value. Informational sites are typically used by consumers to find additional research about a product or service or to check out competing brands before making a purchase. Most informational sites can be customized to specific individual targets, can show links to other related sites, or can offer promotional incentives such as free samples.

Destination sites collect or create content the target can view and interact with. To be relevant and encourage repeat visits, this type of site must alter content on a regular basis. Options might include blogs, coupons, recipes, interesting trivia, links to YouTube videos, and stock or weather updates.

Apart from the type of website employed, initial development of a site can be expensive. However, once initiated, a website is relatively inexpensive to maintain, allowing both large and small businesses to compete both nationally and internationally as never before. Regardless of the simplicity of the design or the technical bells and whistles incorporated, a website should have these characteristics:

1. Easy to navigate.

2. Easy to place an order or ask questions.

3. Kept updated and fresh.

4. Interactive, educational, and engaging.

5. At the top of any search list.

In addition to the traditional website, marketers can incorporate search engines, e-mail announcements, banners, and social media into the media mix to continually entice and engage consumers' interests and feedback. Beyond digital forms of promotion, traditional offline vehicles (e.g., radio, television, and out-of-home) are often used to drive consumers to a website or to support advertising efforts launched on a website.

Figure 6.1

As cost effective and user friendly as the Internet is, it does have a few shortcomings. It is important to understand that not all consumers have the newest or fastest technology available. Creative teams need to ensure that a website offers diversified ways that consumers can view and interact with the site.

Beyond technology limitations, there are still customers who do not feel safe making an online purchase, so it is important to include additional contact options such as a toll-free phone and/or fax number and a mailing address. It is also important that payment options and any warranty or return policies are clearly displayed.

The Reach of Internet Advertising

The Internet is a great way to extend a brand's visual/verbal message and interact with the target. It is also an excellent way to develop or maintain a relationship with the target; inform, entertain, and reward brand loyalty; and increase or maintain brand equity.

Marketers who choose to employ Internet advertising can reach the target no matter where they are locally, nationally, or internationally. It is important that all Internet advertising be easy to use, visually exciting, educational, and interactive. Ads that appear first in a search, received by request, or that promise the target something of value are more likely to successfully produce interaction. Once a target is linked to the sponsoring site, the corporate site should be immediately engaging, match the visual/verbal appearance of any other (on and offline) ads appearing in the campaign, offer some type of incentive such as a coupon, free gift with purchase, information on a contest or sweepstakes, and offer a convenient way to reach a customer or technology representative. Sites that are easy to navigate can simplify both the search and purchase process as well as create opportunities to develop a database of current or interested consumers.

Databases make it easier to maintain or develop new customer contacts. *Database marketing* uses prospected information that is gathered from search and purchase history, opt-in or e-mail lists, and demographic and psychographic information, to name just a few.

A more controversial form of information gathering includes the use of cookies and clickstream tracking. These covert forms of data collection leave an electronic trail behind that marketers use to track consumer movement online. Oftentimes, consumers do not know that they are being tracked, which results in target consumer anger, as many consider these collection techniques an invasion of privacy. Consumer outrage caught the attention of the Federal Trade Commission (FTC) when, in February 2009, they addressed the issue of consumer privacy on the Internet and called for an official "Do Not Track" system in its most recent report.

The Boucher-Stearns bill, a congressional bill sponsored by the House Energy and Commerce Communications Subcommittee is pushing to have all websites post how they collect and use a visitor's private information. Additionally, the FTC proposed that websites add "Do Not Track" technology that would allow visitors a choice to opt-out of having their actions and information on the site recorded.

Not surprisingly, the advertising industry does not look on the "The Do Not Track" proposal favorably. The Interactive Advertising Bureau believes the proposal will "require a re-engineering of the Internet's architecture," and limit what type of content can be offered for free, said authors Jessica E. Vascellaro and her colleagues in a 2011 *Wall Street Journal* online article titled "The Year Ahead for Media: Digital or Die" (Vascellaro, 2011, p. 3).

Additionally, the FTC is currently scrutinizing any product promotions being made digitally through blogs or tweets. The new guidelines state that bloggers, including celebrity endorsers, must disclose any compensation they might have received for writing about a product.

As a result, to avoid offending or aggressively assaulting their target with unwanted messages, many brands are turning to permission-based marketing techniques that allow the target to opt-in, or to agree to receive advertising from brands they find important, valuable, or useful.

Identifying a Medium's Strengths and Weaknesses Reinforces and Highlights the Visual/Verbal Message

Before deciding where Internet advertising fits in a campaign, it is important that both the marketing and advertising teams understand how each vehicle can positively enhance or negatively affect a campaign's message. Let's take a quick look at both its capabilities and limitations.

Internet Advertising Strengths

1. **Cost.** It is relatively inexpensive to maintain a website. Changes or updates can be made quickly and easily.

2. **Targetable.** With the use of databases, it is easier to target small niche audiences.

3. **Creative.** New technology is bringing more creative and interactive ads to the Internet.

4. **Personalization.** Advertising can be customized and personalized to reach the target with a message specific to their interests and designed to elicit a response.

Internet Advertising Weaknesses

1. **Clutter.** Many sites are cluttered with too much advertising, leaving a messy, unattractive, and difficult to read appearance.

2. **Intrusive.** Because consumers are busy actively researching a product or service, they find most Internet advertising intrusive.

3. **Technology.** The Internet is the one form of advertising that cannot be experienced by all consumers in the same way, because of a computer's age and the varied Internet connection possibilities.

4. **Fragmentation.** Without a good database of current and potential targeted consumers, it is hard to reach the solicited audience with a targeted message that they are certain to see.

Great Internet Marketing
Taps the Target's Personal Interests

Let's take a brief look at some of the creative ways that Internet advertising can be used to engage a target.

Chiquita Brands used the Internet to promote an online contest where consumers could place their own customized faces onto the bananas' well-known blue oval stickers.

Knorr Bouillon has ongoing advertising asking consumers for recipes it can use on its labels. Beyond the Internet, Knorr's integrated marketing communication campaign is using print, public relations, signage, grocery store events, and social media.

The Salvation Army has finally taken its bell-ringing campaign online. During the Christmas season they not only streamed a live Christmas concert but also created a mobile app that included a ringing bell to alert interested donors as to where they could send a donation.

Thermador Appliances has found a way to not only demonstrate their product at *Thermador.com* but to give cooking and product demonstrations.

Thermador's "Real Innovations for Real Cooks" web campaign is cooking up a virtual dinner party for visitors. The site offers two kitchens and two parties the target can choose to interact with and visit. In each option, a party is in full swing. Depending on the viewer's choice, they might hear traffic or waves along with guests talking and laughing. Visitors are greeted by the host, who instructs them to mouse over the start icons: to get a close-up view of an appliance, view a dish being prepared, learn how to prepare the dish, get the recipe and detailed tutorial, or get additional information on the appliance featured. Each option incorporates social media elements that allow visitors to save recipes or learn about the appliance in more detail.

To get consumers talking, Edge Shaving Gel created an anti-irritation community forum on its website. Here's how it works: during one NFL football season a New England Patriots fan used the site to complain about how "irritated" he was at not being able to get tickets. Edge responded by sending him tickets to the next home game.

A university of Alabama professor also used the site to complain her husband doesn't listen to her. To ease her irritation, Edge sent her a megaphone. To soften the irritation between coworkers, Edge sent the complaining party a Blu-ray disk player and a DVD of the movie "Office Space." Although the goal of the popular site was to find more interactive ways to build brand equity, the campaign's effect on Edge's profit margin has yet to be determined by the brand owner, Energizer Holdings.

Pepto Bismol, a company that often uses holidays or popular sporting events to push its pink stomach relief is currently concentrating its tummy soothing advertising message on those celebrating Cinco de Mayo. Moving a large percentage of its advertising efforts to the Internet, the creative campaign is focusing on interactive ways to catch the target's attention for fast relief after overeating. Visitors to the site will find a new video gadget imaginatively labeled the Piñata Smash. Interested participants are encouraged to fill a virtual piñata with a variety of spicy food items and then use the gizmo to create a video showing how the piñata was energetically and creatively smashed to bits. Each 30-second video claims: "If you over Fiesta, Pepto has you covered."

TNT Network paired up with Hyatt resorts to promote the "Armchair Detective Mystery Weekend." To spotlight two of TNT's returning cop shows, *The Closer* and *Rizzoli & Isles,* the two sponsors have created a website where interested sleuths can sign up for a chance to solve pseudo crimes. The events, held at two Hyatt Regency resorts, allow winners to assume the persona of a police detective, while professional actors assume the roles of suspects and victims.

In a November 13, 2011, online *New York Times* article, "TNT, in tie-in with Hyatt, will hold 'Armchair Detective' weekends," Tricia Melton, the senior vice president of marketing for TBS, TNT, and Turner Classic Movies, is quoted as saying that the sweepstakes is targeted to "an audience segment that at TNT we affectionately call armchair detectives" (Elliott, 2011c, p. 1).

The article goes on to say, "those viewers are women who have 'an analytical tendency' and 'a real love for solving the cases' along with the characters in the shows." TNT will use both series to promote the mystery weekends as well as social media outlets and a designated website. Hyatt's more elaborate media choices include lobby and restaurant displays, room key cards, e-mail announcements, and social outlets. Melton goes on to say, "there will be menu items at restaurants and bars at Hyatt hotels and resorts to promote the sweepstakes, including chocolate desserts and cocktails" (Elliott, 2011c, p. 1).

To make shopping easier and more interactive, Walmart introduced its Smart Network. Basically, it's a television screen that has replaced shelf-talkers and point of purchase displays to promote various products. Using the Internet, the Smart Network creates an interactive dialogue between buyer and seller. The goal is to help consumers to easily make an informed purchasing decision at the point of purchase.

To promote its Intensive Rescue Skin cream, Vaseline used *crowdsourcing*, or information provided by the general public or target, to find women who were openly discussing their dry skin problems online. Vaseline hired a research company to extensively search the web for conversations about dry skin. After interviewing over 75 women bloggers, three winners were chosen based on the stories they shared. The trio of compensated spokeswomen, known as the "Dry Skin Patrol," were sent samples of the cream to test out before embarking on the upcoming promotional tour.

According to a 2010 *New York Times* online article, "Plucked from their web writing to promote a Vaseline brand," the author, Tanzina Vega, says, "the group will go on a Vaseline Intensive Rescue Mission Tour to promote the brand objective of one million good skin days" (Vega, 2010a, p. 1).

Every stop on the tour will have tents set up where consumers can sample the product and learn about skin care. Consumers who are not near an event or who could not make it to one can visit a Facebook page to watch videos of the spokeswomen on the tour. Visitors to the page can ask questions, request samples, and enter a sweepstakes to win a trip to anywhere the tour stops. Vaseline is also using retail stores to give away samples and to produce up close and personal product demonstrations.

In the same article, Anne Jensen, the senior brand building director for beauty care tells us, "the campaign's strategy [was] broken into three main components: searching and finding the right spokeswomen, kick-starting the mission to rescue women from dry skin, and enrolling other women in that mission" (Vega, 2010a, p. 1).

"The Man Your Man Could Smell Like" campaign by Old Spice is a great example of a traditionally launched campaign that was successfully transferred online, where it continued to produce results.

To attract and hold the consumer's attention longer, Mitsubishi introduced the online test drive to their target. This very engaging idea allowed the target to control and drive an actual car around a track.

Another campaign that attracted attention was Volkswagen's "Fun Theory." Volkswagen took their nontraditional media campaign to a set of stairs in Stockholm, Sweden. To encourage more people to use the stairs, Volkswagen's agency designed a subway staircase to both look and sound like a piano keyboard that created music as consumers went up and down the stairs. The resulting musical collage was featured in their online campaign.

Geico insurance capitalized on their popular caveman campaign by offering a site that featured a visit to the apartment of one of the cavemen. While he excused himself to shower, viewers could interact with varied items in his apartment such as the magnets on his refrigerator. These types of destination sites are great for mature products or as reminder advertising.

Websites Engage and Inform Both Visually and Verbally

Digital marketing or *Internet marketing* or the selling of brands or services via the Internet through options such as search, banners, or e-mail lists, to name just a few, allow advertisers to interact with a large number of consumers on a one-to-one basis, making the web a very consumer-centric media vehicle.

Today's savvy, well-educated consumers, in order to make an informed purchasing decision, use the web to compare products and research claims made by both the brand and their competitors.

The web allows a customer to receive additional information or place an order for almost any type of product or service, no matter where in the country or world they live. It has effectively removed any geographical boundaries, making it easier to define a target audience and determine their personal needs—all for less money.

A good website should be easy to navigate and get the target to their desired destination, all in less than three clicks. It is equally important to provide numerous buttons so viewers can click their way to relevant topics or sections rather than scroll to it. The website should mimic advertising seen elsewhere, both visually and verbally, and strengthen the brand's message by incorporating additional information on complimentary items, testimonials, demonstrations, recipes, optional styles or colors, and so on. It is also a great outlet for requesting price lists, free consultations, brochures, catalogs, coupons, or other promotional materials. Beyond research, it should be easy for the target to place an order or ask for technical or customer service assistance at any time while on the site.

To encourage visits, it is important the site be cross-promoted in other traditional or nontraditional marketing pieces employed throughout the campaign. Consider including website links in print, broadcast, e-mail or mobile alerts, direct mail packages, or catalogs, to name just a few. Many small businesses that don't do much advertising might consider using social media networks to get the word out about their product or service.

It is also important, as previously mentioned, that the site be constantly upgraded to keep viewers coming back for new rather than recycled information. This is when a great mailing list can help to inform loyal viewers when significant or interesting information has been altered.

A great Internet site should

1. Be a place to go for information;

2. Only contact those who opt in to receive correspondence;

3. Include blogs or forums for discussion, not selling;

4. Be a contact vehicle, so e-mail should be checked regularly and responded to in a timely fashion (no more than 24-hours response time);

5. Constantly change to hold viewer interest and keep the target returning to the site;

6. Be carefully proofed to avoid spelling and grammatical errors;

7. Clearly tell the target what you want them to do;

8. Be mentioned in all offline and nontraditional media vehicles to encourage a visit;

9. Promote any press the brand receives or testimonials collected;

10. Not overdo technology just because it's available. It is not a big leap from techno-savvy to creatively tacky. Keep it clean, interactive, and educational, both visually and verbally, as well as readable. Keep scrolling to a minimum, provide appropriate links, and divide the page using headlines and subheads to highlight important points.

11. Make purchase easy, multi-faceted, and provide several payment options.

Additionally, sites that welcome viewers back employ relevant messages, suggest creative uses, and display intriguing images can both excite and hold the target's attention, but note that does not always create brand loyalty.

Loyalty begins or is enhanced by courteous customer service representatives who both remember the target's name and past purchase behavior. Marketers that keep an up-to-date database make retaining a brand loyal target member easier and more convenient.

A Few Thoughts About Site Development

The first step to creating a valuable website is to purchase a domain name, or site name. Keeping it simple by using the business name is often the best way to go, but it could include any word or letter combination.

Second, before finalizing a website's visual/verbal look, it is important to understand the intended target's expectations, requirements, and reactions. For example, business executives are in a hurry and just want a straight presentation of facts, whereas younger 18- to 34-year-old viewers are more likely to engage with an interactive, rich media site. So, before deciding how much audio/video to include or how many pull-down menus to incorporate in a site be certain that the target's profile dictates responsiveness and that the introduced elements ultimately enhance the brand's overall image, build awareness, and reinforce the message.

Beyond the target, the amount and type of rich media used also depends on the age of the recipient's computer and their available Internet capabilities. Sites that are designed to work with the slowest Internet connections and oldest computers ensure that all visitors can find the information they are looking for in multiple high- or low-tech ways.

It is equally important for designers to understand how the overall site is to be used. For example, is it intended: 1) as a primary research tool, 2) as an informational or entertainment outlet, 3) as a way to build or maintain a relationship with the target, 4) as a promotional tool, or 5) as a customer or technical service channel.

Regardless of its purpose, each site should reflect the current campaign, both the brand and target's image, and be quick and easy to use. Each page view should repeat the same layout style, typeface, color or color combinations, copy and headline styles, and images used throughout the campaign's promotional mix to strategically promote the key consumer benefit and accomplish the overall objectives as laid out in the creative brief. In order to stand out, the site should also offer some type of unique feature that competitors' sites do not have.

Additionally, to increase readability, be sure long blocks of copy are broken up with bold headlines and informative subheads and have interesting and educational copy. Good old-fashioned writing skills are still the best way to hold interest and move the reader toward the desired action. Use visuals to tell the brand's story, show how the product or service can be used, or demonstrate results. Visuals that have nothing to say and that do not advance the copy should be eliminated.

Page layout should remain static throughout the site. All navigation devices should appear in the same place and look identical from page to page. An easy to use, intuitive site keeps visitors on the site longer and encourages return visits. It is also important to clearly indicate how the visitor can contact you and place an order. Be sure to give them several options such as e-mail, phone, fax, and mailing address.

Finally, when designing a site do not start out by trying to *wow* visitors with flashy streaming audio and video; go for content first and entertainment second. Once the site creates a bit of buzz because of its witty, informative copy and helpful links, only then should you consider adding the eye-popping technology.

Keep in mind a website is both a promotional and business tool. If you or your company are not web savvy or technologically advanced, don't just throw a site together—the target will notice the lack of quality and professionalism of the site, and in turn attach that negative observation to the products sold, or services offered there. Hire professionals to set up and monitor the site; it will pay off in the end.

Beyond the company website, let's take a quick look at a few of the ways varied brands have integrated the Internet into their media mix to further engage their target and promote both their names and brands.

Finding Creative Ways to Engage the Target

To keep its good name in the public eye, Procter & Gamble is involved in promoting recycling programs. Not only will consumers get points for participating in curbside recycling programs that are redeemable at local merchants, but they can also receive points just for reading, blogging, and watching videos about how to lessen their impact on the environment. Procter & Gamble particularly wants to encourage participants to use blogs and social media to generate buzz in the hopes of driving others to its online content.

Kellogg's Special K cereal wants to interact with their target by not only motivating them to lose weight, but to share their weight loss goals with others. To do this, Kellogg's will be using 30-second television spots, various types of sponsorships, and a heavy dose of the Internet and social media to promote their weight loss program. To get the discussion started, millions of Special K cereal packages have been designed with motivational messages about the rewards of weight loss. On the back of each box, consumers find an empty cartoon bubble where they are encouraged to place their own motivational message. Next, they are encouraged to share their inspirational thoughts, online and then consider posting their weight loss photos on the *SpecialK.com* photography gallery.

Once posted, the program creates a customized version of an inspirational video that shows the participant and their message at the end of the video. Each video can be saved and used as a motivational device when determination needs a boost, and a lucky few will be featured in the campaign's online ads.

Additionally, social media and Internet content not only allows visitors to download coupons but a free mobile app that hands out tips, helps organize recipes, develops a shopping list, and prepares a 2-week management plan.

The Many Forms of Internet Advertising

Internet advertising and promotional devices have evolved beyond the traditional banner and pop-ups and pop-unders to find more practical and engaging ways to reach the target. In this chapter, we illustrate some of the more popular and innovative: search engine and pay-per-click advertising, Internet video options, augmented reality, viral and word-of-mouth marketing, e-mail marketing, and interactive games.

Search Engine Advertising

Search Engine Marketing (SEM)) is where a brand pays a search engine company, such as Google or Yahoo to place their sites high in key word searches in order to increase the chances that the searcher clicks on their website. Search Engine Optimization (SEO) ensures the website includes links to other relevant sites to increase target interest and knowledge.

It is important the search for information be easy and continue to engage the target throughout their initial research and final decision cycles.

Pay-per-click ads are simple text ads that are placed on one or more heavily visited websites. The ad's main goal is to attract enough attention to encourage the viewer to click on the ad and be immediately taken to the sponsoring website.

Types of Internet Video

There are several types of Internet video that marketers can employ, such as online video, virtual product demonstrations, viral video, and webinars.

Online Video

Online video is an inexpensive way to bring television storytelling, product demonstrations, and testimonials to the web.

Past websites that shared homemade videos, photos, and personal anecdotes are quickly becoming a thing of the past. Much of what is seen on the Internet today is coming from professional media companies looking for new ways to showcase a brand's television show, and/or feature stories.

Internet video use follows the same strategy and promotes the same key consumer benefit as the rest of the campaign. Each professionally produced video originates from a storyboard similar to those used in television commercials. It also requires the same type of equipment, lights, camera, music, sound, or special effects, and so on.

Just as when developing a television commercial, it is important to research the spokesperson or voice chosen to deliver the message. For example, a company CEO may seem too dry, a paid actor may appear too slick or precise, consumer testimonials are always nice but may not deliver the whole message clearly, and the use of animated character representatives may not project the sophistication of the product or service offered. As a result, it may take one or more different voices to clearly deliver the message and attitude needed to successfully promote the brand.

Although the thought of producing a web video sounds enticing and the thing to do, the fact is that over 40% of viewers are lost in the first 10 seconds. This fact is known as "viewer abandonment," and just as in the case of television and radio, it is important to grab and retain the target's attention in the first 3 seconds of any advertisement. Give them the key consumer benefit first, and the storied details after.

Erik Bratt, in a February 6, 2011 online article titled "Social media: Adding video to your digital marketing plan," suggests we consider the following types of video options when choosing which type will work best for the client:

1. **Screencasts.** A video screen capture that includes audio—this can be inexpensive and easy to create.

2. **Explanatory Video.** Using old animation techniques, this video format helps very simplistically explain how a company's products or services work.

3. **Customer Testimonials.** A target can never see too many videos showing a satisfied customer praising a brand.

4. **Video E-mail.** Spice up a static e-mail with a video, to demonstrate what is being said.

5. **Viral Video.** A video that is promoted through word of mouth is best known as a webisode or short video that can feature only audio or a combination of audio and video (Bratt, 2011, paras. 5–9).

When a company includes video on a website it takes interactivity to the next level and is a great way to engage consumers. For example, Kraft is hoping to interrupt their target's concentration on being a mom to help build buzz about family life to others in the demographic. In the past, Kraft has pushed recipes; now they want to focus on individuals and how they interact with the brand.

Toy advertising is not always geared toward children; Mattel is tapping adult fans of Barbie and Ken to help them search for "The Great American Boyfriend." Using a digital reality video series lasting eight weeks, eight contestants compete to become the Great American Boyfriend. Each week, celebrity judges eliminate one candidate an episode. In a 2010 online article by Macala Wright Lee, "Why the Fashion Industry Is Betting Big on Branded Online Content," Hamilton South, founding partner of HL Group communications is quoted: "*Genuine Ken*, is the perfect example of engagement through content." He goes on to say, "Mattel was smart to make the investment in this level of production to create a compelling series that authentically reaches and engages an older audience in a relevant, modern way" (Lee, 2010, p. 5).

Online video use is on the rise; prices are coming down and production is getting easier, helping to make it the next big online business tool. Television watching, as we know it, may be slowly replaced with online viewing in the near future.

Virtual Product Demonstrations

Virtual product demonstrations give consumers an interactive chance to experience the brand and its many features before they buy. For example, for consumers who haven't quite made up their minds or found the time to think about buying a car, Mitsubishi found a way to bring car shopping to the consumer. By sitting down at their computers, potential car buyers can test drive the Outlander Sport. Labeled the "Mitsubishi Live Drive," the virtual test drive allows a no fuss, no muss way for busy consumers to operate a real-life Outlander from their personal computers using their keyboards. To achieve this feat, the 2011 Outlander was equipped with multiple point-of-view cameras as well as GPS mapping that gives visitors a chance using an interactive remote control to digitally drive the Outlander across the Mojave Desert.

In an online November 23, 2010 article titled "5,000 people drive real-life Mitsubishi over the web," William Gelner, the executive creative director for 180 L.A., Mitsubishi's creative agency, is quoted as saying, "This was not a simulation or a 'virtual' test drive. You actually got to drive a real car" on a closed track (Quenqua, 2010, p. 1). Although using a computer to make a test drive will never replace the real thing, it is a great way to create interest and to impel those drivers still sitting on the fence to go down to a dealership for a first-hand experience with the car.

Viral Video

No brand can create a **viral video**. This is a video that is promoted through word of mouth. What most people forget is that a video never starts out viral; it ends up that way because it's entertaining and because one consumer shares it with another, and another, and so on.

Two of the most successful viral videos include Evian's "Roller Babies" and Dove's "Evolution." But even these successful brands have not been able to repeat their initial video successes, which gives viral videos an inconclusive reputation.

However, Procter & Gamble's Old Spice ads have successfully reused a formula that keeps consumers logging on to view their videos. The Roger Federer "William Tell" tennis ball campaign by Gillette and Kenny Mayne's *double entendre* campaign about the need to shave have also done very well.

Many marketers are *unsuccessful* at producing a viral video campaign for these reasons:

1. It's not entertaining; it's too much of a sales pitch, and not enough creative storytelling. For example, the Evian's Roller Babies campaign caught over 25 million viewers' attention on YouTube. The video doesn't hide the fact that it is produced by Evian; it is stated clearly at the start of the video when it says, "Let's observe the effect of Evian on your body." That's it. The rest of the video focuses on roller skating and dancing babies. A little talk and a lot of action brought a priceless amount of publicity to the brand. It is usually best to save the sales pitch for traditional media outlets or a website.

2. The video conjures up a "been there, done that" response. If consumers have already seen it, and heard it, it's boring and not memorable. Focus on taking the viewer where they have never been, both visually and verbally. For example, Old Spice was successful because it was new and shocking. Since its release, many have tried to copy its message without success.

3. People can't find you because your metadata does not match content. As a company, spend the time and research to come up with keywords that your targeted consumer can relate to, and they will find you.

4. The video is not promoted and you only tell your Twitter and Facebook buddies to tune into it. This is a start, but chances are that most companies don't have enough influential friends or followers to result in a viral video.

Additionally, consider showing the video to influential bloggers. Be certain to blog about it and post it on your company website and then ask everyone who sees it to pass the word along to friends, colleagues, and family members.

5. The execution is not flawless; the days of amateur videos are gone.

6. Finally, you did not pray for a little luck.

Most successful viral videos have originated from traditional media outlets that included promotional efforts in their campaigns, such as public relations, blog discussions, e-mail marketing and social media posts, to name just a few.

Webinars

The purpose of a *webinar* is to inform, educate, and inspire participation. Before creating a webinar, determine what information your target audience needs to know in order to encourage the action(s) you want them to take.

Using a webinar as a presentation device is more difficult than having a room full of people staring back at you. This type of presentation does not allow the presenter to gauge interest or feed off the room's energy; as a result, the material presented must be engaging, not boring, and presented in a lighthearted way. Normally, an audience cannot run out on, or turn off, a face-to-face presentation, but if bored by a webinar, they can easily log off.

What does it take to hold viewer interest? Consider the following suggestions:

- Tell a good story that has a beginning, middle, and end. Use viewers as characters in the story and familiar scenarios as a plot line.
- Demonstrate what you want visitors to learn; don't just go on and on, telling them in thousands and thousands of words. Use images to move the story along; reading from a power point slide is not entertaining. Show the product or service in action—show results.
- Encourage audience participation and feedback. Web conferencing tools allow all participants to chat during the presentation.

Depending on the audience invited to participate in a webinar, it may or may not be appropriate to include a sales pitch. If it's a general information gathering to create interest in the product or service, a sales pitch is inappropriate. A follow up call with individuals indicating a greater interest in the topic is the best time to consider making a sales pitch.

If you aren't going to sell anything, why host a live webinar? Consider the following points about webinars:

- They are engaging. Attendees don't have to sit and read dry material, they can see and hear the speaker and material delivered, as well as watch a slide or video presentation, ask questions, and receive answers in real time.
- They are interactive. Webinars look and feel like a real classroom or conference room. Beyond the delivered materials, participants can interact with others participating in the webinar through social channels, such as Twitter.
- Webinars can be converted into print articles, podcasts, given away at trade shows, or discussed in blogs.
- They offer a relaxed, educational, entertaining environment.
- Topics can be broad or limited to a single subject. The number of participants is never limited to the number of chairs available or the size of the facility.

Use social media to build interest before the webinar, to keep the momentum going during the presentation, and to encourage a post-discussion of the presentation. You might also consider following up the webinar with a podcast that focuses on the Q&A from the webinar, or questions that due to time constraints did not get covered during the original session.

Augmented Reality

Augmented reality (AR) superimposes real-world images over digital images, text, and graphics to create a 3-D holographic image. It is rarely used to sell anything, playing a largely promotional role in the media mix. Its main job is to engage and extend the time the target spends with the brand.

To achieve this effect, the consumer must hold a 2D image up to a webcam where they will see a 3-D image either reflected on the screen or on the surface immediately in front of their screen.

Like interactive television, augmented reality is bringing interactive properties to print, making it a great way to show how online- and offline-advertising vehicles can be used to engage consumers. When used in advertising, it holds the target's attention by creating an ad that is both engaging and interactive.

When used with a smartphone, augmented reality looks at objects in the real world (e.g., a building) and augments or adds to the image with computer generated imagery, making it interactive and thus realistic, usable, and effective. Let's look at a few examples.

Star Trek fans used augmented reality to receive a "message from Starfleet." All that was required was to print off a PDF and hold it in front of their webcam to get a specialized message they can share with other fans to create buzz about the site.

BMW used augmented reality to get interested consumers behind the wheel of their Z4 model. To increase awareness, the World Wildlife Fund (WWF) is using AR on mobile phones to bring the message of lost habitat and the resulting effects it has on wildlife.

AR was used to launch the Mini Cabris in Germany. Full-page ads in German car magazines were used as the foundation for the AR experience. When participants placed the ad in front of their webcam, they got to play with the 3D image of the minicar on their screen.

General Electric used AR to promote the search for new forms of energy. Consumers were asked to place an image in front of their webcams. The AR resulted in producing interactive 3-D images of wind turbines.

Viral and Word-of-Mouth Marketing

Viral Marketing

Also known as word-of-mouth advertising is a message that is shared with others via the Internet or in person. It doesn't take a creative genius to know that any form of *viral marketing* or *word-of-mouth* advertising is a powerful way of getting a message out through others who have used the product. Family and friends are much more believable than corporate America's self-promoting ad messages.

The goal of a viral campaign is to ensure it keeps going and going. To try to ensure this eventuality, it's important that content be creative and thus memorable. It is also important to ensure you have chosen the correct key words, and to publicize the campaign as well so that interested searchers can find your message and direct others to the online location.

A viral message reaches the target because the target opted to receive it, so the company should be certain that their message and content don't disappoint or annoy their selected audience. Boring, hard-sell advertising tactics quickly change a viral message into unwanted spam, so the message should always include some type of valuable offer. When done well, this form of Internet advertising can be doubly successful—increase brand loyalty and website traffic. Poorly executed viral messages can have the opposite result—affect brand image and annoy and alienate brand loyal consumers.

A message does not go viral on its own. To succeed it has to reach influencers such as bloggers or appear on popular media sites. These tactics increase the number of people who talk about the video. Talking leads to curiosity, curiosity leads to viewing, and viewing increases the discussions, making the idea or message stick.

Word-of-Mouth Marketing

It is a well-known fact that any marketing message that comes from a friend, family member, or colleague is more believable than a paid advertisement. Word-of-mouth comments and reactions, whether delivered virally or in person, can do more harm or build more momentum than a million dollars worth of advertising.

Understanding what promotes discussion is the first step in creating a successful word-of-mouth campaign. Andy Sernovitz in a 2010 online Smart Brief article titled "Andy's answers: The 3 reasons people talk about you," suggests that all word-of-mouth discussions can be reduced down to three basic fundamentals: the 'you' reason, the 'me' reason, and the 'us' reason" (Sernovitz, 2010, p. 1).

The "you" is the brand. It is either so remarkable, unusual, or creatively presented that people start taking about it. The "me" aspect is the individual sharing of what a person knows with others. The relayer may want or need to be seen as helpful, or cutting edge, or trendy because they are the first to pass something along that's interesting or helpful. The "us" is all about being a part of the crowd. To be "in the know" brings group recognition as we pass information along to our friends.

When using word of mouth as part of an advertising campaign, it is a good idea to also create some kind of reward or advantage program. The reward can be product samples, discounts, gift certificates, movie passes, and so on. Beyond that, think about sending a thank you card or e-mail, or posting responsive names in a monthly newsletter. Making a customer feel appreciated builds brand loyalty and brand equity.

E-mail Marketing

One of the most efficient and inexpensive ways to reach an Internet target is via *e-mail marketing*. This "opt-in" or permission form of advertising is a great relationship building and maintenance tool. Permission means the targeted recipients have given their consent for a certain marketer to send them advertised materials. E-mail campaigns are a powerful and personal form of one-on-one marketing. It is the rare form of advertising that is actually requested and anticipated by the consumer. Generalized e-mails, on the other hand, sent without first receiving the target's permission are less likely to be opened and more likely to be considered spam and deleted or blocked.

Thanks to social media, e-mail marketing has changed from a one-way monologue that talks at the client to a more personalized, ongoing two-way dialogue between buyer and seller. Very measurable, e-mail is a quick, inexpensive and effective way to inform and reach current customers. Marketers that employ the use of an e-mail campaign that adheres to a strict code of privacy and permission ethics can drive traffic to a website or brick and mortar store.

E-mail marketing is additionally: 1) easy to create, 2) personalized, 3) inexpensive to produce, and 4) a medium that has fairly high response rates. An e-mail campaign should not contain a hard-sell message. Correspondence should instead work on building relationships and enhancing the customer's experience with the brand rather than concentrating on making a sale. To maintain brand loyalty, be certain to focus messages on the target's needs and wants as well as on their value to the brand. In order for advertising to seem relevant, e-mail campaigns must go beyond just addressing the target by name; they must skillfully tie the product benefits to the target's lifestyle and needs. Understanding why customers make a purchase is more important than what they purchase.

E-mail campaigns keep the relationship between buyer and seller alive and relevant between purchases. A brand that is top-of-mind will be the first product or service the target thinks of to satisfy a need.

To build or maintain loyalty, the target needs a personalized service-based relationship, not an anonymous one. Online interactions must be value oriented, convenient, and immediate. E-mails that offer the target nothing relevant should not be sent; all others are a subtle invasion of privacy. Consumers should be given the option to receive online communication or opt-out. It should be easy to unsubscribe and any such request should be promptly handled. Messages must have a key consumer benefit headline tied to the target's needs, wants, and lifestyle, include copy that clearly states the offer and/or what you want the target to do, and provide some type of viral component. Finally, be sure the message includes a call to action or a request for feedback. Research has shown that any type of interactive component is more likely to induce the required action.

As a rule, a direct e-mail marketing campaign should accomplish the following:

1. Target only those segments most likely to purchase.

2. Clearly state the company will not share information.

3. Clearly identify the company and product(s) sold.

4. Ask how recipients would like to receive e-mail correspondence—for example, in plain text or HTML.

5. Keep visual/verbal messages consistent with other vehicles used in the campaign.

6. Follow up all purchases with a thank you note.

7. Use diverse techniques to engage the reader such as visuals, entertainment options, and creatively written copy.

Unlike traditional advertising methods that require the message be seen several times before it is remembered and acted on, customized e-mails are memorable, personalized, and make purchasing easy.

Building a Database

No e-mail campaign can work without an accurate and up-to-date database list. The days of blanket e-mailing to a mass audience are gone. Today's interactions are personalized and individualized, with the goal of creating a long-lasting relationship.

Database marketing gathers, organizes, and analyzes information about the target that is then stored and maintained in the company's database. Information compiled such as contact information on current and prospective products is used to reach the target with specific offers that are customized to their specific needs and lifestyle.

There are two types of database generated lists: in-house and third party. In-house generated lists, where the target has opted to receive information, often have better results than those lists purchased from a third party. Lists that are purchased from an outside source can target individuals who have not shown an interest in the product or service and are more likely to consider it "spam," thus reflecting negatively on the brand. E-mail advertising sent without the recipient's permission invades the recipient's privacy and questions the ethics of selling private information without permission.

In order to not be considered spam, all e-mail communication must offer the consumer something of interest. E-mail marketing is inexpensive, personalized, and immediate. To avoid any message being labeled as spam, keep away from statements such as FREE, Special Offer, or Best Buy in the headings.

Investing the time to create an in-house list is a great way to begin building a relationship with the target by creating more opportunities to start a one-on-one dialogue. "Each piece of data about every customer," Shannon Kinnard tells us in her book *Marketing with e-mail*, "is what drives customer relationship management" (Kinnard, 2001).

Developing an e-mail list takes time. Be sure to ask for a target's e-mail address whether they are online or in a brick and mortar store. Other techniques to consider include

1. Advertising in the e-zine (online magazine) or newsletter of another company that markets to the same target audience.

2. Making certain that the company's web address is cross-promoted on all advertising generated by the brand.

3. Be certain that all mailings have a viral component as identified above.

4. Make certain that all included information is valuable to the target.

5. Develop a blog where existing consumers can go to discuss the product or service or where new customers can go to learn more about the brand.

Databases offer an invaluable amount of information that can help to make e-mail notices viral in some interactive and engaging way. Ensure that 1) every message sent has something sharable in it and has social icons prominently placed so that recipients can easily share it on Twitter, Facebook, or LinkedIn, 2) the database of e-mail addresses is used to reach the target with a message that encourages them to connect with you via social networks, 3) the e-mail message closes with "a social call to action" (often social icons alone are not enough to get readers to join the brand's social network), and 4) feedback is gathered to create a monthly or quarterly newsletter. Frequently asked questions, or FAQs, are of wide interest and almost always can come with additional information on the topic attached.

A good example of an interactive viral message is the campaign by Direct TV called "Sign up a friend," where they promise to give both the existing and referring customer and the new customer a hundred dollars—a definite incentive worth sharing.

Since most e-mail addresses are not as permanent as physical addresses or phone numbers, it's important to keep Internet databases up to date by purging old addresses and being certain that each recipient is in the database only once.

Writing E-mail Announcements

E-mail messages, just like traditional advertising vehicles, have 3- to 4-seconds to capture and hold the reader's attention before the recipient hits the delete button. Because of this fact, it is important that the name of the brand, service, or organization is clearly used in the web address or subject line. Immediately recognizing the sender can be the difference between success or failure.

E-mail marketing is all about whether the target reacts to the message or not. It has to grab attention but also be informative and relevant. All information included in the e-mail should focus on what the brand can do for the target—how it will make their life easier, make them healthier, create wealth and/or beauty, and so on.

It is imperative that all e-mail notices are personalized and well written. Call the target by name and tie the brand to their lifestyle. The goal of an e-mail campaign is not to make an immediate sale but to inform and encourage the target to take a recommended action. Long e-mails get deleted; nobody has time to read long detailed copy, so it is imperative that the e-mail get to the point quickly and in as few words as possible. To hammer home the point, offer links to relevant information, such as additional websites or blogs, and direct the target to customer service representatives where they can call or instant message for more information.

Give the target a gentle shove, encouraging a response by offering them some kind of added value or incentive, perhaps a coupon or free sample. Don't forget to reward loyal customers with exclusive sales and limited time offers. Always put a time limit on the offer to elicit an immediate response. Don't forget to close the e-mail with a call to action. Remind the target what it is you want them to do, how to do it, and why they should do it—give them response options—for example, web page referrals, phone and fax numbers, and traditional mail addresses. Just before any established time limit is up for an offer, send a second reminder only to those people who have not yet responded. Send a thank you letter to those who have responded, thanking them for their recent purchase.

An automated response that includes a detailed invoice and information on shipping dates and tracking numbers for any purchases should be immediately sent out. Any questions should be answered immediately, or the target should be notified as to when to expect an answer.

Automatic response devices or autoresponders are a great way to 1) impart information, 2) offer customer service, 3) send promotions, or 4) confirm purchases and shipping information.

To be successful, it is important that this form of advertising is unusual and creative enough that consumers will want to pass it along, inundating other mailboxes with the message. E-mails passed along by family, friends, or colleagues are known as *viral e-mails.*

In-game Advertising

In-game advertising or *advergaming* found in video games is an eclectic mix of advertising and entertainment. Basically it can be defined as advertising placed inside of video games that are purchased or provided for free, and played on a computer, television, or mobile device.

There are two places in-game advertising can be found: within social games like Facebook's FarmVille by Zynga that are free, and in traditional computer games. This interactive form of advertising may be static or dynamic in nature. Static advertising is built into the game and cannot be changed, while dynamic ads, thanks to an Internet connection, can be changed or altered frequently. Gamers typically see elements within a game (e.g., cars or billboards that are branded with advertising) or they may actually have to interact with the advertising in order to play the game.

Figure 6.2

Some of the more noticeable corporate users of this form of advertising include Purina's promotion of a trivia game where celebrities competed against online players. The auto industry, including General Motors, Nissan, Honda, and Ford are also one of the biggest and most frequent users to strategically integrate advergaming into their media mixes.

The Internet's diversity has led many experts to believe that a globalization or homogenization of consumer needs and wants will be the Internet's legacy. Consumers from all over the world can buy almost any available product or service on the Internet. Access also allows them to compare prices before making a final purchasing decision. Credit cards make this unlimited exposure to products and services easily attainable, and relatively low-cost global shipping makes obtaining the products fast and easy.

Chapter 6 Exercises

1. Working in the same or new groups, use the brief that was developed for the national brand from Chapter 2. Determine how digital media can be employed in the campaign, or combined with previous vehicles, or used at all.

2. What visual/verbal direction will accomplish the directives laid out in both the marketing plan and creative brief? How will you tie the visual/verbal message together to create a cohesive look across vehicles?

3. Remember the goal from this point forward is to look to competitors to see what they are doing and do it differently—with varied forms of nontraditional media alone, or in combination with other vehicles. Each team must defend their position based on information found in both documents. Tie creative decisions back to the creative brief and marketing plan.

4. Consider whether or not you delete any mediums based on what you now know about digital vehicles. If you do not delete, and continue to use the same vehicles, how can you tie digital media into the existing direction? Either way, be able to substantiate your decisions.

5. Make a presentation of your proposals to the class or marketing team.

6. Repeat this process using the small local business selected in Chapter 2.

Memory Box

Digital Marketing

Internet Marketing

Database Marketing

Crowdsourcing

Augmented Reality

Viral Marketing

E-mail Marketing

Viral E-mail

Advergaming

7

Social Media

Social media unites a buyer and a seller through the sharing of thoughts and ideas or through various types of promotional efforts. In this chapter, we look at the different types of delivery possible with social media as well as some of the ways that marketers and advertisers are using social media to engage the target.

Social Media Bridges the Gap Between Buyer and Seller

Social media also known as *user-generated content* (UGC) or *consumer-generated media* (CGM) is the visual/verbal sharing of thoughts and ideas with others having the same or similar interests that have been placed on the Internet by non-media professionals.

The very term user-generated content puts community news back into the relationship between buyer and seller. For businesses large and small, social media is a great way to 1) generate or increase sales, and 2) lower advertising costs.

In the past, traditional advertising could control content by sending a one-way message to the consumer. Rather than initiate and control the conversation, the type of advertising appearing on social media sites today requires advertisers to join the conversation and develop a dialogue with the targeted audience. By being a part of the discussion, advertisers can quickly address any negative comments and consider incorporating positive comments into future advertising, or learn to use this direct feedback as a way to improve the product's applications and performance.

Companies with the most successful management of social media weave it seamlessly into their media mix. It is not an afterthought, or a separate media goal; it is an extension of the creative message. Typically, the communication objectives for working with social media are simple: to build brand awareness and brand loyalty.

Social media is a great way for brands to interact with their target audience. Kailei Richardson, manager of strategy at PointRoll, in a November 16, 2010 article is quoted as saying that the "website acts as a brochure of sorts for the company, but the social sites they've created promote real dialogue and show a bit of personality behind the organization" (Swallow, 2010, p. 2).

A successful social media strategy should be adapted from the strategy of the entire campaign, including traditional media vehicles. If the brand strays too far from the basic message, consumers are confused about what they need to know about the brand's features and benefits as well as the company philosophy. When strategies for different media vehicles are compatible, they educate, inform, and build both brand loyalty and equity.

To be successful, a social media promotional campaign must take the following into consideration:

1. **Listen.** You can't respond if you don't know or understand what your target is saying.

2. **Focus.** Concentrate efforts around your brand. Efforts aimed at reaching an already loyal target can be more creative than a plan to coax a consumer into trying the brand based solely on promotional efforts.

3. **Be patient.** Success will come over time with patience. Just as in other forms of advertising, it takes consumers a while to catch on before they repeatedly visit your site.

4. **Share.** Creative content helps build a loyal following and sharing then occurs within their social network.

5. **Trendsetter.** Determine Influencers. Build relationships with influencers within your target audience.

6. **Discuss.** Good creative storytelling trumps a dry fact-driven report.

7. **Respond.** Be sure to promptly respond to all inquiries whether negative or positive.

8. **Be available.** If you're going to use social networking, show up every day to monitor what is being said and publish new content, such as third party information.

If you want to take your social media efforts one step further, consider adding video blogging to your marketing efforts. Although still relatively rare, it allows customers to see, to hear, and to get to know you. Visual cues help customers build familiarity with the brand and help to build loyalty.

Engagement can also be attained through a number of imaginative and creative options:

- Giveaways
- Reader-generated content
- Opinionated posts
- How-to ideas
- Humorous, motivational, or personal stories
- Q&A
- Real-time posts
- Controversial content
- Debatable content
- Insider posts
- Contests and sweepstakes

Many brands generate buzz through social media by building a database of loyal followers that allows them to alert the target to upcoming promotions and get feedback on brands or sponsored events, to name just a few of its diverse uses. Many brands also use websites, e-newsletters, search engines, mobile apps, and text messaging, as well as traditional media outlets to advertise their brand.

Never forget that social networking sites are business tools which are used most effectively to inform—not as hard sales vehicles or places to push competitive differences. Marketers should not use social sites as an advertising forum, but instead as a forum to engender word-of-mouth communications. Social networking sites are great for promoting brand awareness, personalizing a national brand, building leads, and as promotional outlets.

Before developing a social network it is critical to follow some basic principles: listen to what the customer has to say; ask them questions; know what they like, dislike, and their lifestyle; be open and honest; be certain that all internal and external messages are aligned, and that all employees are educated on the advertising message being sent as well as the anticipated or conveyed response.

When advertising on a social networking site, advertisers must understand that they cannot control content but can become an integral part of the message by talking *to* visitors, not *at* visitors. Marketers and their agencies are always looking for interactive ways to engage consumers in their brand, and to prompt them to turn around and share information with their network of friends. Brands that constantly monitor what is said and become a part of the conversation can control any negative postings and can help accentuate and relay the positive messages.

Brand-sponsored sites often allow the audience to give an honest opinion about their experience with a product or service, but, as you can imagine, this can make advertisers nervous. Therefore, most sites require users to honor a standard user agreement of conduct before posting any material. These agreements prohibit the use of profanity, defamation, or other types of inappropriate content. Posters are informed up front that they are legally responsible for anything they post. As a precaution, many sites also have someone who monitors content and has the authority to remove anything they deem is in violation of the agreement.

Although no site can guarantee advertised products will not receive a negative posting, they can reasonably assume the posting offers an honest assessment of the target's experience with the brand.

Social media is the cornerstone of information shared between family and friends; it has redefined how companies interact with consumers, receive local, national, and even international news—sometimes even before the media know what is happening. For example, Twitter and Facebook have helped move political change in the Middle East, and Twitter was used to alert the world about the initial sights and sounds of the United States' raid on the Osama bin Laden compound in Pakistan.

Identifying a Medium's Strengths and Weaknesses Reinforces and Highlights the Visual/Verbal Message

Before deciding where social media advertising fits in a campaign, it is important that both the marketers and the advertising teams understand how each vehicle can positively enhance or negatively affect a campaign's message. Let's take a quick look at both its capabilities and limitations.

Social Media Advertising Strengths

1. **Builds relationships with the target.** Social media is a great public relations tool.

2. **Builds brand loyalty.** The target can keep up with what the brand is doing as well as document their own personal experiences with the brand.

3. **Generates traffic to a website.** Promotions, games, and so on can drive current and potential consumers to a site.

4. **Effective branding tool.** Great way to explain uses and showcase consumer experiences.

5. **Credible.** Reading unbiased comments projects advertising credibility.

Social Media Advertising Weaknesses

1. **Word of mouth.** One unhappy customer will tell ten friends while one happy customer will tell very few.

2. **Information may be bland.** Compared to third-party sites, a branded site may seem contrived.

3. **Negative feedback.** Comments are not always regulated so anyone posting can say anything about a product or service whether true or not, which can put the company in a crisis management mode.

4. **Time-consuming.** Although social media is relatively inexpensive to launch, it is time-consuming to maintain.

Creative Use of Social Media

Let's take a brief look at some of the creative ways social media can be used to engage the target.

It is not a surprise that social media supports almost every car launch. For example, the new Chevy Camaro and Dodge Durango RT were first launched on Facebook and Twitter. The night before a big car show, Volkswagen posted photos of its new EOS model on Facebook, giving its target an exclusive sneak peek. Porsche got in on the social media action by hosting a live tweet chat with one of its product managers. Audi used a live chat featuring its head of design, as well as producing a live blog of its launch on Tumblr. Ford used social network stars with strong followings to talk about its new models, while Land Rover used celebrities to tout their brand's attributes.

Many social media campaigns draw on loyal target members or even employees in their social media campaigns. For example, Snapple tapped their receptionist to be their spokesperson based on her experience responding to fan mail. Intrigued by her success, Snapple's ad agency developed a campaign around her activities. Her lack of acting experience and real life activities and knowledge of the brand made her one of the first nonprofessional advocates for a brand.

Subway used consumer Jared Fogel to share his experience with the brand. Subway chose Fogel as their spokesperson when they found out about his astounding weight loss, which revolved around eating almost nothing but Subway sandwiches.

Coke used the Internet to select the spokespeople for one of their campaigns. By means of online voting by Coke fans around the globe, three winners were named. Their job is to travel to every country where Coke is sold, create videos, shoot photos, tweet, blog, and use Facebook to interact and discuss their travels with Coke fans the world over.

During their adventures, "The Mix" team (as they are called) use their interactions with fans to find lodgings, restaurants, and interesting places to see. The campaign is not totally about drinking Coke but also about sharing the love of Coke in different cultures.

Walmart chose to use moms who shop at Walmart to give advice on ways to save money, to organize a budget, as well as give product reviews and tips on how to save and live better. The online discussions are led by five moms whose job it is to talk to other Walmart customers about what is going on in the world, in their communities, and in their own families.

Coach is one of the first luxury fashion brands to use social media. To promote its Poppy line of affordable fashions, they used hundreds of blogs that are part of a network promoting the new line.

The idea was when social media fans landed on a blog featuring poppy flowers they would see the message "you've found a poppy," along with an invitation to follow the poppy trail. Every fashion blogging site visited added a small piece of code to their poppy that supplied insider information along with information about a game. The game allowed visitors to grow and enlarge the poppy image on the site based on their number of visits or tweets. Coach chose to use social media instead of using traditional

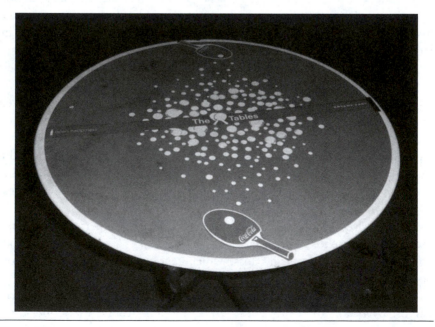

Figure 7.1

magazines that feature air brushed models and high-fashion images so that they could involve the target in the brand from the first introduction. Coach also used social media to conduct a highly successful contest to design the best tote bag for Coach.

Burberry used social media to promote its "Art of the Trench" site, where viewers were asked to upload photos of themselves wearing trench coats. Burberry encouraged further interaction by asking visitors to rate and comment on the trenches shown on the site.

Brands such as Starbucks have a built in following in their brick and mortar stores. To encourage some kind of interaction online, Starbucks developed the "My Starbucks Idea" website. The goal was to encourage consumer-generated input on such topics as reward cards and flavors that should be introduced or resurrected. Once discussions were complete, participants could vote on the necessary next step(s), making for promotion that incorporated the audience as an active part of the Starbucks brand.

The "Idea Storm" website by Dell Computers also brings brand advocates together in one place. Participants can post feedback on new products, comment on a perceived need for improvement, and introduce any product ideas they might have.

The soft drink manufacturer Mountain Dew serves a niche audience who love highy caffeinated beverages. To bring their brand loyal target together, Mountain Dew created the "Dewmocracy" contest that gives their high-energy fans the opportunity to pick the newest flavor. The yearlong contest began with its online advocates and concluded with the general public. The first phases began with 50 of its most devoted fans receiving seven new flavors and a video camera.

Each lucky participant was asked to film his or her reactions, both pro and con on video. As a result, three flavors were chosen for further review by 4,000 of its "Dew Lab Community" of soft drink lovers. Their job was to determine a name, packaging, and the best way to market the new flavors. The final three flavors were made available to the general public and the final decision was made via online voting.

Starbucks and Dell drew consumer input from all of their targeted consumers setting up sites to encourage input. On the other hand, Mountain Dew approached its most loyal consumers offline first, and then set up a site where they could discuss ideas and organize testimonials and feedback. Each brand relied on Facebook, Twitter, and YouTube to assemble like-minded individuals for a common cause.

More and more marketers are using social media sites as a customer service outlet. Comcast Cable, for example, has an employee dedicated to handling customer problems and complaints via Twitter.

Many companies are avoiding social sites and instead are adding social components to their own sites where customers can share ideas and experiences. For example, Esurance decided it was better to create a social site than advertise on an existing one. As part of a public relations campaign created for their sponsorship of the 2009 summer Star Trek release, they created their own home pages on Facebook and MySpace and asked "Trekkies" to submit videos promoting their devotion to the ongoing storyline.

Not all planned social media campaigns work. Take the Skittles campaign for Mars candies, for example. Skittles redesigned its website to work like a Twitter page, allowing fans to send tweets about the popular candy. Unfortunately, those tweets could not be controlled and included many profanities and inappropriate language, which forced Mars to shut down the campaign.

Another social media campaign that didn't fare as well was by Gucci. Dubbed the "EyeWeb," viewers on this site were asked to upload their personal photos of themselves or others in Gucci sunglasses. The problem was not the idea, but the point—there wasn't one. Gucci's campaign not only lacked objectives but a required strategy to drive home Gucci's brand to their target.

Types of Social Media Interaction

Some of the more well known social media promotions include wikis, widgets, brand profile pages, and branded wrappers. Let's take a quick look at each one.

Wikis

Wikis are collections of information posted on a website about specific topics. Many are open to all willing to add content while others may require a membership to add information, which is usually made up of topic-qualified individuals. Wikipedia, for instance, is open to anyone from the general public to post. The general community of readers then edits content for accuracy.

Widgets

Widgets, according to the Interactive Advertising Bureau (IAB), are "portable applications that allow both users and sites to have a hand in the content." Users can easily include an interesting widget on their site or send it to friends and family. Widgets are a great outlet for advertising content. IAB defines widgets as "small programs that users can download onto their desktops or embed in their blog or profile pages that import some form of live content." For example, a blogger interested in stocks can place stock quotes from the New York Stock Exchange on their sites. The goal of widgets is to offer visitors something to do at a site to encourage them to frequently return or stay and become an interactive part of the site's blogging community (IAB, 2008, pp. 7, 10).

Brand Profile Pages

The most common form of promotion on social sites is the brand profile page. This page is created by the advertiser for a specific brand. Usually full of interesting informational and educational information, users can download graphics and widgets to their personal sites, watch demonstrations, participate in games, and so on. A good site can create great viral discussions as users share their experiences with the site.

Branded Wrappers

This promotional device is placed on the home or opening page of a social site. Everyone who logs onto the site is exposed to the message. This type of promotion allows advertisers to buy space on the social site's home page. One single ad dominates the page. Interested users can further promote the brand by transferring the image or "skin" to their own pages. Uninterested viewers are not detained by the image in any way, as opposed to an overlay or pre-roll, and can easily move on to their online destination.

When all is said and done, marketers are still trying to isolate what social media brings to their brand. Terms for this form of marketing are being created to reflect its place in the media and marketing mix and to make it more business relevant (e.g., social media, social marketing, social buzz, social influence marketing, and social response management), to name just a few.

David Baker, in an October 4, 2010, online article appearing in *Media Post.com* titled "The New Social Marketing Paradigm," points out that "Social [media] is more than a reach vehicle for marketers. It's more than a response management channel for customer service people. It's more than a perfect viral storm for salespeople. It's more than a listening platform for product and brand people." The article also points out that "A world of marketing and customer relationship as we know it today is changing and the new paradigm of social marketing will be defined by velocity, not scale" (Baker, 2010, paras. 9, 14).

Next, let's take a look at some of the most popular social media sites: Facebook, Twitter, blogs, and YouTube.

Facebook Gets the Target Involved in the Brand

Anyone on the fence about whether to have a presence on Facebook is missing out on the chance to build their client base, keep the channel of communications with existing loyal customers open, promote new products, get feedback on existing products, and deliver diverse types of sales promotions that can encourage trial or repurchase. As a marketing tool, Facebook can not only add to a brand's value but is also a great engagement tool, public relations tool, and buzz-generating tool.

Research has shown that traditional advertising is the main informational tool that drives consumers to brand pages. Coming in second are recommendations by friends and web searches. Fans of brands do not want their visit to a brand page to be mediocre. They want more than just a coupon, they want to feel special and important; they want exclusive and elite content; insider information on new products; the chance to be the first to own or to benefit from the product or service; and to play a role in improving product performance, or to give feedback on possible new product offers.

Research has also shown that most consumers who join a brand's fan page use the product at least occasionally, if not regularly, and repeatedly use the discounts they find there. However, promotions alone do not keep the target coming back, so it is important to update the page often with content that fans find relevant to the brand and their lifestyle. The main reason that fans lose interest in a brand is that the content becomes static, boring, and uninteresting.

Before jumping immediately into promotions, educate the consumer about the brand. Fail-safe rules for engaging your target on Facebook include the following:

1. Be certain before posting that all comments reflect positively on the brand and its image.

2. All posts need to close with a call to action (i.e., encourage them to "like" a brand, etc.). What do you want the target to do?

3. Support discussion. Start a conversation by asking questions and suggesting ideas. This is not the place to sell the product or service; it's a place to build a community around the brand.

4. Post comments/articles. The community wants to know what outsiders are saying. Offer diverse types of content that originates from different sources—people as well as multimedia features.

To take engagement one step further, Facebook offers a location-based feature they call "Facebook Places" that lets Facebook users see where their friends are and share their location. Marketers have jumped on the new tool with campaigns designed around its check-in service to reach and reward the customer where they are located. Facebook Places is a type of viral tool for marketers because every time a user checks in at a real-world location, Facebook notifies their friends with news feeds. It is also a great promotional tool, rewarding those fans who check in with some type of incentive when they decide to visit a store.

For brands considering employing the use of Facebook Places to dispense a simple coupon or sustain a more complicated loyalty program, consider the following:

1. **Check-in incentives.** To get consumers into the store, reward them for stopping by with items such as a free cup of coffee or a two-for-one coupon. Incentives are a positive way to get consumers thinking about your store or brand when they leave and a great incentive to encourage them to return.

2. **Promotional events.** Use promotional events (e.g., a 10K run or sidewalk sale, etc.) to encourage a check-in. For greater rewards than a coupon, perhaps the fan is required to sign in multiple times or sign on to different events to qualify. For example, Onitsuka Tiger shoes by Asics used the Sydney Bicycle Film Festival for their Facebook Places campaign. The goal of the promotion was to make the current location of the Onitsuka Tiger brand the place to be at each of the events taking place during the four-day festival. Each venue had a branded Facebook Places checkpoint where event goers were asked to check in. Upon checking in to a booth or logging in to the Onitsuka Tiger Facebook page, three of the event locations asked questions of the participants for a chance to win a customized bike and Onitsuka Tiger merchandise.

Consider some of these other creative check-in ideas:

1. Consumers who check in one time receive a free item or discount. This is a great way to encourage consumers to share the promotion with others.

2. Multiple check-ins are a great way to build consumer loyalty. Turn the old loyalty card idea of getting 10 card punches and you receive a free item into 10 check-ins geting you a free item.

3. During slow traffic times, brands can use timed check-in deals. This is a great way to increase foot traffic at a brick and mortar store.

4. Attract a crowd with group check-ins. One business owner used Foursquare to increase traffic by providing a discount if enough customers triggered the swarm badge, which is activated if you get 50 people to log in to the website simultaneously.

Other examples include the University of Kentucky, which used the Facebook Places check-in tool for recruiting efforts and as a way to educate students about online privacy and the pros and cons of location-based tracking software. All students had to do was check in at any of the giant wooden Facebook icons stationed around campus every day. Each check-in showed up in the student's news feed.

To increase traffic, one mall used Facebook Places to promote discounts for checking in, such as a 15% discount at one of the mall's retail clothing stores or a chance to win a pair of concert tickets.

Creative Ways to Interact With the Target

One of the most successful ways that brands are using Facebook is as a distribution hub to give away coupons—when more consumers click on

Figure 7.2

the *like* icon for the brand, the value amount of the coupon grows correspondingly. For example, to increase the value of a digital coupon, fans of Healthy Choice, Jack in the Box, and Wasa Crispbread had to jump on each brand's fan page and declare they *liked* the brand. Company representatives claim it's not a bid to get more followers but to create a more engaging way of interacting with their target audience.

Healthy Choice started out with a coupon worth 75 cents off their next purchase. Within a day, their fan based nearly tripled and as a result the coupon's value grew to $1.25. After three days, the numbers grew enough for loyal fans to receive a BOGO, or a buy one, get one free offer, the initial goal of the promotion.

Jack in the Box is using a similar type of Facebook promotion called "Be My Rich Fan." Here's how it works: every time a consumer joins its Facebook page, Jack in the Box places a virtual nickel in a jar. At the end of the promotion, one winner will collect the pot.

The first social media campaign for Jack in the Box was tied to its Super Bowl XLIV ad where their character representative, "Jack," unfortunately gets hit by a bus. To support Jack's recovery, fans were asked to post get well wishes, and contemplate possible conspiracy theories. Anyone who participated in the campaign was awarded a coupon at the conclusion of the promotion.

The Facebook promotion for Wasa Crispbread also offered coupons that increased in value based on the number of consumers who joined their page.

Each of these examples mimics the strategy used by Groupon (a name derived from "group coupon"), a popular deal-of-the-day website that features discounted gift certificates.

In a 2010 *Brandweek* article titled "Why more brands are dangling incentives on Facebook," Genevieve Mazzeo, public relations and social media manager at ConAgra, is quoted as saying, "By allowing the value of the coupon to be directly linked to the amount of people who want and reserve it, we've created a sense of community" (Wong, 2010, p. 1).

Creating and managing a Facebook fan base requires offering the target a benefit they cannot get from other media outlets or competitors. Let's examine a few other ways that Facebook can engage a selected target.

A children's clothing retailer, who wanted to drive up visits to its website, used Facebook's *like* button to let shoppers vote on their favorite items. The winning garment then went on sale the next day.

"AirTran U," a program offered by AirTran airways, used Facebook to attract 18- to 24-year-olds willing to fly standby at a discount. To be eligible, consumers had to submit a photo to "AirTran U Creeper" by midnight. It would then show the photos online. The first person to spot their photo and contact the airline won the discounted fare.

Nestle created a branded Facebook game around its Purina PetCare Products. Players assume the role of store manager of their own virtual pet resorts where they care for and entertain virtual pets. The game begins by requiring players to choose their pet, either dog or cat, and then determine the breed and sex. Just as in real life, other virtual pets come by to visit the resort. Each player cares for their pet by interacting with them and purchasing virtual food and toys as well as grooming supplies. Players can accumulate game coins and popularity points for adding new stations and keeping food and snacks available.

Warner Brothers used a destination page on Facebook to promote their 2007 movie, *Fred Claus*. Visitors to the page could view a short promo of the film, participate in a discussion group, post both negative and positive reviews of the movie, and download graphics to their own Facebook pages.

Jim Beam is using Facebook to promote its "8 years changes everything" advertising campaign for Black Double Aged Bourbon. The message is all about spotlighting its 8-year aging process. To accomplish this objective, they are metaphorically using a bonfire to promote an online game and sweepstakes.

Interested consumers (of legal age) can go to *Beamfire.com*. Upon entry to the site, the voice-over explains that by tossing photographs, or copy describing a person, place, or thing into the virtual bonfire, a visitor can symbolically eliminate varied aspects of their lives that they have tired of over the last eight years. Every time something is thrown out, it earns the player one point and an automatic entry into a sweepstakes. Each week a winner is drawn to vie for a prize package. At the end of the contest, eligible players are automatically entered into a drawing for three grand prizes.

To join Beamfire, consumers can use Facebook to link into the site. To help the promotion pick up a little viral speed, a consumer's participation is posted on his or her Facebook wall for friends to see. Facebook will also be used to update participants on both the game and contest.

Along with the print campaign, the social media aspects are designed to reach Jim Beam's target of 30- to 35-year-old men who are entering into the next stage of their lives and looking for products that can help them do that.

To initiate participation in the bonfire toss each week, *JimBeam.com* suggests theme challenges to participants, such as "my old job" and so on. Players who participate can earn "badges" that help elevate their placement in the game rankings. Those who want to skip the challenges are still able to toss out old interests.

And finally, Super Bowl advertisers can now get more bang for their media buck by extending the message of their expensive ads beyond the initial 30-seconds through discussions and contests and sweepstakes on Facebook or Twitter. This extended conversation allows marketers an opportunity for an ongoing two-way dialogue with consumers.

Facebook COO Sheryl Sandberg, quoted in *Real Time Advertising Week*, said, "The most effective marketing programs have integrated traditional mass-market media pushes with the personalization that social-media offers. Effective marketing on Facebook has those big pushes, but [also] has those daily interactions." As an example, Sandberg referenced the Facebook promotion for Oreo cookies which asked their fans "to imagine what an Oreo would say if it could talk to a glass of milk. This is the small interaction that makes [the brand] part of our daily lives" (Parpis, 2010, p. 1).

Twitter Makes Short Work of a Social Interaction

Twitter, the Internet's version of KISS—keep it simple stupid—allows consumers to interact with a brand, service, company, or other consumers in little bite-sized discussions. This great word-of-mouth vehicle can make or break a brand. Social sites like Twitter give the general public a forum to give their opinions about a brand; because of this, marketers must constantly monitor the chatter to offset negative postings with facts and support positive ones with additional information. Most importantly, it gives marketers a glimpse of public opinion and the insight to use this free research to improve their product or service.

Marketers can use Twitter to build and maintain relationships, create a two-way dialogue with their target, or as a branding tool. Its goal is to engage and increase a brand's target base, boost brand awareness, and drive traffic to a website and/or a brick and mortar store.

Twitter is also great at

1. Pacifying unhappy customers. Since it is used and read in real time, it can solve problems quickly.

2. Expanding positive conversations and helping to keep a brand abreast of any negative discussions. Oftentimes, when problems arise, instead of waiting for complaints to come in, a brand can start the conversation and begin any commentary with truths rather than with gossip and innuendo.

3. Forestalling complaints by not allowing any to go unanswered. Always respond even if the customer is right. Admit it publicly and fix it.

The short and to the point messages required by Twitter make it a great attention-getting device that can quickly reach the target wherever they are. It offers an opportunity to keep a continuous dialogue going with the target, receives immediate feedback not only on a brand but also on the competition, and often uses clever and creative promotions to engage the target.

The most common reasons given for following a brand on Twitter include: a) getting updates before the general population on new products, b) keeping up with what the brand is doing, c) saving money via discounts and promotions, d) receiving advanced notice on upcoming sales, and e) getting freebies such as coupons or buy-one-get-one-free offers.

Using Twitter to promote events and offer consumers some type of benefit is successful because it can reach more consumers, it builds a foundation for an ongoing relationship, and it creates positive public relations.

The "no frills" approach of Twitter to social networking is the basis of its popularity. However, this same simplicity can be limiting and often frustrating to marketers. Rather than using Twitter as an advertising vehicle, many brands see it as a more profitable interactive opportunity. This doesn't have to necessarily be a bad thing. A short message is easier for consumers to remember and to pass along. A message written in the manner of a headline has teeth; it offers a feature and a benefit, which is all the consumer cares about.

Tweets, or updates are a great way to add a viral component and public relations boost to any campaign. Marketers like Twitter because it's an inexpensive way to engage their target, and consumers love it because it's a fairly easy way to be awarded some type of incentive or easily enter a contest or sweepstakes. Although its use as a public relations tool has proven successful for those marketers looking for an advertising outlet, Twitter has introduced three different ways for marketers to advertise and interact with Twitter users: promoted tweets, promoted trends, and promoted accounts.

The author Pascal-Emmanuel Gobry, defines the three types of ads in the following way:

Promoted Tweets

Promoted tweets are tweets that are ads. They show up at the top of searches on related topics and at the top of a user's timeline when the user follows the account.

Promoted Trends

Promoted trends places a sponsored topic at the top of Twitter's "trending topics" box, which reflects the most-discussed topics on Twitter at any given time.

Promoted Accounts

Twitter suggests brands for people to follow; ***promoted accounts*** puts these accounts at the top of the queue and are a way for brands to gain more followers.

A *FastCompany.com* article by Austin Carr titled "Twitter Crushing Facebook's Click-Through Rate: Report" tells us that if you're not sure of the best digital platform to employ to reach the target, research shows social networking as leading the way. The results by marketing firm, SocialTwist, showed that e-mail is responsible for 55% of referrals; click-through rates, however, were higher on social networking sites, grabbing 60% of the market share. The most popular social networking site for sharing is Facebook, at 78%, but when it comes to click-through rates, Twitter produces almost triple that of Facebook. Research has found that Twitter users were more than twice as likely to purchase a brand after actively following the brand via the social network. Because of their loyalty, Twitter fans were more likely to recommend a brand to others than e-mail subscribers or Facebook users (Carr, 2010).

Research has also shown that Twitter users are most often influencers or trendsetters while Facebook users mirror the average consumer more closely. Facebook users usually become a fan of a brand because they are already users.

Creative Promotions Using Twitter

A creative idea that breaks through the clutter and reaches the target with an interesting and compelling message can unite today's media fragmented audience. Here are a few examples.

A new flatbread pizza by DiGiorno will be launched using traditional print, broadcast, and Twitter. DiGiorno is tapping into the social outlets' strong following by offering food in exchange for tweetups (a gathering or meeting). For every tweetup hosted by influential tweeters, Kraft will deliver their new flatbread pizza to the event.

"We've always been out there with a lot of different media touch points, with a combination of online and offline," said Tome Moe, Kraft director of marketing for the DiGiorno brand, quoted in an online *Advertising Age* article. "We're always looking for the newest and most relevant places to be in both areas, and we thought this would be a great offer to combine with Twitter" (York, 2009, p.1).

Publishers Clearing House (PCH) is looking for a younger target audience. Many may remember seeing their television advertisements announcing sweepstakes winners with a big check, balloons, and a prize patrol on the winners' front porches. Today's sweepstakes is going digital in order to reinvent its image and attract younger contestants.

Sweepstakes entrants are directed to check Twitter or their smartphone to see if they are winners. The reinvented look hopes to attract attention by surprising the intended audience with its "hip" new appeal. Interested consumers who register for the PCH contests on Twitter have the chance to win $100 a month and get updates on www.twitter.com/pchwinningways.

Consumers using their smartphone applications find two different games available from PCH: PCH trivia, which asks questions about entertainment, history, and so forth, and PCH slots, which resembles a typical slot machine. PCH is not only looking for contest entrants, the longtime direct mail company is also looking to sell and showcase ads, and to build their mailing lists.

Using special discounts to attract attention, Virgin America used Twitter to launch its new service to Toronto. Movie studios have jumped on the Twitter digital bandwagon to promote their upcoming movies using both Promoted Tweets and Promoted Trends.

High-end restaurants such as the Ritz-Carlton have used Twitter to alert their fans about specials, and to get their input on what items should be added to the holiday menu. To encourage participation, a contest was held soliciting input from fans on the newest dessert item. The winner received a dinner for two.

If you're open to where you want to go on your next vacation, then taking part in *LuxuryLink.com* and *FamilyGetaway.com* mystery auctions is for you. Here's how it works: consumers bid for discounted hotels without knowing the details of the trip they are bidding on. To increase excitement, each site posts clues about the hotel or area on their Facebook and Twitter sites.

To make holiday shopping easier for consumers, the Mall of America used Twitter to offer shoppers reserved parking on Black Friday, with its "Big Secret Parking Party." To make the offer even more appealing, they also offered a $25 gift certificate to the first five people who logged in to Foursquare. An additional promotion by the Mall of America Youth Foundation is using Facebook Places to host a charity event where $1 will be donated for each check-in to preestablished charities, with a limit of up to $500 through December 24th.

To create excitement and encourage interaction during the holiday season, the retail chain GAP hired eight GPS collared reindeer to fictitiously race to the North Pole.

The 5-day promotion lets the winning reindeer pick the discount of the day. For example, if Chloe crosses the faux finish line first, all accessories are only $5; if Emma takes the blue ribbon, it's worth 40% off the shopper's entire purchase. Each of the eight reindeer represents a different offer; the winning promotion is determined by how far the reindeer travels that day. The retail chain is using Twitter (each reindeer is assigned a hashtag) and Facebook to announce the day's reindeer winner and also the promotion of the day.

KFC is using Twitter as a way to award $20,000 to one lucky high school student to apply toward their college tuition. Winners will be selected based on the best tweet KFC receives, followed by their need and drive as represented in the submitted application.

To celebrate its 10th anniversary, JetBlue used Twitter to give away 1,000 round-trip tickets. The promotion was in New York, and the tweets drove interested travelers to three different locations in Manhattan to collect the free tickets.

Hugh Jackman, as part of the promotion for his film *X-Men*, proposed a Twitter challenge that was for charity. The winning participant's favorite charity was to receive $100,000, if they could plead for their cause in a single tweet. The passionate pleas resulted in two winners splitting the pot between their respective charities.

Twitter has also been successfully used to counter negative issues. When a YouTube video surfaced supposedly showing two of Domino's employees unfashionably desecrating a pizza, fans were outraged. Twitter users demanded to know what was going on and what Domino's planned to do about it. Seen by Domino's management, it was quickly ruled a hoax, before it blew up into a public relations disaster.

Ford also responded to rumors that surfaced on Twitter about sending a legal notice to a blogger who had been talking negatively about a Ford Ranger. Rumor had it that Ford asked the blogger to surrender his URL. Ford's social media leader, Scott Monty, quickly addressed the issue, labeling it untrue, and successfully ended any further discussion.

Blogging: Let's Talk About It

Blogs are an online discussion or information site publishing personal commentaries, diaries, and conversations between the seller of a product or service and multiple consumers. They are a great way to drive traffic to a website, receive feedback on new product launches or upgrades, and build or maintain brand loyal consumers through dialogue with customer or technical service agents or a public relations representative.

The best way to promote a blog is to place it high in the priority list of a search engine, attach it to the brand's website, or post a link to related and relevant content. All of these efforts should include a short paragraph describing why you feel the blog is important and relevant to the target. For example, if you're a financial planner, you may want to link to information on retirement or saving for your child's college education.

Blogs are not the popular destination they once were for the general population. Many are losing ground as more people, especially younger people, turn to Facebook and Twitter to voice their opinions.

It is important to point out, however, that blogs have not lost their allure to middle-aged adults who are using the Internet as a business or research tool. These hard-core enthusiasts are looking for more detailed discussions that offer value-based content. Discussions on social or entertainment topics are more likely to be found on a social networking site. More comprehensive discussions are also found on blogs. Valuable content is crucial. Visitors to blogs expect to find honest and straightforward discussions. Any misleading information posted on a blog results in negative publicity.

For example, ConAgra Foods invited food and mom bloggers in New York City to enjoy a four-course Italian dinner at a local high end restaurant run by a well-known chef. Attendees were promised a surprise at the evening's conclusion, and also two extra tickets they could pass along to their readers. At the close of the event, the only thing diners were surprised at was that they had been misled. There was no delectable Italian food prepared by a celebrity chef, only lasagna and pies that were compliments of Marie Callender, a line of ConAgra frozen foods.

Hidden cameras were used to catch diner's reactions to the food served. According to a *New York Times* article by Andrew Adam Newman, their goal was to use the footage for promotions on their website and YouTube, and "for bloggers to generate buzz when they wrote about being pleasantly surprised" (Newman, 2011, p. 1). Once the deception was exposed, the diners were not pleasant, but they were surprised, at being so openly duped. The bloggers did write about their experience, but not positively as ConAgra had hoped.

However, many blogs do report favorably on brands, corporations, and organizations. The following examples show how blogs that are integrated into to a brand's promotional mix can deliver positive word-of-mouth benefits for a brand.

Want to get your trade show presentation to reach more people? Consider using a blog. The Consumer Electronics Show used a slew of bloggers hired by varied exhibitors who wanted them to recruit visitors to the show by writing about what was going on during the event.

Bloggers did more than just write reports; in order to move the discussions beyond the showroom floor, they also did interviews with company principles, developed assorted audio and video content, and posted reports on the brands various social network platforms. Some attendees created check-in points to drive participants to a blogger's site while others hosted integrated events, such as Kodak's cupcake "Tweetup."

General Mills is using blogger moms to talk about their experience with General Mills' products. Participants can receive anything from samples to coupons in exchange. Bloggers are free to write anything they wish and are encouraged to inform readers that they do receive products for review as compensation for their input.

YouTube

YouTube has come a long way from its roots—homemade videos of surfing dogs. Today's major players include Kellogg's, McDonald's, and Ford, to name just a few companies who are spending big bucks to bring a slick and hopefully viral message to the site.

A video-sharing website that is very popular, YouTube has grown almost entirely by word of mouth with very few dollars ever spent on advertising. As an advertising vehicle, YouTube is a relatively inexpensive way to repeatedly reach a selected target with new or revamped products or services and to expose the brand to a newly identified target group.

As with all social media, feedback is almost immediate. The best way to create a viral video is to ensure it is entertaining, funny, engaging, and contains no hard sell advertising pitch; those attributes translate into viewers sharing it with their friends, family, and colleagues. Let's take a look at a few successful examples.

Ray-Ban scored big on YouTube with a video titled "Guy catches glasses with face." Clearly identified as a promotional device for Ray-Ban, the poor quality video shows a guy repeatedly catching a pair of Ray-Bans with his face from varying heights and distances. Viewers watched this video repeatedly, securing its viral status, as they debated how he did it. Interesting content that speaks creatively to the target, in a language they understand and about a topic they are interested in, creates results.

Another creative video was produced by Kellogg's. Wanting to promote the virtues of a healthy breakfast, Kellogg's used a split screen to humorously show how your day will go if you eat breakfast. On the left side, the character starts his successful day with a Kellogg's breakfast while the same character shown on the right side skips breakfast, resulting in a day full of calamity.

Another success story using YouTube comes from Dove, called "Dove Evolution." The video shows a model sitting in front of the camera before her make-up is applied and her hair is done. The video fast-forwards through her amazing transformation. The kicker is that she looks great, but compliments of a photo retouching program we get an inside look at the air-brushing used to remove imaginary flaws, and the faux plastic surgery that transforms her into a super beauty who did not exist when the video opened.

Brands can elect to create a special topic or dedicated channel in order to feature special content. These focused video channels are a great alternative way to reach the target, often offering various types of activities. For example, Pepto Bismol created a contest site that asked visitors to create a one-minute personal video where they sang about the product's virtues in solving various types of digestive distress problems. To make it more engaging, Pepto Bismol provided a few props and music options. At the conclusion of the contest, winners were chosen by other viewers.

Using Social Media for Crisis Control

Beyond its function as a successful marketing vehicle, social media is also a great public relations tool for a company to use if something goes wrong and negative publicity results. A crisis can range anywhere from an environmental disaster to packaging that is hard to open. However, regardless of the level of discontent, it is important to understand that in the digital world negative publicity can travel quickly if left unmonitored. Companies with a crisis management plan in place are prepared to address any issue head on, as quickly as possible, and with accuracy and professionalism. A crisis allowed to fester is ripe for innuendo and assumptions that can result in long-term consequences or even permanently destroy a brand's overall equity within its product category. For example, in 2008 when an old story was picked up by a news outlet that United Airlines was going to file for bankruptcy, mayhem ensued. The bottom dropped out of United's stock price when the digital world started talking and speculating. Although United was not at fault for the false news leak, they were caught sleeping. Had they been properly monitoring the digital arena, they could have reacted to the misinformation with a statement of their own and successfully avoided a situation that proved to have very negative consequences.

When monitored and used properly, social media can increase awareness and initiate a positive interaction between the brand and the consumer. Brands with a solid reputation survive a crisis better than an unknown brand or even a well-known brand that is slow to respond and allows word of mouth to rule what consumers think and feel.

Taco Bell is a good example of a company that responded quickly and successfully when a crisis occurred. After an accusation was made that the "seasoned beef" used by the fast food chain did not meet USDA requirements, the company's response was immediate and enacted through legal and social media means. Using its influencers as its front line of defense, Taco Bell managed to slow down the *naysayers* making it difficult for them to be heard. By actively maintaining its brand image over the years and catering to its brand loyal consumers, Taco Bell kept the need for damage control to a minimum.

To ensure consumers heard their side of the story first, Taco Bell launched an SEM (search engine marketing) campaign that placed their stories first with initiation of a web search. In a February 17, 2011, online article for *Mashable.com*, Patrick Kerley tells us, "Clearly, Taco Bell appreciates the role of search engines as de facto gatekeepers of information. The company understood that the first story told is the story that is believed. As a result, the plaintiffs now have to swim against a rising tide of public opinion" (Kerley, 2011, p. 2).

To prove they used real beef, Taco Bell offered consumers a free taco to prove it. The promotion was designed to convey a "no fear" mentality. As a final response, Taco Bell president Greg Creed appeared on a YouTube video appropriately titled, "Of course we use real beef."

Taking your message directly to the public is the way to go, if you are confident that your brand's claims will prevail. For those brands with a smaller following, this in-your-face approach may be inappropriate. Products that are used more by businesses rather than consumers should consider using LinkedIn as their online voice.

Two good examples of poor crisis management can be seen in scenarios with Toyota and BP (British Petroleum). Each was very slow to respond to a crisis surrounding their brands. Instead of immediately informing consumers about how the company would fix the problem, the delay in communication allowed consumers and competitors to interject speculation and innuendo into the resulting information gap. Successful management of a crisis is easiest in its early stages. The fastest response mechanism is Twitter. Use it to track discussions and answer questions honestly. Misleading consumers at the beginning of a crisis with misinformation or conjecture just adds fuel to the fire.

To avoid inadvertently igniting more controversy, always pause and think before responding to a critical post. Do not respond to any post without having all the facts. If you are still waiting for information, tell that to the target and go further to say that as soon as you have any additional information, you will let them know. Determine whether the complaint is a personal attack from someone with their own agenda or one that could apply to other users. Problems that affect the largest sector of the target should be addressed publicly by the company, but suggest that issues of a more personal nature can be dealt with directly.

Consider the following steps for managing a crisis:

1. Take immediate action. It doesn't take long for negative publicity to become the hub around which negative press revolves.

2. Be a part of the conversation. Give the facts that are available and keep consumers updated on changes as they happen.

3. It (whatever *it* is) happened; admit it. Be a part of the solution; let the target know the steps that are being taken to avoid such a mishap in the future. Monitor the ongoing conversation to nip baseless accusations in the bud and to clarify points.

4. Do not issue a scripted apology. Social networks are not press conferences, and personal interaction is necessary.

5. Ask for a solution. Find out what it will take to make amends. This proactive approach lets consumers know that you take responsibility and care about what they think. It is also a great way to maneuver the discussion from a negative one to a more positive one.

6. Solve it.

7. Build on it and move on.

As a mouthpiece, social media gives brand-loyal consumers the opportunity to stand up for a brand, and at the same time gives angry consumers a forum to give their opinions, spread rumors, or advocate for change or action. A brand's value to an individual consumer is always hard to define and very difficult to change or maintain. Warren Buffett once said, "it can take 20 years to build a reputation and only five minutes to ruin it" (Lux, 2010, p. 1).

Technology-based media options make it simple to measure click-through rates on the web, the number of impressions or time an ad was viewed in mobile ads, the number of tweets received on Twitter, and the number of "likes" recorded on Facebook. Notwithstanding, it is still not enough to effectively determine its impact on sales or its success at building brand loyalty or brand equity.

Chapter 7 Exercises

1. Working in the same or new groups, use the brief that was developed for the national brand from Chapter 2. Determine how social media can be employed in the campaign or combined with previous vehicles.

2. What promotional direction will accomplish the directives laid out in both the marketing plan and creative brief? How will you tie the visual/verbal message into social media to create a cohesive message across vehicles?

3. Be sure to keep your eye on what competitors are doing and do it differently, with varied forms of nontraditional media alone or in combination with other vehicles. Each team must defend its position based on information found in both documents. Tie creative decisions back to the creative brief and marketing plan.

4. Consider whether or not you will delete any medium based on what you now know about social media vehicles. If you do not delete and continue using the same vehicles, how can you tie social media into the existing direction? Be able to back up your decisions either way.

5. Present to class or to the marketing team.

6. Do the same thing for the small, local business selected in Chapter 2.

Memory Box

Social Media User-Generated Content

Consumer-Generated Media

Engagement

Widgets

Facebook

Twitter

YouTube

Blogs

8

Mobile Media

A variety of forms of mobile advertising are on the rise. It is the one media vehicle that travels with the targeted audience wherever they go. Since the target opts-in or elects to receive mobile advertising, it must have a purpose and a message that the target determines is constructive and valuable. The ability of mobile advertising to reach a target near the point of purchase makes it a popular, geographically based marketing tool and an excellent consumer-oriented promotional tool.

Mobile Is a Form of Nontraditional Media That Is Always Accessible

Today, advertisers and marketers alike are looking for new and entertaining ways to reach their target audience. Increasingly, as we have seen, they are turning to nontraditional media as a way to capture attention and engage a target that is often distracted, leery, and distrustful of traditional media options. Mobile as a viable alternative to traditional advertising is one of the strongest and most publicly accepted vehicles to emerge from the nontraditional pack. Consumers have endorsed receiving locally initiated advertising via their mobile phones, admitting they find this ad delivery more engaging and memorable. The Mobile Marketing Association reports that at least half of all mobile users who interacted with a mobile delivered ad responded to it favorably, especially if they received some kind of promotional incentive.

Additionally, consumers who opt-in to receive advertising from popular retailers can also be notified about store openings, receive notices about advanced or private sales, obtain additional information about products as they shop—such as using a QR (quick response) code to look up nutritional information, or check product reviews, to name just a few. Another important perk for consumers with smartphones equipped with a GPS feature is that they can be immediately notified of product sales or events as they drive or walk by local establishments.

Mobile works because consumers usually carry their phone with them. Because of this, it is important for any marketing program not to inundate the target with generic and nonpersonalized messages. Just as with the use of other forms of nontraditional marketing, mobile advertising is a great equalizer, allowing businesses large and small to connect with their target where they are, with a message of specific interest to the target. In an *Advertising Age* article titled, "Check-in Apps' next stop: Your supermarket aisles," Mark DiPaola, CEO and cofounder of CheckPoints feels that "mobile will be bigger for brands than the Internet was, because mobile goes with you to the store. We drive feet to the product, wherever it's sold in the store, even if it's all the way in the back on the bottom shelf" (Zmuda, 2010, p. 2).

Before employing mobile advertising, any brand thinking about using this form of advertising needs to make certain that it is an extension of their current strategy and integrates seamlessly into their current visual/verbal message. If a message is not well thought out, brands who jump on this newest of media trends can suffer the consequence that a target can perceive the company as a copycat and the brand as second-rate.

For mobile efforts to be successful advertisers must research and understand many elements:

1. *When* will the target be reached? The advertising efforts are directed to a targeted consumer who is constantly moving. The upside of this reality is that the target can be reached with a current and timely promotion when they are at or near the point of purchase of the product or service.

2. *What* is the target doing? Is the target shopping, traveling, on business, or looking for local establishments or entertainment venues?

3. *Who* is the target? How do they use their mobile phones? Where do they shop, eat, play, and so on?

4. *Why* do they use a mobile phone? To make calls to business associates, friends, play games, watch videos, search the web, or as a way to receive e-mails?

The ability to reach the target in almost any location automatically raises several privacy issues (e.g., mobile spam, GPS finders, personal phone numbers, and wireless security). Because of this, it is important to double check that not only has the target opted-in to receive messages, but that the messages are relevant, kept secure by the sender, and not sold. Additionally, to ensure consumers continue to accept mobile advertising, mobile ad agencies have worked on creating more interactive and engaging ads. Many of these new visual/verbal ads incorporate the use of rich media that fills the cell phone's screen with both video and game options. HBO for example, creatively used mobile to highlight the third season of their popular sci-fi show, *True Blood*. Niraj Sheth, in a *Wall Street Journal* article, explained HBO's promotion: "When users opened up the apps for Variety magazine and Flixster on their iPhones, bloody fingerprints started appearing as they tapped around. Blood oozed from the top, eventually covering the screen with an ad for the show and a link to watch the trailer for the upcoming season" (Sheth, 2010, p. 2).

More and more consumers are now using their smartphones as a convenient way to visit websites and communicate and shop online, so be certain that your company's website can be adapted to the mobile screen. If it cannot, you may want to create an app for each of the varied types of smartphones, including iPhone, Android, and BlackBerry, and encourage the target to download it from your website directly to their wireless providers' app store. Adaptation is increasingly important with the introduction of 4G mobile technology, which is slowly making its way across the country. Consumers can view branded messages and any accompanying rich media content faster than ever before. Marketers hope that the faster a target can open a website, the longer the message holds the target's attention and the greater an increase in click-through rates.

Because of its portability and adaptability, wireless or mobile advertising use is rapidly increasing; however, it is still uncertain exactly how the format will evolve. Mobile devices already are used to not only make a call or surf the web but start our cars and make cashless purchases, to name just a few. What is known is that consumers are open to receiving advertising via their cell phones, pagers, or personal digital assistants (PDA).

Identifying a Medium's Strengths and Weaknesses Reinforces and Highlights the Visual/Verbal Message

Before deciding where mobile advertising fits in a campaign, it is important that both marketers and the advertising teams understand how it can positively enhance or negatively affect a campaign's message. Let's take a quick look at both its capabilities and limitations.

Mobile Advertising Strengths

1. **Opt-In.** Consumers choose to receive advertising through their mobile phones.

2. **Targeted.** Consumers are interested in the product or service based on past research or use, making it easier to personalize the message.

3. **Interactive.** Mobile advertising requires the target to interact with the message in varied ways, making it more memorable.

4. **Portability.** The target takes their phone everywhere with them.

Mobile Advertising Weaknesses

1. **Opt-Out.** Consumers can opt-out of mobile advertising as easily as they opted-in, making quality and engagement a critical aspect of message development.

2. **Short messages.** All correspondence must be short and to the point.

3. **Attention deficit.** The target is active, typically doing something else when the message is received.

4. **Irritating.** Even though messages are permissible, the target can be overwhelmed by the sheer number of them.

Mobile Apps With a Purpose

Apps or *applications* are buttons that direct the mobile user to a specific Internet site. There are two basic types of mobile apps: native and web. Native apps are either preinstalled on a phone, such as calendars and calculators, or they can be downloaded from the Internet for free or for a small fee from an app store. Web apps are also downloaded from the Internet but are designed for a more specific purpose such as playing a game, videos, or listening to music.

The decision to add an application to your media mix should be both engaging and informative. It should not be another sales channel. Before adding mobile apps to your promotional arsenal, ask yourself: 1) How hard can it be to engage the intended target? 2) What sets one app apart from another? 3) Why do you need to add a mobile app to your existing media arsenal? 4) What outcomes are you looking for?

To determine the answers first requires an examination of the communication objectives of a marketing plan; what is the plan trying to accomplish and will adding mobile advertising aid in accomplishing those objectives? To show ROI, or return on investment, it's imperative that each media vehicle in the marketing campaign have a specific purpose, such as fulfilling a currently unmet consumer need. For example, can this vehicle choice solve a recognized problem, answer a researched question, entertain, or save the target time and money? Ultimately, if this vehicle is selected, can the company exceed its closest competitors in this market?

Second, look at other ads currently in use in the campaign. To present a cohesive look across the media mix, an app needs to cleanly mesh with the current visual/verbal look; it should be simply designed and easy to read and use.

Third, be certain to include promotion for the new app. Excite the target with its attributes and ease of use. Cross-promote it in all media used in the current campaign. Consider tying the download of the app with a coupon, contest, or sweepstakes to encourage the target to check it out. To further strengthen a promotion, consider joining forces with one or more compatible advertisers in a cooperative arrangement, where the cost of advertising is shared, doubling each brand's exposure. Apps that offer useable information and can solve the target's current problems help to build both brand loyalty and brand equity.

Unsuccessful apps are ones that do not solve a problem, or repeatedly attract the target's attention, or do not encourage the target to come back a second or third time. Similar to websites and traditionally used media, apps need to have an ever-changing visual/verbal message to help hold interest and create multiple impressions.

Most successful apps also have some type of viral aspect that interests the target, lets them do something they have always wanted to do, or offers them something relevant. For example, Kraft created the iFood assistant. This app is successful because it is useful to the target, allowing them to check out recipes—either by category or based on the occasion—and makes it easy to add the ingredients to a shopping list. The app also allows users to download coupons and store their favorite recipes in a file box.

These types of interactive apps increase the amount of time the target spends with an ad, making the ads more memorable and engaging enough that the target wants to use social outlets (i.e., Twitter or Facebook) to share them, therefore building buzz about the product or service.

Apps will fail that are not well thought out or are created for all the wrong reasons, such as the fact that everybody else in the brand category has one. There are other reasons why an app may fail:

- If it is nothing more than a fancy sales tool. The target will not return to a thinly disguised sales pitch. Loyalty can be affected if they feel you were deceptive in your promotion of the app and its inherent attributes
- If it is poorly designed. It looks great but is not legible at first glance

- Doesn't work or consistently crashes. Either one reflects negatively on the brand, and encourages impatient and disgusted users to unceremoniously delete it
- Does not match the profile of the target audience
- Does not solve a current problem or is not perceived as useful by the target
- Has not been actively promoted in other media used throughout the campaign. It is imperative the target not only know about it, but they must know what's in it for them if they download it.

The once static app that could only take a target to a specific website has undergone an amazing transformation. An app can now recognize its owner's voice and verbal patterns and immediately locate where they are physically. Here's how it works. Let's say that you're sitting having drinks with a friend and discussing what movie to see and where they are playing. The app recognizes the speaker's voice and brings up a laundry list of movies and the nearest location of each theater.

Consumers who have downloaded a brand's app can have the phone deliver coupons for the nearest drug store or restaurant they are walking or driving near, or have it *ping* or notify them with a push or special alert when they are within a few blocks of the location. Using a GPS locator, these very targetable and useful apps can tell if the target is walking or driving based on speed. This action then determines the type of alert that is sent—coupons, or directions, for example.

Beyond location-based options, ads, and promotional offers, smartphones can also be used to make a purchase. In select locations, Starbucks accepts payment by cell phone. All consumers have to do is download the app currently available for iPhones or BlackBerry devices and then swipe their phone at the register. The Starbucks card mobile app allows consumers to hold the barcode over a scanner at checkout to pay for their purchase. Users can also check their card balance, add to their balance using a credit card, track purchase history, and find the closest Starbucks that accepts mobile payment.

Mobile can also replace traditional "pay at the register" purchases with what is now labeled "contactless" payments. Users can transfer funds by waving their phone at retailer-installed card readers. Blaze Mobile Wallet uses RFID, or radio frequency identification stickers, which support MasterCard's Paypass protocol to allow any smartphone that runs that application to literally pay by phone. This newest perk not only makes purchasing easier but makes it easier in the future to reach the target with further advertising and sales promotion offers.

Other pay by phone companies can send an electronic receipt by e-mail or text that shows a picture of the purchase, how many times you have visited the store in the past, and a map of where the purchase was made.

Electronic receipts are also a great place to showcase further promotions or deliver a coupon or two.

The popularity of mobile apps creates a lot of brand clutter. So to stand out, Pizza Hut made their app interactive and entertaining enough to encourage repetitive use by allowing its target to use the app to create their own pizza. The ingredient specific app allows the target to shake, drag, and pinch their favorite toppings onto to a virtual pizza crust. The creative app then lets the target know which of Pizza Hut's stores is nearest to their current location. The app allows the target "to engage in the ordering process which is typically mundane and not all that exciting," said Brian Niccol, the chain's chief marketing officer in a 2010 online *Technology Review* article (Jones & Ryan, 2010, p. 2). To promote the new app, Pizza Hut used the Internet, print, and television outlets, as well as co-op ads with Apple. At the time, the innovative idea was only available for iPhones so Apple promoted the app in their commercials as well.

Pizza Hut's successful integration of new and traditional media channels ensured their target knew about the app, where to find it, and how to use it, creating buzz every step of the way that stimulated interest and eventually action.

Purina's "Petcentric" mobile app was created as a way for pet lovers to receive news, video stories, and photos that revolve around ownership. The app also included a GPS function where their target could find pet sitters and pet friendly places near their location, as well as share ratings and comments about their experiences.

In a comparable manner to other types of brands, sports franchises are creating apps that bring topical news items, game schedules, players and game statistics, current lineups, team standings, instant replays, and a Twitter option to fans. For example, the NHL got in the mobile frame of mind when the Pittsburgh Penguins created a campaign that encouraged fans to sign up for their "mobile fan club." By opting in to the club, fans were privy to news updates, recaps, and various offers via their cell phones (e.g., free tickets to the Pittsburgh auto show). The Cleveland Cavaliers basketball franchise went one step further by including fan requested content, such as game schedules and team statistics, along with varying promotions. According to an online *New York Times* article dated September 20, 2010, "Mobile has a lot of tentacles, from building a database of fans, reaching commercial sponsors, selling tickets and merchandising," said Michael Falato, vice president of sales for Txtstation, an Austin, Texas, mobile marketing company (Olson, 2010a, p. 2).

The Penguins also incorporated a guerrilla marketing event to enhance their mobile promotions. The franchise teamed up with American Eagle Outfitters to create the American Eagle Student Rush Club. Here's how it worked: the team contacted members via their cell phones about a "student flush" event they were hosting. The first 400 members to respond would not only get a T-shirt but an insider's look at the new arena, if they helped test its restroom facilities. The goal: have all participants flush the toilets at once "so we could see if everything worked," said Jeremy Zimmer the team's director of new media.

The Miami Dolphins have incorporated mobile into the team's daily radio show. Fans are encouraged to text in questions, comments, and even suggestions for the team's most valuable player. Texts can also be used to register for prizes such as free tickets.

Location-Based Applications Reach the Target Near the Point of Purchase

Location-based marketing is all about sending your target a message based on where they are located when they see it, what their current location reveals about their habits and lifestyle, and how easy or difficult it is for them to interact with the brand.

Users of *location-based marketing* use location-based services with GPS technology to locate the target and send them promotions near their location. To receive these types of alerts users must opt-in or agree to receive them. Location-based social apps (i.e., Foursquare, Groupon, Gowalla, Loopt, and Facebook Places, to name just a few) offer marketers creative and diverse ways to reach and interact with their target. The popularity of these social applications makes employing location-based marketing a very effective way to deliver a geographically based message to the target, hopefully with a message that sparks their interest.

Local businesses can decide the type of promotion, and how to direct or position the offer, whether to the individual, friends, based on loyalty, or for charity. Individual and loyalty options typically include digital coupons and loyalty cards. The friends option is tied directly to Facebook and requires the participants to check in friends and family in order to get the current incentive. The charity option allows businesses such as PepsiCo to donate a set amount of money for each check-in to a specified charity. Let's take a look at how a few of these location-based apps work.

Mobile phone users who had an app from the social mapping network, Loopt were alerted to a special offer from Virgin America, about its new service to Mexico. For a chance to win a two-for-one ticket offer to Los Cabos or Cancun, all the recipients had to do was get to the airport in San Francisco, or Los Angeles, or to a local taco truck that Loopt had rebranded for the promotion. On a smaller scale, a restaurant having a slow night might use Loopt to let users know there was a last minute dinner promotion immediately available.

SCVNGR, a location-based application takes the check-in idea that is popular with sites such as Foursquare to a new level. They created some of the more innovative, engaging, and interactive promotions that tap in to the consumer's love of games, by incorporating their mobile phones into scavenger hunt challenges. Some tasks are tied to purchases, such as taking a picture of the meal you just ordered, while others are a way to gather clues. The point is to directly involve the target in a particular location or event.

To participate in a SCVNGR sponsored hunt, consumers only need to scan the designated QR code with their smartphones to receive the next clue. Because scanning is a part of the game, participants do not have to worry about anything beyond solving or finding clues, simplifying and demystifying its use. Players can earn points or merchandise on completion of each task and check-in.

Figure 8.1

Kidrobot, a small New York firm, decided to build even more interaction into a traditional contest when they chose to use a mobile scavenger hunt they dubbed the "Dunny Hunt" to launch the newest collection of limited edition Dunny action figures, toys, and apparel. The hunt incorporated QR barcodes into the action, requiring interested players to first download the software that matched their particular type of smartphone. The software allowed players to photograph the codes, which exposed a clue and virtual image about their highly collectable Dunny figures.

To play, participants could either opt-in to receive daily mobile clues or locate them on Twitter, in Kidrobot newsletters, in stores, or on the street where the required promotional codes were located on posters, pedicabs, T-shirts, and/or stickers. Players who located the coded material were required to photograph or scan the QR barcode to be automatically entered into a drawing for Dunny toys. Those who were the first to locate and photograph the code each day were eligible to win additional prizes. To keep players involved, a new code was released on each of the five days of the promotion.

Attracting a niche market of affluent, "first to own" creative types, Kidrobot chose the scavenger hunt because it was an interactive, engaging, and viral way to keep savvy consumers involved in the brand for a longer period of time than a simple "sign up and forget about it" contest ever could.

Of all the location-based social networks, Foursquare provides the best way for a brand to interact with their target. Beyond being interactive, it is a great way to reward and virtually interrelate with loyal customers. Foursquare, unlike its earlier predecessors such as Loopt and Brightkite, is probably the most responsible for expanding the acceptance of location-sharing applications by consumers. Hess Corporation, for example, used Foursquare to promote a Brisk iced tea and Frito-Lay product combo give-away to consumers who checked into any of their hundreds of gas stations. The promotion also included entrance into a sweepstakes to win a year's supply of free gas and Brisk iced tea. Although Hess initially used in-store signage to promote its program, they believed that additional advertising was not necessary once consumers make checking in a habit.

Shooger is another location-based app that delivers coupons via the target's cell phone. They specialize in helping consumers locate both local and national coupon offers that users can then redeem directly off their mobile phone. It also allows users to share coupons with friends via Twitter and Facebook. Recently, Shooger added the ability for retailers to add QR codes to their mobile coupon offers. As an added bonus, business owners can track in-store redemptions and limit the number of times a consumer can redeem a coupon.

Facebook "Deals," an offshoot of its Places mobile feature, allows global brands such as McDonald's or Starbucks to deliver location-based offers to anyone open to sharing their locations in status updates. This "Deals" application allows businesses to announce a "deal" or incentive on their Facebook Places page. Participants only have to check in to a specific location using their mobile phone in order to receive the current deal. "Deals" combines the location check-in services used by Foursquare and the local group offers associated with Groupon or LivingSocial.

Gowalla, a check-in based social network service, also similar to Foursquare, integrates Facebook and Twitter user accounts into their promotions.

Yelp initially gained fame as a local directory where consumers could get recommendations and see reviews of local merchants. It has recently added a check-in feature that alerts friends to the specific location of a user.

All of these location-based promotional offers are effective ways to reward brand loyal consumers who have opted in to receive advertising messages. This type of promotion is the next step in creating a more personalized message.

Beyond its use as a promotional tool, PepsiCo, for example, uses location-based marketing to gather both target demographics and psychographic data by researching where and how often the target checks in.

Quick Response Codes Are Both Entertaining and Informative

Barcodes have been a part of computer technology for decades. Every time we purchase a loaf of bread, a sheet set, or can of bug spray, the cashier at our local retail establishment scans the code for the price. Now this same technology, known as *quick response codes* (QR) or QR barcodes is being used as a way to entertain and find information via our cell phones. QR codes allow visitors to quickly and wirelessly connect to websites and view photos or videos from a sponsoring advertiser. To interact with information inside the code, interested consumers must use their smartphone to photograph or scan the black-and-white or colored graphic square to be delivered a multitude of options: receive an online message or coupon, be taken to a website, see a video or photograph, find clues for games, learn nutritional information for grocery items, or gain access to free giveaways. As a marketing tool, QR codes can also be used to direct participants to an event or website, process tickets with QR codes, organize a list of attendees at events, and keep track of the participants attended, to name just a few.

Additionally, when consumers download a QR code they are looking to find additional information on the product or service, such as where to purchase, consumer opinions, and specifics on how the product performs, what it weighs, the range of available colors, and so on. QR codes can appear anywhere and on anything and because of this diversity, they can offer many advertising and promotional opportunities for both consumers and businesses.

For example, the Albany New York transit system used QR codes to promote a contest where visitors could register to win an iPad. Lamar advertising placed the barcodes throughout Albany's two rail stations using not only the walls, but floors and kiosks to attract attention. Waiting passengers could also view the codes in bus shelters and on the ceilings of buses.

"The ads look like modern art," said Margo Janak, transit authority spokesperson, in an October 25, 2010 online *New York Times* article. She goes on to say, "People are definitely noticing" (Olson, 2010d, p. 3).

A July, 2010, article in *mashable.com*, "Why QR codes are poised to hit the mainstream," by Jennifer Van Grove, presents other good examples of the use of QR codes as employed by the Smithsonian and the *Boston Globe*. The promotion

> 'goSmithsonian,' used SCVNGR and barcodes to build a trek through several of the Smithsonian museums that required solving clues and completing challenges. More recently, the *Boston Globe* introduced a trek involving five different content-driven, city-based challenges. Treks are about mobile challenge-based discovery so they're certainly Foursquare and Gowallaesque in nature, but as the Smithsonian and the *Boston Globe* examples demonstrate, there's more here than just check-ins. (Van Grove, 2010, p. 4)

QR codes have created a new way of reaching the target, which is known as context-sensitive marketing (CSM) or virtual impulse buying. QR codes make on the spot buying easy since the brand is right in front of you.

Consumers find CSM an irresistible and timesaving convenience. Because they elect whether to scan the code, they are engaged in the buying experience. Consumers can click to search a brand's availability or click on

Figure 8.2

a link to find a wealth of crowdsourcing information to aid in the decision-making process, thus eliminating self-serving or ill-informed salespeople or the need for a lengthy Google hunt for a manual. Especially handy is the ability, with just a quick scan of the barcode, to easily download a manual or how-to video to a cell phone.

Consider the following sales-generating examples using QR codes:

1. After a long search, you notice the perfect side tables for your living room, not at your local furniture store or the mall, but in the lobby of your bank. Luckily for you, each table is equipped with a QR code. You scan it with your phone and click on the link that enables you to buy it on the spot.

2. Short on time, you call ahead to confirm your local nursery carries river rock for your garden. Assured that it is available, you travel miles out of your way to purchase this stony garden border. Unfortunately for you, they did not inform you that they close early if it rains. To make amends, they post a sign that says, "If we missed you due to rain, please accept a rain check on your next visit of 20% off any purchase, plus a free plant of your choice costing $5 or less, after scanning this message."

3. For the first time in years, you attend a basketball game at your college alma mater. The next day discussing the game with colleagues, you produce the program and while perusing its many stats and conference updates, you notice a QR code that you can scan to see the next home game for half price, if you order within the next 24 hours.

In the future, items purchased repeatedly will come with a scannable QR code printed on the label. Copy will direct the target to "scan to reorder." Participating consumers should receive some type of money-saving offer. Not only can this be done quickly and easily but it comes with some type of financial reward.

The acceptance and increased use of QR codes depends on whether the often hurried and distracted American consumer takes the time to interact with them. First, they must stop what they are doing, grab their smartphone, load up an app, and scan or take a picture of the code. Repetitive, inventive, and entertaining results should ultimately answer the cynical question, "why should I take the time to scan this?" So, if you have nothing of value to offer the consumer, do not use QR codes. It has to be worth the target's time and effort to scan the code. It should be creative, engaging, and enhance the target's lifestyle in some way.

Let's take a look at a few more examples.

Starz entertainment marketing is using QR barcodes to promote its new series "Spartacus: Gods of the Arena." Participating consumers will receive both special offers and insider information.

Fox is using mobile codes that give consumers additional access to current programming. Each code incorporates a new scanning technology that Fox has dubbed, "Fox Codes." Once consumers photograph the code, they are transported to a designated website that highlights additional "material-videos, first look photos, behind-the-scene footage and exclusive cast interviews," said Wayne Friedman in an online article for *Media Daily News* (Friedman, 2010, p. 1). Paramount Pictures used mobile barcodes to promote a variety of movie trailers for upcoming releases, such as *How To Train Your Dragon* and *Dinner for Schmucks*.

Macy's is using QR codes that they creatively labeled "Backstage Passes" to serve up consumer-oriented video content that includes tips, trends, and overall fashion advice. Since consumers cannot always make it into their stores, they believe the barcodes are a great way to bring designers and their lines to consumers.

Additionally, during the holiday season Macy's asked customers to photograph the barcode and text the photo to Macy's; in return they received a holiday-themed video. In the same manner, their Spring barcode promotion incorporates a more integrated approach by using television, print, and in-store signage.

A local bank used the Denver airport to promote the free download of an e-book to any passenger scanning the code found on posters throughout the airport. Once scanned, participants are taken to a webpage listing the e-book choices. Bored passengers could also download free crosswords and Sudoku games.

Additional examples include Ford Motor Company and the University of Maryland, using the Washington Metro Area Transit Stations for their barcode promotions. Participants who downloaded Ford's barcode are educated on the technology of its EcoBoost engine, while the University used a number of ads to promote its various educational programs.

Another brand successfully using QR codes is Lionsgate Films. To promote the film *For Colored Girls*, Lionsgate used both QR codes and short message service (SMS) tactics.

Once downloaded, this very engaging Internet campaign treats viewers to a movie trailer, information on the film, photos of cast members, and a text alert that reminds viewers about the film's premiere. Those consumers who are not interested, or are unable to download the QR code can text "colors" to 30333 to reach the mobile site. Promotions for the mobile campaign used bus shelters, wild postings, or postings placed around the city or town, and were featured on all theater posters promoting the movie.

To promote its contest for a trip to Napa Valley, Aloft Hotels placed three QR codes throughout the hotels on items such as postcards and room keys, to name just a few. To enter, patrons scanned the codes with their smartphones and signed up to win. Guests were informed about the contest on e-mailed reservation confirmations, via the website, or on the electronic ticker located in each participating hotel lobby.

For marketers, "this is the holy grail of advertising—interactive media in public places," said Michael Becker, North American managing director for the Mobile Marketing Association (Olson, 2010d, p. 2).

Text Messaging Still Gets the Word Out

Currently *SMS* or *text messaging* is the largest and most common form of mobile delivery. Future trends focus more on search and display, mainly due to the growing number of smartphones in operation today. This trend is aided by Google's AdMob and Apple's iAd, which put more focus on the use of rich media (e.g., streaming video and applets or programs that interact with the user, such as altering the look of an ad when the user's mouse passes over it).

Since there are no visual aspects to standard mobile advertising, it is important that all correspondence incorporate the same tone of voice used throughout the campaign.

Messages that are limited to no more than 160 characters require that advertising either gets to the point quickly or provides the targeted consumer with a link for more detailed information. Although the messages are limited, it is important to remember that the intended receiver is constantly on the move with little time for details.

Text messaging is a great mobile support device within a traditionally based advertising campaign and is an inexpensive way to reach the target. Multimedia messaging service or MMS allows for more sophisticated messages that include not only text but also slideshows, as well as audio and video capabilities.

Mobile Augmented Reality

Basically, the definition of *mobile augmented reality* is the same as the definition given in Chapter 6 for augmented reality (AR), which superimposes real-world images over digital images, text, and graphics to create a 3-D holographic image. The only real difference between the two definitions is in how it is used. Let's take a look at a few illustrations.

Relatively new to marketers, Cadbury is one of the first food brands to enter into the mobile augmented reality sphere with the introduction of an interactive game. According to a 2011 online article in *ConfectionaryNews* *.com*, Lynda Searby tells us, "The Kraft-owned confectionery producer is the launch partner for blippar, a new smartphone app that generates virtual experiences by superimposing graphics, audio and other sense enhancements onto physical products" (Searby, 2010, para. 2).

Basically, what blippar does for Cadbury is to transform one of their candy bars into a free augmented reality game that can be played on a consumer's phone. The article goes on to tell us that "the 'Qwak Smack' game can be played by anyone with a smartphone. When the app is running, pointing the phone's camera at a Cadbury countline launches a 30-second game in which quacking cartoon ducks emerge from the bar on an augmented overlay on the screen. The idea is to tap as many of the ducks as possible and players can submit their score to be entered into a drawing to win prizes" (Searby, 2010, para. 5).

Bloomingdale's, in a cooperative arrangement with NBC, is using mobile augmented reality in a way that allows their customers to virtually have their picture taken with stars from NBC's new fall season shows. The "Look the Part, Be the Part" campaign is discussed in a *Media Daily* article by Steve Smith, "[Bloomingdale's] uses the GoldRun augmented reality app, which superimposes images and data atop phone cam snapshots" (Smith, 2011, p. 1). Those willing to share their virtual photos are entered into a contest for a free trip to the set of one of the new television shows.

As an advertising vehicle, mobile is just getting its feet wet with marketers who are wading in to see just how much advertising versus promotional materials their target audience will tolerate. In the end, digital content expert Lee Bogner in an *Open Forum* article advises "that, no matter what, you need to be where your customers are—so if they are on the web, be on the web, if they're on Facebook, be there too. The same goes with e-mail, SMS, mobile apps and mobile websites" (Ray, 2010, p. 1).

Chapter 8 Exercises

1. Working in the same or new groups, use the brief from Chapter 2 that was developed for the national brand. Determine how mobile can be employed in the campaign, or combined with previous vehicles, if at all.

2. What visual/verbal and promotional direction will accomplish the directives laid out in both the marketing plan and creative brief? How will you tie the visual/verbal message together to create a cohesive look across vehicles?

3. Does the competition use mobile? If so, how can you create more engagement in your approach? If not, why will it increase awareness in your brand,

and attract the target's attention? Tie any decision regarding mobile use to the various forms of nontraditional media and any additional vehicles already being used in the campaign. Each team must defend their position based on information found in both documents. Tie creative decisions back to the creative brief and marketing plan.

4. Consider whether or not to delete any mediums based on what you now know about mobile media. If you do not delete and continue to use the same vehicles, how can you tie mobile into the existing direction? Be able to back up your decisions either way.

5. Present to class or to the marketing team.

6. Follow the same process for the small, local business determined in Chapter 2.

Memory Box

Mobile Marketing

Applications (Apps)

Location-Based Marketing

Quick Response (QR) Codes

Text Messaging

Mobile Augmented Reality

9

Out-of-Home and Transit Media

This chapter lays out the different forms of out-of-home advertising and illustrates additional creative ways to transmit a memorable message. When appropriately used, this type of advertising can both engage and create an encounter that can be shared beyond the target's initial exposure to the message.

A Diverse Canvas Gives Out-of Home a Unique Appeal

Out-of-home advertising can be simply defined as anything seen outside of the home. The definition may seem a bit broad, but the canvases most often associated with out-of-home include traditional and electronic billboards, wallscapes, and street furniture. For the purpose of this text, although transit is technically considered an out-of-home vehicle, we examine it separately in order to discuss its many diverse and creative options.

There is not much to say about out-of-home that is not already known, but the creative use of the chosen display space is what can make the advertising so successful. Because out-of-home vehicles are so diverse, there is no limit to the standard size or surface shape that can be used to deliver a message. Because of this, each design is not only visually and verbally unique to the brand but often physically diverse as well. Whether large or small in stature, no successful out-of-home message is verbose. The goal is to capture attention with an arresting visual that is accompanied by not more than five to seven words. The objective is to get to the point quickly and memorably since the assumption is that most viewers are distracted, tired, grumpy, or on the move.

Most out-of-home is commonly posted along interstate highways, in or near major metropolitan cities, and inside or outside of commuter transports (e.g., taxis, subways, buses, or airplanes). Messages strategically placed inside of public transportation or along roadways reach a captive audience, since most commuters travel back and forth from home to work or play along the same route. The large or unusual canvases are fixed and cannot be ignored—the daily commuter cannot fast forward, delete, or turn off the message—accurately defining them as in-your-face messages.

Any type of out-of-home vehicle is easily adapted to a local, regional, national, or international market. Rural areas use road signs that direct travelers to hotels and restaurants, and larger cities throughout the world have various types of mass transit, shelters, and terminals that can creatively deliver culturally adaptable messages and images.

All forms of out-of-home are considered mass media vehicles by virtue of the static properties of the medium: they cannot be personalized, cannot build a relationship with the target, and cannot tell a brand's story with in-depth copy points. It serves as a reminder vehicle, relying on additional advertising vehicles to entice and engage. However, it is a great vehicle to build or maintain interest, to alert or direct consumers to a specific business location, announce events or promotions, and reinforce other visual/verbal messages that are incorporated into a marketing campaign. With a few words, out-of-home must capture the target's attention through visually powerful images and get the target talking about the brand beyond their initial exposure. Images that change out regularly keep the conversation in play as consumers are attracted to an ongoing storyline. Nobody does this better than Chick-fil-A. Not only is the cow and chicken idea amusing, the 3-D cows placed on outdoor boards across the country capture attention through their changing costumes, local adaptations, and clever quips.

Rarely is out-of-home used as a primary media vehicle in any campaign, but it can be used to successfully launch a brand, as a teaser to build interest, to extend a brand's message or as a cooperative vehicle with other local or national brands.

Marketers who are deciding whether or not to include some form of out-of-home in their marketing mix should consider what it can bring to the message and overall media mix:

1. The ability for marketers to reach their moving target and grab their attention.

2. The targetability of its geographic location. Marketers who vary their messages can reach the target multiple times with a new message as they move about their day.

3. A great way to build brand awareness by showcasing their logo or relevant images.

4. Its overall effectiveness when used within an integrated marketing campaign.

5. Digital and interactive options allow marketers to easily change out their message and engage the target for longer periods of time than ever before.

Marketers need to decide during the development or evaluation of their marketing mix whether the use of out-of-home effectively reaches the target with the right message, in the right place, at the right time, within or on vehicles they are likely to see, hear, read, or view, if possible interacts with the target, does not convey any negativity to the brand's image, and ensures a profitable ROI. It is also important to determine how out-of-home can cohesively be injected into the existing visual/verbal message of the promotional mix, its effect on sales, and whether its role contributes to the campaign's overall call to action.

One of the greatest assets of out-of-home is that it can reach the target geographically, whether they are walking, driving, riding, or just looking out their office windows or storefronts. Because of this movement, it is a great option for retail products, local services, entertainment options, and tourism. Fine-tuned geographic targeting and placement allows advertisers to tailor messages based on store location, as well as to ensure that messages are placed near the point of sale or near the site of a brand's use or target interaction.

New digital capabilities allow out-of-home to be more creative and interactive. Messages can be changed out frequently, thus guaranteeing freshness and avoiding a stale, static image. It is also a great way to reinforce the visual/verbal message used elsewhere in a campaign, and offers further engagement possibilities by tying any message to the Internet and mobile devices.

The numerous options available when considering out-of-home advertising are:

1. Outdoor boards

2. Transit (inside and out)

3. Mobile billboards

4. Video projection

5. Wild postings

6. Aerial advertising

7. Golf carts

8. Valet parking tickets

9. Parking permits

10. Pedicabs

11. Carriages

The choice of media mix must be both visually and verbally synergistic, regardless of where consumers encounter a message. Any individual vehicle choice can be effective but the combination of multiple vehicles reinforces the message and encourages action on the part of the target. So it is important marketers and their agencies work together to ensure marketing objectives and strategies are cohesively intertwined with advertising objectives and strategies in order to accomplish the marketing sales goals. To accomplish this, the visual/verbal message associated with out-of-home must strongly project the key consumer benefit. Its strength lies in its ability to show and tell with little or no copy, as the upcoming examples illustrate.

Identifying a Medium's Strengths and Weaknesses Reinforces and Highlights the Visual/Verbal Message

Before deciding where out-of-home advertising fits in a campaign, it is important that both marketers and the advertising teams understand how it can positively enhance or negatively affect a campaign's message. Let's take a quick look at both its capabilities and limitations.

Out-of-Home Advertising Strengths

1. **Captures attention.** Geographic flexibility is a great way to target and attract attention near the point of sale.

2. **Repetition.** Messages can be seen repetitively because commuters travel the same routes on a daily basis from home to work and back again.

3. **Strengthens brand awareness.** Because messages can be placed near the point of purchase, out-of-home keeps the brand top of mind.

4. **Costs.** All types of out-of-home are affordable.

Out-of-Home Advertising Weaknesses

1. **Clutter.** Messages can often be hard to see when placed near other forms of outdoor advertising or obscured by tall buildings, electrical wires, and so on.

2. **Public spaces.** Any advertising placed outside can be affected by weather, vandalism, and pollution, all of which can affect brand image.

3. **Limited copy.** It has little space to tell the brand's story, so copy must get to the point in as few words as possible.

4. **Fleeting messages.** Many out-of-home surfaces are seen while the target is distracted and on the move.

Taking It to the Streets

The popularity of out-of-home is growing as more people commute and spend more time outside the home or office. The varied sizes, shapes, and creative options associated with out-of-home ensure a powerful, impactful delivery. The design should be simple, bold, and creative in order to visually and verbally tie back to other messages used throughout the campaign. It is a creative way to talk to the public and more precisely your target, based on its location. This form of message is a fairly inexpensive way to 24/7 say something big, or point consumers to a location, or advertise a local event.

Messages placed on any outdoor board are rarely seen for longer than six to eight seconds unless placed near a stoplight or in an area with heavy pedestrian traffic. Because of this, messages must imaginatively scream out the key consumer benefit in an unexpected yet memorable way. With the introduction of digital technology, outdoor can say more than ever before. Providing great engagement and interactivity, creative teams can take advantage of the new technology (such as tying a mobile alert to the advertising seen on an outdoor board) and let the target know that the advertised store or brand is nearby and that a coupon has already been delivered to their phone.

Although used as a supportive vehicle, out-of-home does not need to take a back seat creatively. Many of today's outdoor boards are often movable, incorporate the surrounding landscape, have 3-D additions, or are lighted. They are creative, attractive, eye-catching—often placed in high traffic and public places, such as shopping malls, subways, buses, or airport terminals or placed on top of buildings or hung off the sides of structures.

Message delivery can also be affected by size. Depending on the location, outdoor boards come in a variety of sizes: for example, interstate highway signs are the largest at 20 x 60 feet, signs placed within city limits are typically 14 x 48 feet, while mall or terminal boards are sized around 12 x 24 feet. Regardless of where boards are placed, they are almost always surrounded by visual clutter so be certain that the visual images are big and colorful, that the text can be easily read from 500 feet away on roads and highways, and from 5 to 10 feet away by pedestrians. To adjust for surrounding conditions, check to make certain that the board is not only readable from a specific distance but from all angles, lighting, and weather conditions.

Since outdoor advertising is relegated to specific but always high traffic locations, it makes it harder to target a specific group of individuals. To guarantee the notice of the targeted group, the visual/verbal message must highlight their specific needs and/or lifestyle and be placed in a location that the target frequents. Let's take a look at a few highly creative examples.

Products, especially foreign produced goods and services with a difficult name to pronounce need to find a way to get their name onto their target's lips and firmly planted in their minds. For example, Chicco (pronounced KEE-KO), the Italian producer of baby products wanted Americans to not only be able to correctly pronounce its name but become involved in pronouncing its name. Built around the tag "If you say it right, it makes you smile," Chicco's name campaign encouraged parents to teach their babies how to pronounce their unusual brand name. All enterprising parents had to do was to make a video of their baby saying Chicco, and it could appear on a Times Square billboard.

Beyond billboards, the campaign also included print and a website. Online ads effectively reinforced the message with a special webcam banner where videos can be uploaded as well as providing access to social media sites.

An interactive board, which also appeared in Times Square several years ago, advertised a phone number pedestrians could call using their cell phones to play a game with another viewer that could be seen in real time up on the board.

The YMCA decided to take a very simple approach with an all white board that sported only a 3-D basketball net and their logo to push its local basketball courts.

To exhort the need for backseat passengers to wear safety belts, one creative advertiser placed a huge slingshot on the ground that was hooked on to the billboard on either side of a visual that shows a man sitting in the backseat of a car. The slingshot is so taut it looks like it is ready to shoot him forward. The copy confirms the illusion, saying, "The Back Seat's No Safer. Belt Up."

To advertise the dramatic effect of its natural hair colors, one company used a transparent board that showed the graphic silhouette of a woman's eye, nose, mouth, and flowing head of hair. The ad worked like a negative, depending on the time of day and location of the sun, the changing colors of the setting and rising sun appeared to change the color of the hair.

To advertise its quality care, a hospital used a billboard with a woman sitting on a gurney in the foreground along with the logo. The background showed two cars smashed during an accident. One car had real-time smoke pouring from it, compliments of a smoke machine hidden behind the board. Copy reads: "*WhyImAlive.com.*"

A local pizza company also used a smoke machine to show the steam rising off a very large pizza. On the left a huge, round, delicious looking pizza extends off the board. On the right placed on a red background is the copy reversed to white that reads, "New Hand Tossed Pizza. Big On Taste," followed by the logo.

A promotion for the movie *Kill Bill 2* not only used a billboard on the side of a building to promote the movie, but props. The visual on the board showed a picture of Uma Thurman with her sword and the movie's title on the far right side. Blood from the sword held over her shoulder is not only splattered across the board but onto the wall that holds the board, the street below, and onto two white cars parked in the direct path of the blood.

Using existing electric wires, an ad for a nose hair trimmer dramatized the need by using a vertical board that showed a cartoon illustration of a man's face with the actual electrical wires passing through his rather large nostrils (simulating nose hairs). The bottom of the ad held a picture of the trimmer with copy that reads, "Nose Hair Trimmer Safety Cutting System."

To showcase the perils of tailgating, the Colorado state patrol used a billboard that showed a visual of a car rear-ending a semi-trailer. To dramatize the impact, the billboard crinkled up in the same way a vehicle would after a crash. The billboard's accordion look partially extended off the top of the board, leaving the impression that the board and both vehicles were damaged. The copy on the upper left reads: "Tailgating Isn't Worth It." Smaller on the upper right was additional copy that reads, "Give Trucks Room. It's The Law," followed by the logo.

In an ad touting the dangers of drinking and driving, one attention-grabbing ad painted a white rectangle the size and shape of a car around a tree. Half of the rectangle was painted on the street while the other half was up on the sidewalk. Copy painted in yellow on the opposite end from the tree read, "Reserved For Drunk Drivers," followed by the sponsor's logo.

A self defense school used a wall mounted board and rip-away posters to advertise its classes. The visual was a cartoon of what appears to be a man wearing a mask that covers only his eyes; the only other part of the face that is visible is the upper lip. The rip-away acts as the illustration's teeth. All interested consumers had to do was rip off one of the teeth and contact them for a free lesson.

Wallscapes, Building Wraps, and Rooftop Advertising

A *wallscape* or banner is a huge out-of-home advertising vehicle that can be painted directly on vinyl or onto the outside of a building or hung off a structure. A building wrap is just that, an advertisement printed on vinyl used as an enormous outdoor board that typically wraps around a building on two or more sides, and which often uses the building's windows in the design. ***Rooftop advertising*** places bigger than life 3-D logos atop tall buildings where they can be seen for miles.

A local gym used a huge wallscape that hung off the side of a building under construction. The visual is black-and-white and shows a sweaty buff guy preparing to lift weights. The only copy is the logo.

Allstate used a circular high-rise parking building to show its customer service capabilities by hanging a smallish blue banner featuring its logo and familiar copy, "Are you in Good Hands?" Not that creative until you look just above the banner where a real car looks as if it has broken through the safety railing to perilously dangle off the garage, high above the pedestrians below.

An ad for a milk producer in India placed a large banner on the side of a building to dramatize the superhuman powers that milk drinkers can achieve. The banner extended off the right side of the building and showed a man

Figure 9.1

pushing a horizontal slice of the building out into the open sky. The only copy is the logo—a great example of how it's always better to show than tell.

Pepsi and Nescafe used the tops of buildings to showcase their 3-D ads. Pepsi placed its name on a circular pedestal that featured a 3-D version of its graphic red, white, and blue logo sitting on top. Nescafe also featured its logo prominently on the top of a building complete with a big, red, 3-D coffee mug sitting on top of it.

Digital Out-of-Home

The static billboards of old are all going digital. Messages that once could not be changed or altered for anywhere from one to twelve months can now be rotated between several different advertisers a day. Digital outdoor boards, also known as **digital billboards**, *LED billboards* and *electronic billboards,* are a great choice for marketers with a relevant, even time-sensitive message. A simple click of a mouse can quickly change or update images that once required a team of workers and multiple hours to dismantle and replace old messages with new ones.

Able to be seen from great distances, these spectacular, brightly colored boards can show one image or ad at a time, show a loop of multiple ads, or project computer-animated content, while still others might digitally show the time or current gas prices at the next exit. Marketers can pick from one of two basic types of digital boards: digital outdoor and on premise LED signs. Digital boards are the ones seen along the interstate or local streets and highways that can display up to six to eight different messages from one or more advertisers on the same board. Depending on state and local regulations, each image rotates every four to ten seconds. On premise LED signs are located outside of a business showcasing its name and/or logo. Boards can either be attached to the business itself or placed on stilts high above it, so as to be clearly visible to a pedestrian.

Transit Advertising Is Always Working

Transit advertising is any brand-sponsored message appearing in or on public transportation (buses, taxis), on benches, in shelters, waiting areas, and terminals. A mass media vehicle, transit reaches consumers of all ages, income levels, and professions. Messages are not only visible to commuters but pedestrians, bike riders, drivers sitting in traffic, and anyone looking out the window of their store, home, or office.

Advertising surfaces come in very diverse shapes, sizes, and technology fueled delivery options. Similar to outdoor, transit as a medium has a limited amount of space in which to capture the target's attention. Although transit advertising is not hard to miss, consumers spend very little time reading and digesting their meaning. Because of this, images must be powerful, colorful, bold, and supported by brief but educational copy. Minimized messages are confined to either pushing the key consumer benefit or showcasing the slogan or tagline and logo. The additional use of recognizable images such as packaging, character representatives, or spokespersons, is a great way to say more than the limited space allows. Transit, unlike other forms of mass communication, does not entertain or tell a detailed story; its job is to entice through memorable images that serve to remind and support messages seen elsewhere in a campaign.

All transit advertising relies on a captive audience repeatedly seeing the message to increase recall and encourage action. Perhaps one of the biggest downsides to transit advertising is its ability to deliver only a one-way message to the consumer, but one of the biggest assets of a transit message is that the advertising is viewable twenty-four-seven. To offset this downside, many brands create advertising that is interactive to increase memorability and engage consumers while they wait for a ride. These types of ads are successful because people travel the same route to work on a daily basis, increasing the viewing frequency of the message and increasing the recall potential. Transit advertising placed on vehicles, benches, and in terminals that is close to the point of purchase makes this option a great vehicle to promote impulse buying.

Bus Advertising Covers a Lot of Ground

Advertising on city buses, in shelters, and on benches is a sure way to get your message noticed. Buses dominate the landscape in cities large and small, and due to their size and sheer numbers, the ads they carry can dominate as well. Of course, buses can cover great distances, thereby impacting a huge audience.

There are several different types of bus ads, including full wrap, half wrap, bus back, king, queen, and tail light. Full wraps cover the entire bus, car, or truck with colorful images that can be seen from all sides. Designs can be either air brushed directly onto the bus or applied with a self-adhesive vinyl. These digitally created advertisements are both weather and fade resistant and can last up to a year. This bold surface is a great reminder vehicle for local sports, news, or cultural events.

A full wrap also covers the vehicle's windows. To allow passengers to see out, the design often features punctures in the images covering the panels that are not noticeable from a viewable distance.

Half wraps cover the side of the bus and stretch from front to back, not including the windows. Bus backs are noticeable because there will always be someone sitting behind the bus, making this is a great place to boldly advertise or display something. King-size bus ads are panels that are placed on the street side of the bus, usually measuring around 30 inches x 140 inches. Queen-size ads are viewable from the curb facing side of the bus and measure the same size as king-size panels. Tail light panels appear on the back of the bus and typically measure 21 inches x 72 inches.

Most interior bus advertising is placed on interior cards that are mounted directly above the seats. Each card measures around 11 inches x 40 inches, allowing for several to be placed the length of the interior of the bus. These billboard shaped advertisements are colorful, sporting big images and little copy. Let's take a look at a few creative and eye-catching examples of bus advertising.

To advertise its current snake exhibit, a smallish zoo in Tennessee used a bus side to promote its largest visitor, a reticulated python named Buttercup, by showing its girth (bigger than a man's hand) and length (23 feet) with copy that reads: Actual Size.

The Copenhagen zoo also used the image of a giant snake that stretches from one end to the other that appears to wrap completely around and squeeze the bus. Between wraps is the logo.

For cities boasting large skyscrapers where consumers work or live high above the city streets, *Careerbuilder.com* commandeered the use of bus tops to promote a short but to the point message: the featured black copy on a stark white background read "Don't Jump."

To promote a line of its cameras, Canon used a bus side that focused all eyes on the wheel wells. Painted on the side was the camera; the lens was represented by one of the bus's wheels. Bus sides that focus on wheel wells have also been used to portray a turntable, as the front wheel of a motor-cycle and as the iris of a human eye.

To promote its weight loss program, Weight Watchers used the back of the bus as its advertising canvas. The visual was tilted down on one side. The lowest side showed the back of a woman supposedly seated inside the bus, her weight appearing to be the cause of its current tilt. The only copy was the logo.

National Geographic, to announce its Shark Week series used bus sides to show an up-close view of a shark. His very large and slightly opened mouth grew wider each time the bus's double door opened, where passengers appeared to be entering the shark's mouth. The copy read, "Built for the kill. Now on National Geographic Channel," accompanied by the logo.

ToysDirect.com used the sides of a double-decker bus to place a visual showing a battery compartment complete with three batteries placed end to end to make it appear as if the "toy" looking bus was battery powered.

A wonderful insurance ad placed on the back of the bus employed a visual of a bus driver who appeared to be looking behind him instead of straight ahead to where he was going. That would scare any driver—if for a split second they thought the bus was actually coming toward them rather than driving away. Copy reads: "Just Call Us."

ALL Detergent completely wrapped a city bus with real pieces of clothing. Copy reads: "How Much Can One Small Bottle Clean?" The only other "visual" is a picture of the product.

Interior Hand Hold Adverting

Bus and shelter advertising are not the only places that passengers can encounter creative advertising. Once on board a bus, standing travelers can do so while holding onto something more creative than just a simple bar. What could be more interactive than holding on to an advertisement as the subway train or bus speeds you to your destination?

A brand of hand lotion hung arms off the horizontal bars on a bus. Standing passengers could hold onto the faux hands to help them maintain their balance.

One beer company placed actual sized beer cans around the vertical poles. Those who held on looked like they were holding the foamy thirst-quenching beverage.

A beauty salon wanted to promote their new hair-strengthening product by hanging a braided ponytail made of real hair (or what appears to be real hair) off the straps. The top of the tail has a picture of the product and the bottom sported a pretty red bow.

Amnesty International used the circular straps on a bus to represent a noose and then they hung cutouts of people with their hands tied behind their backs.

Harley Davidson, to announce the arrival of a new model, mounted motorcycle grips to the upper bars on buses.

A fitness company decided to use the horizontal poles as faux barbells by placing simulated weights about three-feet apart down the length of the poles.

Bus Shelters and Benches Are a
Creative Way to Extend the Message

Consumers have to sit when they wait for any kind of public transportation so why not make their seats a part of an advertising message. These stationary surfaces are an excellent way for local and national advertisers to reach a moving target. These often creative designs can extend messages seen on other transit vehicles, or continue a theme used throughout a campaign.

Bench advertising, also known as street furniture advertising, can consist of advertising on benches, bus, or train shelters, freestanding newspaper distribution racks, and mall or terminal kiosks, to name just a few. Commonly used surfaces for this type of advertising can be found in local parks, restaurants, malls, college campuses, and subway or airport terminals. These surfaces are popular advertising vehicles because they are often found in areas with a large amount of pedestrian traffic.

When marketers choose to use city property that serves the local community such as shelters and benches, they are often responsible for upkeep and sometimes even the construction of the vehicles. Because visual ads are more memorable, picture the following very creative examples:

To promote the virtues of reading, the city of Istanbul created benches that look like a partially open paperback novel. Each bench comes complete with numerous poems from well-known Turkish poets.

Denver Water Company wanted to ensure that consumers understood the importance of conserving water. To do this, they removed all but a quarter of a wooden park bench's seat and backrest, leaving just enough of the bench intact to seat one person. Copy was placed on an orange seatback with white lettering that read: "Use Only What You Need. Denver Water."

IKEA, always inventive, covered benches, and almost any other everyday item that pedestrians might encounter with fabric slipcovers to promote their campaign called "A little fabric makes a big difference."

To draw attention to the movie *District 9*, transit bench backs were creatively used to let anyone or anything considering sitting that this "Bus Bench Was For Humans Only." Additional copy read: "Report Non-Humans. 1-866-666-6001. Beware: Non-Human Secretions May Corrode Metal. *D-9.com*." The only visual showed a non-human inside a big red circle with a big red line slashing through it.

Platform, Shelter, or Terminal Advertising

Platform or shelter posters can be located in any terminal or shelter where a commuter waits for public transportation such as at entrances and exits, platforms, even bathrooms.

The goal of all transit advertising is to be so creative it encourages viral and word-of-mouth sharing to increase its often limited reach. The imaginative ideas illustrated in the following examples are limited only to the advertising team's creativity and, of course, the client's budget.

United is selling ad space on its fleet of planes and within its terminal locations to outside retailers. Each ad campaign is an integrated multiplatform initiative. Chase Bank, for example, will use the in-flight magazine and tray tables to promote travel to fun or exotic locales, as well as use the overhead monitors for video spots. Campaigns can be geographically targeted based on flight destination or based on seating, such as first class, business, or economy.

On another airline flight, Wrigley's handed out samples of Altoids Smalls breath mints to passengers, along with an informative card about the product and an overhead video spot that expounded further on the mint's virtues.

One German restaurant used a freestanding shelter poster made of glass to advertise the freshness of their seafood. The poster sports a blue background that shows a single place setting. The fresh part is brought to life by the real fish swimming inside the display. Copy reads, "Fresh As Can Be," followed by the logo.

Another creative advertiser used one of the glass sides of a shelter for its message. The poster is solid black with a big white arrow pointing down to the very small copy at the bottom. In order to read it, the intrigued viewer must bend over. Copy reads: "At this moment your bum is completely exposed. If it were in a sexy pair of jeans, it would attract attention all the time."

An ad for the movie *UP* used a shelter side and a light post for advertising. Directly above the promotional poster, which featured the Wilderness Explorer Russell, was a light pole that held a batch of helium-filled balloons that mimic those used in the movie.

In Sweden, Norwegian Airlines used a shelter poster that featured a real kilt and a photograph of feet sticking out from underneath. Riders and pedestrians who wanted to see what the kilt was hiding could lift it up and find an ad for the airline's newest travel destination—Scotland, of course.

The MacBook Air not only used a shelter side to advertise the laptop but also installed a swing for the waiting riders.

An advertising agency in Italy placed a white curtain over their shelter poster. Consumer curiosity being what it is, they knew bored riders could not keep from opening the curtain and taking a quick peek. When they did, they were confronted with the silhouetted image of a man holding a knife above his head. Copy read: "How does it feel to be involved in a crime?"

Sony Playstation used a bus shelter in Malaysia to promote its PS2. To engage consumers, they covered each panel with bubble wrap. Each bubble featured either an X or an O. Advertisers knew that consumers could not resist popping each and every one of them while they waited.

A zoo in British Columbia used shelter signage to promote the Victoria Bug Zoo. The sign used a plastic sheet that had been divided into a grid. Each box was made up of small magnifying lenses. When pedestrians or waiting passengers stood in front of them, it gave them the same bug's-eye, multilens view as the creepy, crawly, multilegged insects on display at the zoo.

A South African company, to demonstrate their energy saving light bulbs, placed them in a shelter to light only when someone entered in order to prove their point, "Only use electricity when you need it."

Coca-Cola, to promote its new grip bottle, created posters made out of red Velcro that showed the new bottle with copy that read: "New Grip Bottle." This very successful campaign actually caused the clothes of viewers to stick to the posters.

Amnesty International was the first service to use shelter posters with a camera that kicks into action when people look at it. The black copy placed on a yellow background reads: It Happens When Nobody Is Watching." The first visual shows a man preparing to hit a woman. When waiting passengers look directly at the poster, it changes to the same couple posed and smiling as if waiting to have their picture taken.

Ecko clothing used a single freestanding glass panel to advertise its unique brand of clothing. Passersby could use the Bluetooth capability on their cell phones and "spray paint" their own message on the all white board using the cursor on their phone. The only text permanently on the board was the clothing line's logo in the lower right corner.

A vending machine in a Shinagawa, Japan, train station does not immediately show thirsty commuters the bottled or canned drinks found inside; instead, it encourages consumers to interact with its 47-inch touch screen monitor. Anyone standing in front of the monitor will not only have their picture taken, but a sensor determines their sex and approximate age. Based on the data collected the alien machine recommends the appropriate drinks for that particular profile.

Toshinari Sasagaioa, general manager of sales at an East Japan Railway subsidiary, in a 2010 *Wall Street Journal* article is quoted as saying, "with this machine, we can actually see who is buying what, instead of relying on educated guesses" (Wakabayashi & Osawa, 2010, p. 1). Will we see any of these intrusive machines in the United States? Privacy issues being what they are, probably not any time soon.

Mini Cooper placed an ad for its unique looking little car at the entrance to a train station. The visual shows a cutout of the car with the driver's side door open. As riders enter the station, it appears that they are getting into the car.

Taxi Advertising Can Be Geographically Targeted

Taxi advertising is no longer confined to just the roof of the car. Many are now wrapped, use the trunk, or are equipped with interior video screens or exterior digital technology. Just as in the case of bus advertising, these vehicles cover a large territory where the messages receive a great deal of exposure. It is a great vehicle for reaching consumers with repetitive messages that increase brand recognition and support or extend messages advertised in another medium. Based on the location of the cab, vehicles that have rooftop advertising with GPS capabilities are ideal for delivering a geographically targeted message, making it an excellent advertising choice for large and small locally based advertisers to promote their message close to the point of sale.

Some of today's newest technology appears on taxi tops where digitally displayed messages give sponsored weather and stock reports. More technologically advanced features can employ three- and four-sided digital toppers that show full-motion video and even holograms. One of the more creative 3-D examples of taxi advertising was used by ColdStone Creamery.

This very tall display captured the attention of consumers with a sweet tooth when they placed a large waffle cone and a single dip of ice cream featuring bits of fruit upside down on the roof of a taxi. The chunky, creamy looking scoop is slowly melting down the window; the door panels sported the logo. Pretty enough to make you salivate.

Nontraditional Out-of-Home
Takes Memorable One Step Further

Many types of out-of-home advertising are very new to the marketplace. Those using digital technology not only grab attention but also create word-of-mouth opportunities, or even in some cases become interactive. Let's take a look at some of these more captivating forms of nontraditional out-of-home opportunities.

Coastal cities or cities with waterfront development can incorporate the use of sails on sailboats and the exposed portions of large cargo or cruise ships to display their advertised message.

One of the new inventions, building illumination, is spectacular for nighttime exposure and allows a brand to project their logo or name down the side of buildings. Easy to see by drivers, commuters, and pedestrians alike, if the view is unobstructed these huge illuminated messages are often over 300 feet tall and can be seen for miles.

If you need a more complicated or detailed projection, think mobile projection. Using the side of a building as a screen, the advertised message can be moved daily or hourly to spotlight the action. It works by placing the projection equipment on the top of customized vans. The images are mobile as the vans move up and down the city streets, or stationary if the van is parked.

Images that are on the move can be 30 to 40 feet in diameter. Stationary images can top out at 200 feet square. There is also the option to project more than one image at a time. In high pedestrian areas to make the imaging more spectacular and attention grabbing, multiple images can be panned from one side of the street to the other.

Digital interactive advertising is a unique advertising vehicle that allows the target to interact with a digitally projected message. Sensors capture the target's movements; in turn, the data trigger the display's reaction mechanisms that then allow the message to be manipulated by the target in real time.

This very adaptable vehicle can be projected almost anywhere—onto the floor, walls, and windows as well as on plasma screen displays and interactive kiosks. The diversity of size and interaction capabilities makes it very portable and easy to deploy in a variety of locations such as malls, stadiums or arenas, hotel lobbies, airports, tradeshows, and so on.

Out-of-Home Engages and Informs Both Visually and Verbally

Because of its supporting role in a campaign, it is important that any form of out-of-home strongly push the key consumer benefit, repeat color or color combinations, headline styles, typeface(s), character representatives or spokespersons, or employ other images such as packaging to help synergistically tie the message into an existing campaign. Furthermore, to keep it simple, rarely is more than one image used, so it is important it speak loudly and as boldly as the budget and local and national restrictions permit.

Most out-of-home is limited to delivering a single, high impact message in a short period of time, so be sure that the image screams out the key consumer benefit and that copy is easy to read and understand from a distance. The most memorable out-of-home ads are composed of three distinct visual/verbal elements: 1) a powerful image, 2) the key consumer benefit, and 3) the slogan or tagline and logo.

Many marketers are leery of out-of-home vehicles because they cannot fully explain the brand's features and benefits (e.g., uses, colors, shapes, sizes, etc.). To overcome this skepticism, it is important to keep in mind that one impressive and creative image can say more and is more memorable than a page full of copy.

Images that are bold and colorful and are high in contrast attract attention. Choices of visual imagery are unlimited, ranging from color or black-and-white photographs, to illustrations, to animated figures or graphic images, depending on the strategic direction employed, and the brand's overall image.

On most out-of-home surfaces, images do not need to be confined to the surface on which it appears. Many can extend beyond its boundaries or be enhanced by 3-D or digital images.

Type should be large to be easily read and understood. Be certain that the logo is easy to find and viewable from a distance. Copy on larger vehicles is limited to no more than five to seven words; smaller vehicles rely on the brand's slogan or tagline and logo as their only visual/verbal message.

Color combinations should not overwhelm the images or type employed. It is also important to assure that color choices do not blend into the surrounding area. For example, avoid using a sky blue color on outdoor boards placed along open highways or greens if placed along wooded areas. Boards that blend into their surroundings and are hard to see cannot be effective or interactive.

Out-of-home has become a vibrant, creative advertising tool that not only attracts attention but can often interact with the target, thereby lengthening the life of a message through viral and word-of-mouth sharing. Thanks to the advances in technology and wireless capabilities, out-of-home can entertain, engage, and reach consumers through their cell phones with promotional devices to further increase exposure for the advertiser.

Chapter 9 Exercises

1. Working in the same or new groups, use the brief that was developed for the national brand from Chapter 2. Determine how out-of-home can be employed in the campaign, or combined with previous vehicles, if at all.

2. What visual/verbal direction accomplishes the directives laid out in both the marketing plan and creative brief? How will you tie the visual/verbal message together to create a cohesive vision across vehicles?

3. Do competitors use any form of out-of-home? If so, how can you create more engagement in your approach? If not, why will it increase awareness in your brand and attract the target's attention? Integrate all proposals with the various forms of nontraditional media and additional vehicles already selected

for the campaign. Each team must defend their position based on information found in both documents. Tie creative decisions back to the creative brief and marketing plan.

4. Consider whether or not you delete any mediums based on what you now know about out-of-home vehicles. If you do not delete and continue to use the same vehicles, how can you tie out-of-home into the existing direction? Be able to support your decisions in either case.

5. Make a presentation to the class or to the marketing team of your findings.

6. Repeat the same process for the small, local business selected in Chapter 2.

Memory Box

Out-of-Home Advertising

Digital Out-of-Home

Transit Advertising

Wallscapes

Building Wraps

Rooftop Advertising

10

Direct Marketing and Sales Promotion

This chapter defines the ways that direct marketing can be used to build a relationship with the target. Its various forms are dissected one-by-one to show how this customized media vehicle can reach the selected target with a message that reflects and embodies their lifestyle. Discussions also cover how sales promotions can be used as an enticement to further research a brand, visit a brick-and-mortar store, or increase brand awareness and brand value.

Direct Marketing Makes Reaching the Target Personal

As previously discussed, marketers and advertisers have typically used traditional advertising vehicles to launch or reposition a brand, build awareness, define image, and announce a sale. Unlike mass marketing's generic approach to message delivery, a personalized, relationship-building tactic is possible with direct marketing, in order to further enhance the relationship between buyer and seller. These highly customized messages call the target by name and tie the sales message directly to the target's interests and lifestyle. Because of this, the cost to reach the target is relatively expensive but extremely measurable.

One of the most encompassing definitions of *direct marketing* comes from Daniel Cortes: "a promotion and communication strategy that allows you to target a specific market using different media in order to stimulate your customer's behavior in a way that you can measure, track and analyze all the information involved in the process and store it on a database for future use" (Cortes, 2011, p. 1).

Direct marketing—also known as *relationship marketing*—is a great way to develop and maintain a relationship with the target over time. It ignores the middleman or retailer and allows the manufacturer to interact and sell directly to the targeted audience. It is a great way to individualize mass media tactics, thus making it a great relationship-enhancing tool.

The goal of relationship marketing is to not only sell a good, consistently reliable product and to personalize the sale by addressing the client by name, but to extend the sale by including personal experiences between the customer and the company's customer service representatives, sales personnel, or technical advisors. All marketing plans need to incorporate some type of relationship development vehicle to keep the lines of communication open and further build or maintain brand loyal customers.

Direct mail or e-mail marketing are some of the best vehicles to assist in developing this personal relationship by allowing for direct interaction with the target on a one-to-one basis. In the case of vehicles such as catalogs, the Internet, brochures, and interactive television, the consumer picks up or watches by choice these direct messages. Sometimes, the direct mail message is combined with other information that the target is guaranteed to interact with—for example, advertisements in statement stuffers, or in the mail (magalogs and poly packs).

Whether a brand incorporates offline direct marketing tactics into their media mix or not, almost all brands use some form of online direct marketing tactics. Online, there are essentially two categories of direct marketing, including 1) those products that are sold exclusively online like Amazon and eBay, and 2) as an additional marketing tool for offline brands that can be purchased at traditional brick-and-mortar stores, such as IKEA or Coldwater Creek.

Direct marketing has flourished over the last several decades because of its ability to personally address the target by name, both on and offline, and to talk directly about any specific needs, concerns, and interests of the target. With this form of advertising, success relies on the production and delivery of a well-made product—a product that repeatedly performs as advertised and is backed up by a solid warranty and easy return policy. The objective is to successfully take the worry out of purchasing what the consumer cannot see or touch.

Employees are also a big part of brand management; efficient customer and technology service teams help to solidify a relationship and encourage future purchases. Today's savvy consumer understands that often the only differences between one brand and another are customer service initiatives, so it is important that every contact point meets or exceeds the target's expectations. High turnover or product-ignorant service efforts that result in unhappy, poorly treated consumers can, and will, negatively affect customer interactions.

In order to successfully continue to build or maintain a brand's image, brands need to value employee feedback and use those insights to determine future product requirements and upgrades, improve customer and technical assistance, and monitor overall brand performance. Image can be negatively affected by employee rudeness, inattentiveness, or dismissive behavior. Common courtesy is one of the best and least expensive ways to make a lasting impression on new or repeat customers. The small things that a company does to build or maintain brand loyal customers and increase brand equity are often the most memorable: sales personnel and customer service representatives who call the target by name when they call or walk in, attendants who offer helpful assistance, a direct thank you after a purchase, and a follow-up contact to gain feedback.

Using a Database to Reach the Right Target With the Right Message at the Right Time

In order for a company to personalize a message using direct marketing, they must keep a cache or database of relevant information on their targeted audience. Messages that rely on a compilation of specific data to reach the right target audience with the right message are often referred to as *database marketing*.

A database stores the targeted audience's demographic and psychographic profiles as well as past purchase behavior. A database can track those who have purchased before and made inquiries or opted in to receive information on the product or service. An accurate database is essential to maintaining a relationship with the target and can ensure that the advertised message reaches those most likely to buy with a message they are interested in and can relate to.

It took marketers a long time to realize that selling to existing customers was a lot cheaper and more profitable than constantly finding new ones. Consumers who have an existing relationship with a brand require less advertising to convince them to repurchase, while new customers need to hear or see an ad repeatedly before making an initial purchase or inquiry. Advertising that is sent to loyal consumers is able to tap into consumer lifestyles, making it easier to maintain the relationship.

The best ways to elicit a response from a target is to pique their interest and request an action: 1) enter a contest or sweepstakes, 2) join a loyalty program, 3) opt-in to receive e-mail promotions, 4) join a brand's Facebook page, 5) ask for a direct mail package, 6) try a sample of the brand, 7) fill out a reply card, 8) return a warranty card, and so on.

Because most engagement options require the target to input personal information, it is important that companies and organizations promise to not sell personal information to outside parties. Brands that do not protect the privacy of their target run the risk of alienating them and opening the door to their switching to a different brand.

The advantages to database marketing as a sales tool:

1. The ability to target only those most likely to buy

2. The ability to build and maintain a long-term relationship

3. The ability to personalize messages

4. The ability to offer a more personalized relationship based on increased knowledge about the target

Keeping a database updated is essential to the success of a direct marketing campaign. Updating requires consistent vigilance to ensure that individuals who have opted-out or moved are immediately removed from the list. The consequence of inaccurate data or unsolicited materials is the alienation of the receiver.

Identifying a Medium's Strengths and Weaknesses Reinforces and Highlights the Visual/Verbal Message

Before deciding where direct marketing and sales promotion fit in a campaign, it is important that both marketers and the advertising teams understand how each vehicle can positively enhance or negatively affect a campaign's message. Let's take a quick look at both its capabilities and limitations.

Direct Marketing and Sales Promotion's Advertising Strengths

1. **Feedback.** Many direct response and promotional vehicles encourage the target to report on their experiences with the product or service.

2. **Reach.** Guaranteed to reach the target that research has identified as most likely to buy.

3. **Relationship building.** The target can interact in some way with brand representatives 24/7. This one-on-one dialogue builds brand loyalty and encourages repeat purchase.

4. **Trial for new product launches.** Gets the product into the hands of consumers who are the most knowledgeable and qualified to give valuable feedback.

Direct Marketing and Sales Promotion's Advertising Weaknesses

1. **Loss of brand value.** Too many promotions can damage a brand's image in a consumer's mind.

2. **Database development.** It takes time to build a database of loyal consumers that ensures those most likely to buy are reached with the right message.

3. **Cost.** Promotions and personalized messages are expensive.

4. **Junk advertising.** A promotion is considered junk if it's poorly written and designed and offers the consumer nothing of value.

The Use of Traditional Media as a Direct Response Vehicle

To increase memorability, traditional media vehicles are regularly employing some form of direct response device to attract and hold the target's attention by asking them to do something, such as visit a website or Facebook page, enter a contest or sweepstakes, try a free sample, or redeem a coupon.

This interactive form of advertising may use any or all of the traditional mass media vehicles to reach the target. Both print and broadcast vehicles allow the consumer to respond to the message by pushing a few buttons, clicking a few keys, or dropping an order form in the mail. This medium is great for more generically used products and services; the goal is that once the target is exposed to the message, they will pick up the phone or run to their computers to place an order or request additional information. Let's take a quick look at some of the more popular direct marketing and sales promotion options.

The most often used direct response newspaper vehicle is known as a *freestanding insert* (FSI). A form of direct response, freestanding inserts are inserted into a newspaper after printing—these often four-color, single or double-sided inserts feature multiple coupons or offers.

Magazine options include simple business reply cards or more detailed multipage, multicolor inserts that mimic a small catalog. These vehicles are often bound into the magazine and appear alongside a more detailed and informative ad. These nationally distributed flyers or inserts are also known as *supplemental advertising*.

Most direct response offers used on radio are introduced by a local DJ and are associated with either a remote broadcast or locally sponsored event. Because they are read live, it is easy to update or change content relatively quickly. Probably the best known direct response vehicle is television. Infomercials are excellent at demonstrating product features and backing up claims with testimonials or studies. The announcer's exuberance and ability to show and tell how the product works makes it the ideal medium to encourage the target to act quickly. All forms of direct response offer some type of incentive to encourage the target to act immediately.

An *infomercial* is an informative commercial that can be found on network and cable television, the radio, and on the Internet. They are successful if the price is low, the product has some kind of wow factor, is easy to demonstrate, and has a likeable, believable spokesperson. The job of the spokesperson is to deliver the key feature and benefit with testimonials or demonstrations in a way that encourages the target to respond.

Infomercials (usually 60 to 120 minutes long) are a fact-based type of advertising that drills the brand's message home with demonstrations, testimonials, and often a celebrity spokesperson. Consumers are encouraged to order immediately in order to take advantage of low prices and any additional offers before they expire. Consumers are offered various ways to purchase and a 100% guarantee of satisfaction, or they can return the product for a full refund. Infomercials should include the following:

1. Before and after demonstrations

2. Highlight features and benefits using testimonials and demonstrations

3. An identifiable and appealing spokesperson

4. Regularly repeat key features throughout the presentation

5. Show the toll-free number on the screen throughout the presentation

6. Repeat the brand name about every three to five minutes

7. Regularly remind the target what action you want them to take

8. Highlight statistical information on graphs or pie charts to visually assist with the delivery of any technical information

9. Use actors that reflect or mirror the psychographics and demographics of the target

This type of direct response advertising is successful because there is little or no competition diverting the target's attention. There is also little or no creative flair in a direct response message. The goal is to grab the target's attention in the first three to five seconds, present the offer, and simply and often repeat the call to action. The message has more validity if claims can be backed up by research studies or delivered by experts or people who have used the product or service. Finally, give the target several ordering options such as a web address, toll-free number, or post office address, and any credit cards, money orders, or other financial options accepted by the seller. Thanks to the connected world of today's technology, the contact is personal and the sales immediate.

The Varied Visual and Verbal Faces of Direct Marketing

There are too many forms of direct marketing to cover here so we will take a quick look at some of the more popular forms of delivery, including direct mail, brochures, e-mail alerts, catalogs, loyalty programs, and telemarketing.

Direct Mail

Direct mail is a highly targetable personalized promotional device that reaches the target through the mail. Its job is to entice the consumer into making a purchase or to make further inquiries.

Direct mail when properly targeted to those consumers who have already shown a past interest in the product or service and are therefore the most likely to buy will return the most positive results, and will keep the piece from landing in the trash as junk mail. It is important to remember that direct mail is only considered junk mail when the design is poor and the message misdirected.

A great direct mail campaign should employ the following:

- A creative and personalized outer envelope
- A personalized letter
- Testimonials
- Interactive devices such as scratch offs, multiple folds, games, samples, and so on
- Price list
- A clear offer
- Information on warranties, guarantees, or return policies
- Offer multiple ways to respond and pay
- A response device such as order forms or reply cards that can be combined with coupons or shipping discounts and a preaddressed envelope

Once a decision is made to use direct mail in a campaign, do not scrimp on quality and use bright colors and graphics when possible, as well as creative copy. Use the envelope to attract attention, or if using a self-mailing piece be certain it is die cut, or cut into an unusual but relevant shape. The more visual the piece, the longer it holds the target's attention. Always ensure that the key consumer benefit is the first thing the target sees and repeat that benefit throughout the copy. Use testimonials to validate claims and make the product easy to return. Be certain that each piece is appealing and easily leads the reader through each piece. If the target doesn't need a piece to make a purchasing decision, leave it out. Every image and color used should help set the tone and sell the product or service.

Due to the significant price for production and distribution of a direct mail piece, using direct marketing to reach a mass audience is cost prohibitive. On the other hand, using direct mail to reach a niche audience can not only increase awareness but also build knowledge and loyalty, which ultimately leads the targeted consumer toward the final goal—purchase.

To reach this niche audience, it is important for marketers to have an accurate and up-to-date database of names. These targeted consumers may have purchased the product before, called or visited a brick-and-mortar store, or searched for more information via the web. Lists created in-house are much cheaper and more accurate than purchased lists from an outside source that can only be used for one mailing. Consumers who do respond to the mailing can be legally added to a marketer's in-house list. The quickest way to waste money is to send an expensive mailer to the wrong person or to a brand loyal customer of a competing brand.

Sending a package to one of your existing brand loyal customers about the launch of a new product or upcoming sales event will fail to entice if the package is little more than a traditional letter, brochure, or catalog. These folks need an eye-catching, multidimensional package with an incentive available only to loyal users, or a first-to-own offer. The objective is to entice the consumer to open the package, but most importantly, read and act on its message. Make the packaging big, colorful, or an unusual shape— even better, make the design all three. The key is to assure that the design matches the key consumer benefit; in this way, it is relevant to the consumer and a cohesive member of the visual and verbal campaign message.

Most poorly designed direct mail packages, even if they are sent to the correct target are never opened.The more fun the envelope looks, the more curious the target. Make it lumpy or oddly shaped by placing some kind of retainable or take-a-way inside to ensure that the target opens it to inspect what's inside. For example, BT Blackberry, to promote "Stress free business communications," placed a squishable blackberry phone inside the mailer box designed for businessmen and women to squeeze when facing an abnormal amount of stress. A letter attached to the foldout box lid accompanied the squeezable.

To draw attention away from traditional casino gambling, an online casino designed packaging in the shape of a wallet. Inside the target found not only a VIP pass but also a faux hundred-dollar bill. Inside the wallet's protective plastic window was a card with copy that read: "We'd like to offer you $100 free to give our Casino a try." That's the way to hold a target's attention and perhaps induce action.

Do not forget to clearly state payment options and include any information needed to place an order or get a question answered. Finally, make returns easy by offering some type of guarantee or warranty.

Ensuring the direct mail package reaches an interested target is critical. Direct mail can cost anywhere from $10 to $100 per person, depending on the overall design and contents. Once the package is delivered, it is imperative that customer service representatives follow up in some memorable way, such as calling, e-mailing, or by sending a post card. Be sure the package also identifies the multiple ways the target can find out additional information on their own such as employing both online and offline efforts by visiting a website, calling a toll-free number, or visiting a brick-and-mortar location.

To be successful, direct mail needs to be seamlessly integrated into the promotional mix. No matter how inventive or interactive the mailing, if the campaign message is not continuously reinforced, then the message will not be memorable. A repetitive message seen in multiple media not only is remembered, it also engages.

Brochures

These very colorful and informative pieces are a great way to advertise a new product or service and highlight a brand's specific features and benefits. One of the more accessible and accepted forms of advertising, brochures can visually and verbally tell a product or service's story in a creative, engaging, and even interactive way.

A brochure's job is to educate the reader about any relevant facts or claims that can be backed up by testing, scientific studies, or testimonials. Each feature should detail relevant information on prices, colors, sizes, uses, and contain a schedule of events depending on the key consumer benefit to be emphasized and the overall objective and strategy employed.

Delivery of a brochure can be either controlled or uncontrolled. A controlled delivery ensures that the brochure will reach the target by including it in a direct mail package, or by personally handing it out at trade shows or on showroom floors. An uncontrolled delivery means the piece is placed in a publicly accessible display case surrounded by other advertising and promotional pieces. If brochures are displayed in this manner, they must find a way to stand out and be noticed, such as having an unusual shape, use of a prominent color or color combinations, or verbally deliver the key consumer benefit in a very creative and powerful way.

Design options depend on whether the brochure is used as an advertising, promotional, direct marketing, or public relations device. All are colorful and feature multiple visuals, diverse folds and cuts, and come in an array of sizes. What typically distinguishes one from another is the descriptive, colorful, and persuasive inside copy.

E-mail Alerts

A form of e-mail marketing, e-mail alerts are personalized, inexpensive, fast, and a great way to support a direct mail package by announcing its imminent arrival. Include the outer envelope or catalog cover in the e-mail to help the target identify the promotion. After delivery, send follow-up e-mails as reminders and to encourage purchase. Placing coupons within the e-mail or including a directive to the website to download one is a great interactive device. If the budget is tight and does not support using a direct mail package, consider using e-mail alone as an announcement device and use a coordinated postcard to follow-up a few days later. To encourage immediate purchase, be certain to include some type of sales promotion device. Once the target has opted in to receive the alerts, messages can easily be tailored to match their special interests.

Catalogs

Catalogs have been around a long time, successfully presenting all types of goods, large and small, to consumers all over the world. Since the target chooses to interact with the showcased products, it is a very successful form of direct marketing.

Today, catalogs can be viewed on mobile devices, tablets, e-readers, via the Internet, and (still the most popular) in paper form. These colorful, multipage "magazines" can sell a category of items such as sportswear, or a diverse range of products from soap to barns.

Beautifully photographed images, descriptive copy, and boldly showcased prices promote the item to a small but loyal niche market of users. Thanks to credit cards, purchase is fast, and ordering is easy and available in multiple forms—on the web, via a toll-free number or fax, or through the mail.

Loyalty Programs

Loyalty programs are a form of customer service that rewards the target for their repeated loyalty with incentives, priority service, first-to-own opportunities, and gifts such as free products or discounts. Offered as a courtesy to targeted consumers who opt in to take advantage of the program, these types of long-term promotions can be offered by a single company or through a cooperative venture between multiple companies. For example, the Hilton Honors program rewards free night hotel stays based on the number of points accumulated, and Delta's Sky Miles program offers free tickets based on the number of miles flown. A cooperative arrangement between these two vendors might include two nights free at a Hilton Hotel anywhere Delta flies. The goal is to retain brand loyal consumers and encourage repurchase. This is a great way to build a lasting relationship with the target and to make a brand with few differentiating features the target's first choice when purchasing.

Telemarketing

Telemarketing uses the telephone to reach a predetermined target on a one-to-one basis. This type of sales technique relies on a defined calling list, an effective script, and a well-trained sales staff. Because the call originates from a sales center, this type of advertising is known as *outbound telemarketing*. Telemarketers use databases to reach those consumers who have a

Figure 10.1

known interest in the product or service. When consumers use a toll-free number to make a purchase, it is known as *inbound telemarketing*.

Telemarketing is not a creative sales pitch; it relies on the use of a prepared script and the tone of voice of the telemarketer to make the sale. It is important that each telemarketer is aware of any promotions that are being advertised elsewhere in the campaign. They must also be totally versed in the importance of the key consumer benefit to the target or any other relevant features and benefits associated with the brand.

Sales Promotion Can Increase Interest in a Brand and Promote Purchase

Sales promotion is often defined as a sales tool that increases interest in a product or service in order to increase a brand's value and achieve a set of marketing objectives. The use of sales promotion is usually a relatively inexpensive way to create awareness, reach new buyers, or reward loyal users. It is also a great way to give the target something extra for making a first time or repeat purchase. Marketers determine what promotional activity will bring the target the most value, such as reducing the purchase price through sales, offering coupons, or by attaching additional value-added material (e.g., bonus packs or two-for-one offers).

The American Marketing Association (AMA) definition of sales promotion, as reported in *eNotes*, the online encyclopedia of small business is described as "media and non-media marketing pressure applied for a predetermined, limited period of time in order to stimulate trial, increase consumer demand, or improve product quality." *eNotes* goes on to say that this definition does not capture all the elements of modern sales promotion:

> It should be noted that effective sales promotion increases the basic value of a product for a limited time and directly stimulates consumer purchasing, selling effectiveness, or the effort of the sales force. It can be used to inform, persuade, and remind targeted customers about the business [brand] and its marketing mix. (eNotes, 2012, p. 1)

Sales promotion can effectively be used to draw the target away from competing brands by offering an added incentive that temporarily stimulates demand. It is a great way to induce trial of a new or reinvented brand, or as an enticement to make an unplanned purchase. Every brand has an established or perceived value; as an enticement to buy, marketers may employ sales promotion to temporarily alter this price/value relationship by increasing the take-home value or lowering the price. Unlike other vehicles within the promotional mix (i.e., advertising, direct marketing, or even personal selling), sales promotion is usually available to consumers for a shorter amount of time, employs a more rational appeal, encourages immediate purchase, and increases sales in the short term.

The amount of importance given to the role of sales promotion in the marketing mix depends on several factors:

1. The overall marketing budget

2. The target to be reached

3. The brand's lifecycle stage

4. Price

5. Competitor's promotions

6. Type of product or service offered

Sales promotion is a great addition to the media mix when a brand needs to create awareness, increase interest or demand, inform, persuade, support a new product launch, upgrade or reinvent a mature product, direct attention toward a languishing brand in a crowded market category, or convince retailers to carry the brand or improve its shelf location.

To be effective, sales promotion is best used on products whose quality and effectiveness can be judged at the point of purchase rather than on larger, more expensive, or more difficult to use products that might require additional research, or a hands-on demonstration.

Growth in the use of sales promotion can be traced to 1) the current economic environment demands that brands find creative ways to encourage purchase based on their value in comparison to competing brands, 2) promotions are becoming more prevalent because consumers often do not purchase without an incentive, especially if their preferred brand is slightly more expensive, 3) marketers have an ongoing tendency to focus more on short-term results to provide an influx of cash or to reach a preset sales goal, and 4) computer technology is making it faster and easier to distribute coupons and to receive feedback on sales promotion results.

The use of sales promotions depends on what marketers need to accomplish with their communication objectives. For example, brands purchased on a more rational basis may want to build or increase awareness about a new product during the early stages of its lifecycle. There is no better way to build awareness than to get the product in the hands of the target. For mature brands, sales promotion is a great reminder device. For brands that are being reinvented the goal may be to introduce a new use or improved formula.

However, strategically sales promotion may not always be a good choice. Certain types of brands (usually more expensive, emotionally based brands) should avoid using sales promotion efforts in order to avoid damaging the brand's image and perception by the target. But for long-standing consumers, sales promotion can be used as a reward for their continued patronage by offering unadvertised pricing, first-to-own opportunities, and loyalty programs. Other reasons to strategically *reject* sales promotion as part of an advertising campaign might include any of the following:

- Depending on the number of sales promotions going on at any one time, in any one product category, the promotion could easily be overlooked.
- It is not unusual for competing brands to attempt to match existing promotions or to outmaneuver competitors with more creative and unique incentives.
- Consumers are not above exploiting promotional offers—for example, brand switchers who purchase based only on the current promotion rather than settling for any one preferred brand.
- Even brand loyal consumers may wait for the next promotion in order to stock up on brand favorites.

It is not unusual for marketers to launch a last minute sales promotion in order to reach quarterly sales goals. However, these *one-off efforts*, as they are known, have little or no long lasting effect. Sales promotions that are effectively woven into the marketing and communication strategies are more likely to reflect the visual/verbal voice of the campaign and deliver not only a longer lasting impression, but also bring in a more educated target.

Advertising and sales promotions can work together or independently. For example, magazine advertising that includes a promotion might announce a contest, sweepstakes, event, or even offer a sample. In order to entice consumers to try a product and/or get immediate feedback, newspaper advertising may include a coupon, television may offer "buy now" incentives, while radio might announce an event or a taste test or demonstration taking place at a local brick-and-mortar store. Other nontraditional options include using direct mail packages, bonus packs, street teams, fliers, tear-aways, telemarketers, shopping bags, sales personnel, the Internet, or mobile phones.

The easiest way to distinguish the difference between sales promotion and advertising has to do with limited time offers. An advertising campaign may run for months or even years while a sales promotion involves some type of limited time, value-oriented proposition that has an expiration date. The other differentiating factor is that sales promotions require an action on the part of the target, such as entering a contest, redeeming coupons, or filling out a rebate form. Sales promotion is all about getting the target to act within a certain time period. Action to an advertised message, on the other hand, often requires that the target is exposed to a message five to seven times before the expectation of an action by the target, whether in the form of a request for more information, an active purchase, a log-in to a website, or a visit to a brick-and-mortar store.

Just as in the case of advertising, a sales promotion cannot save a bad product or service, or overcome ineffective advertising and an inadequate sales force. A sales promotion can enhance a brand's already established image or reputation by calling attention to the product or service in an interactive and usually memorable way; after that, it is up to the brand performance to trigger a repeat purchase. Cooperative efforts are also enhanced by sales promotion efforts—for example, when companion brands like milk and cookies pair up to offer a free gallon of milk with the purchase of a package of cookie dough. This type of cooperative promotion not only opens the door to new customers but can get consumers to reimagine the brand in a new way—or even refocusses the brand so that the target experiences and views a new pairing of the brand.

The more appealing the promotion, the better the chances of increasing foot traffic or even instigating an impulse or unplanned purchase. There is no better method to create interest and word-of-mouth or viral exchanges than getting the target to interact with the product or service in a meaningful way.

Technically, the goal of sales promotion is to encourage the target to take some kind of desired action, not provide additional information. However, consumers may be able to ask for a direct mail package or catalog. Some brands even offer a free in-house trial before purchase, allowing the consumer to experience each of the features and benefits of the product at home without any accompanying high-pressure sales tactics.

Consumer Incentives Attract Attention and Increase Awareness

The most well-known forms of sales promotion are those promotions that consumers interact with every time they go into a grocery or retail store, see on a television commercial, or begin an Internet search. If asked, most consumers would define sales promotion as a simple coupon or sale offer, but it is so much more. Let's take a quick look at some of the more popular consumer sales promotions that are employed today: product sales or promotional pricing, bonus or branded packs, refunds and rebates, coupons, contests, and sweepstakes, event sponsorships or promotions, premiums, and sampling.

Product Sales or Promotional Pricing

These are the lower price options aimed at saving consumers money when they purchase the product or use the service. The most commonly seen price deals include percentage off deals, bonus pack offers, refunds and rebates, and coupons. Most marketers employ a price deal to encourage trial of a new or reinvented product, to increase usage of a mature brand, and to encourage current users to stock up on the product. Reducing the price of a brand works best when price is the ultimate value motivator.

There are two ways consumers ultimately learn about price reduction deals: either at the point of purchase or via advertising. Point of purchase reductions may be posted in stores, on shelves or window signage, or on the package itself. Advertising options might include direct mail, newspaper ads, freestanding inserts, mobile, Internet, or e-mail coupons, or radio or television offers. A price reduction strategy is only effective if all members within the distribution channel (manufacturers, distributors, or retailers) buy into the promotion. Loyal consumers perceive incentives as rewards for their continued loyalty and will often stock up on their favorite brands or employ a service they may have postponed using.

Promotional pricing is a successful, often used form of sales promotion. These short-term price reduction promotions are best known as sales. A sale can immediately increase demand. It is important to employ this form of promotion infrequently; otherwise, consumers anticipate the sales and, as a result, wait to purchase until the next price reduction occurs.

Bonus or Branded Packs

Another commonly seen promotion includes the offering of bonus or branded packs. A bonus pack offers consumers an extra or bonus amount of the product when it is purchased at the regular retail price. It is employed most often with beauty or personal hygiene products and cleaning products to introduce a new formula, color, or size. This is a great way to reward loyal users but offers little incentive to switch brands to the consumer who uses a competitive brand. Branded packs are a fancy way to sell two products for the price of one. However, some marketers deviate slightly from the standard approach by offering two products that can be used together for the price of a single item—for example, pairing shampoo and conditioner.

Refunds and Rebates

Refunds and rebates offer the consumer a return of some portion of the money spent. Almost all brands offer a refund or 100% money back guarantee if not completely satisfied, while still others agree to meet or beat a competitor's price if the consumer finds the product at a cheaper price. To receive a refund, most brands request that consumers show proof of purchase before any money is refunded or credited to their account. However, today many businesses will accept returns without any proof of purchase.

A rebate temporarily lowers the price of an advertised brand. This form of promotion is usually associated with larger or more expensive purchases such as computers or appliances. Most rebates require consumers to fill out a lengthy form and return it along with an accompanying proof of purchase receipt before receiving the discount. Rebates are not immediate and can take up to six to eight weeks before any percentage of the purchase price or delivery charge is refunded.

Coupons

Although over 90% of all households use coupons, only a small fraction (less than 1%) are actually redeemed. A sluggish economy always brings renewed interest in coupons and other types of promotional discounts. However, in recent years, coupon use has declined with the introduction of grocery store incentive cards and shortened expiration dates.

Coupons can be offered by either the manufacturer or retailer and usually suggest a percentage or certain amount deducted from a particular brand's retail price. Most incentives have a specific time limit, and although consumers are interested in a bargain, the statistics show that many offers expire or go unused.

Coupons can arrive in local newspapers, be found on packaging, be downloaded off the Internet, and arrive via e-mail or cell phone. Consumers looking for unadvertised coupons can use the Internet. It is now easier than ever to locate coupons on the web, with a large assortment of sites for consumers to compare: couponmom.com, coupons.com, 8coupons.com, couponcabin.com, fatwallet.com, shortcuts.com, and couponcode.com.

A less popular coupon delivery method arrives with a grocery receipt known as Catalina Marketing checkout coupons. These are not as successful as traditional coupons because they cannot be used immediately; instead, they require a return visit. Distribution is somewhat random so that instead of matching the current purchases exactly, a competitor's product is substituted for the current purchase. The goal is to build awareness of many products in the category and to encourage trial.

Contests and Sweepstakes

Contests and sweepstakes are a great interactive form of sales promotion. To enter a sweepstakes all consumers have to do is sign up. Winners are chosen at random or by chance. A contest, on the other hand, requires the consumer to do something in addition to registering that will be judged by others before a winner is declared. Because of this, participation in a sweep-stakes is usually higher than those of contests.

Event Sponsorship or Promotions

Event promotions link a product or service to a specific event such as film festivals and 10K runs. Events are a good way to showcase a product—for example, a car give away, food and beverage samples, or branded items such as T-shirts, hats, coffee mugs, or water bottles, to name just a few. Events tend to attract a similar demographic in their attendance (people of the same age, interests, etc.) so it is important that the brand is suited to the event and that the planned event allows the target to get up close and personal with the brand, ask questions, or sign up to receive more information.

Premiums

Premiums are rewards that are based on the performance of a specific task, usually nothing more complicated than purchase. Premiums can be given away or offered at a discounted price. The premium may be included in the packaging (known as a *direct premium*) or offered as free gifts to the first one hundred store visitors. This type of premium is known as a *traffic-builder*. Direct TV offers what's known as a *referral premium* that rewards both new and existing customers (e.g., a $100 premium for signing up and for the recommendation).

Sampling

Product sampling gets the brand directly into the hands of the consumer by personnel who are familiar with the brand's features and benefits. Samples can be delivered by street teams, given out after demonstrations or taste tests at retail or grocery stores. This is a great way to get a new or reinvented product directly into the hands of the consumer.

Samples can also be delivered through the mail, inserted into newspapers, and magazines, or included in a direct mail package. It may be as simple as a scratch and sniff panel, or it may require placing an order online or via a toll-free number. Sample packages are often distributed on college campuses by brand ambassadors to promote trial and boost name recognition to a concentrated demographic.

Business Incentives Help Promotional Efforts at the Point of Purchase

Business-to-business sales promotion efforts are a smaller niche form of promotion that is used in many industries. Trade-related promotions help "push" a brand through the distribution channel by encouraging businesses to not only purchase a brand, but also promote it. For example, promotions that are focused on retailers may encourage their sales staff to promote a certain brand over another.

Most business-to-business promotions use a similar format to those offered to consumers, such as giveaways, sales and contests, or sweepstakes. Other promotional options may include

1. Point of purchase displays

2. Advertising support programs

3. Short term allowances

4. Sales incentives or push money

5. Promotional products

6. Tradeshows

Point of Purchase Displays (POP)

These specially designed displays are most often placed in brick-and-mortar locations. Often freestanding, these three-dimensional displays prominently showcase a brand in aisles or other high-traffic locations, in order to attract attention, increase sales, and tempt the impulse buyers. Other popular types of POP displays are known as *end-caps*, or displays that are placed at the end of an aisle. No campaign can rely on POP alone, but it's a great reminder and reinforcement device when paired with primary media vehicles. Well-planned and educational POP displays can also help retail sales personnel promote the product or service.

Advertising Support Programs

Advertising support programs offer channel members or retailers financial assistance with their advertising; in return, retailers use the money to promote the marketer's brand in their advertising efforts. Marketers may pay the entire cost, or more commonly offer partial support, known as *cooperative advertising* or co-op advertising funds. This form of advertising usually partners two like brands to promote them together and also to share the cost of advertising. These programs can also include packets of advertising material sent by marketers for display in the store, such as posters, stickers, or buttons used by the retail store and their sales staff.

Short Term Allowances

These allowances offer channel partners a reduced price for selling the brand. Additionally, the allowance is also meant as an incentive to offer additional promotional efforts—for instance, eye-level shelf placement or convenient store placement, promoting the brand in the store's advertising, or allowing company representatives to enter the store as brand ambassadors in order to hand out samples or give product demonstrations.

Short-term allowances also cover price reductions (off-invoice promotions) and buy-back guarantees that permit any merchandise that has not been sold within a certain time frame to be returned.

Sales Incentives or Push Money

These incentives are used within a company to reward sales or customer service personnel for selling the product or service. Often referred to as "push money," this type of incentive rewards employees for reaching their preset sales goals with cash, prizes, or trips.

Promotional Products

Promotional products are free gifts that are given out as rewards for performance or as a reward for participating in some kind of sponsored event. All promotional products have the company, organization, or brand logo, slogan, or tagline printed on them.

Trade Shows

Trade shows, whether catering to businesses or consumers is all about getting the potential buyer up-close and interacting with a brand. Representatives can answer questions, give demonstrations, or help with placing an order. This one-on-one interaction between buyer and seller not only increases awareness but also is a great way to build a relationship with consumers or businesspersons who can place an order on the spot.

Now that we have examined the different types of promotions, let's take a look at how some brands have creatively employed them.

Sales Promotion Can Move a Brand

With the economy in a funk, Heinz is capitalizing on the current eat-in trend by promoting a cooking video contest. The "Shine at Dinnertime" promotion places the Heinz brand, Lea & Perrins Worcestershire sauce, front and center. The individual who submits the best video showcasing the sauce wins $10,000.

This is Heinz's first foray into user-generated content. Consumers will select a winner from six finalists. To promote the contest, Heinz is using public relations, e-mail, banner ads, blogging sites, as well as a sponsorship with *FoodBuzz.com*.

Instead of spending $3 million for an ad during the Super Bowl, Papa John's Pizza decided to spend their money on a promotion that could give a free large pizza to every American. The rules were as follows: the game had to go into its first-ever overtime and, in order to be eligible, interested consumers had to presign for its loyalty program.

Andrew Varga, Papa John's marketing chief explained, "We'd rather give away millions in free pizzas than spend millions on a spot" (Horovitz, 2011, p. 1). An additional promotion allowed consumers who ordered online on Super Bowl Sunday to automatically enter to win a free pizza.

The thin line between an intrusive message and an entertaining one is a difficult line to walk. Gillette chose to use a Yankees game to showcase its "Here's to confidence" campaign. Via the big screen and using the services of famous sports names, Gillette gave out free samples in hopes of reaching a multiage target audience.

The spot directed consumers to *Gillette.com/walk,* where they could sign up to win a free Fusion razor. The spot featured recognizable visuals and sounds from the classic film *Saturday Night Fever.*

A Few Nontraditional Response Devices

For those brands wanting to step out of the traditional direct response box, consider employing more nontraditional types of promotional vehicles: magalogs, package insert programs, poly packs, flyers or blow-ins and bind-ins, to name just a few.

Because these types of vehicles are not personalized, they are often overlooked or dismissed by the targeted consumer. So it is important that each piece is visually stimulating to attract and hold the target's attention. Let's take a look at a few examples.

Magalogs

A magalog is part magazine and part catalog, but unlike a catalog most magalogs focus on just one product. These high quality looking "magazines" arrive through the mail with stunning four-color photographs and graphics and are full of feature stories that use a simply written conversational tone to deliver the message. An *esbjournal* article by Mike Klassen tells us, "A magalog communicates image and brand by telling the story behind the product using magazine-like techniques. A catalog tells you what the fabric is made of. A magalog explains how it makes you look and feel. The result is a more emotional connection to the products being sold" (Klassen, 2010, p. 3).

Package Insert Programs

Ads that are inserted into packages sent from the seller to the buyer or are included in catalogs or magazines are known as *package insert programs* (PIPs). Advertisers who are attempting to reach the same or similar target audience most often use these low-cost, noncompeting, and often freestanding direct marketing pieces.

Although most package inserts are accompanied by up to eight other advertised products, none are direct competitors, making them a great way to reach small, loyal niche markets.

Poly Packs

Poly packs are small 3 x 5 cards bound together that arrive in the mail and feature advertising for a diverse number of noncompeting products. These interest-generating promotional pieces are often colorful and double-sided. Recipients are directed to a website, toll-free number, or can send in an attached reply card for more information.

Fliers

Fliers are an inexpensive way for small businesses to reach their target around the point of sale. Fliers do not have to be printed on standard sized paper but can be reproduced on napkins, plates, business cards, tissue packs, photographs—or just about any imaginable surface just be certain to attach a coupon to encourage trial. Redeemed promotional devices are also a great way to determine ROI. These low cost promotional devices are not a great choice for specialty products but work well for generic products and services sold locally.

Blow-ins and Bind-ins

Blow-ins are small (often 4 x 5¾) promotional devices that are blown between the pages of a magazine, whereas bind-ins are bound into the magazine and are perforated for easy removal. The objective is to serve as a reply card for products or services, often mimicking brands and product categories seen in the magazine. Interested readers can drop the card in the mail to have more information sent directly to them. Blow-ins capture attention by falling out of the magazine directly into the lap of the reader when opened. On the other hand, as readers flip through the magazine bind-ins automatically open to the placement pages.

Both direct marketing and sales promotion engage the targeted audience by getting them to interact with the advertising. Both help to create interest and build relationships through personalized messages and privileged rewards for their continued loyalty. Both are great vehicles for demonstrating the key consumer benefit, whether creatively showing and writing about the product or service's virtues or encouraging trial through free samples or other types of promotional devices.

Chapter 10 Exercises

1. Working in the same or new groups, use the brief that was developed for the national brand from Chapter 2. Determine how direct marketing and/or sales promotion can be employed in the campaign, or combined with previous vehicles, if at all.

2. What visual/verbal direction accomplishes the directives laid out in both the marketing plan and creative brief? How can you tie the visual/verbal and promotional message together to create a cohesive look across vehicles?

3. Do competitors use direct marketing and/or sales promotion? If so, how can you create more engagement in your approach? If not, why will it increase awareness in your brand and attract the target's attention? Tie your findings to the various forms of nontraditional media and any additional vehicles you have already incorporated. Each team must defend their position based on information found in both documents. Tie creative decisions back to the creative brief and marketing plan.

4. Consider whether or not you will delete any mediums based on what you now know about direct marketing and sales promotion. If you do not delete, and continue to use the same vehicles, how can you tie direct marketing and/or sales promotion into the existing direction? Be able to back up your decisions either way.

5. Present to class or to the marketing team.

6. Follow the same directives with the small, local business selected in Chapter 2.

Memory Box

Direct Marketing

Relationship Marketing

Database Marketing

Freestanding Insert

Supplemental Advertising

Infomercial

E-Mail Marketing

Inbound and Outbound Telemarketing

Sales Promotion

Business-to-Business Sales Promotions

11

The Most Unusual of All Are Often the Most Memorable

Innovative nontraditional media vehicles are so diverse that they often defy classification. In this chapter, we look at some of the more unusual ways and creative surfaces that marketers and advertisers use to capture and hold a target's attention.

Taking Innovation to the Next Level

There are some forms of nontraditional media that do not fit cleanly into any of the media boxes discussed thus far—think round peg/square hole. Because of this, whenever using this type of nontraditional media, it is even more important that the visual/verbal voice maintains a consistency and ties back to the brand and current campaign message. As is true with most nontraditional vehicles, these unique or unusual media outlets cannot promote the key consumer benefit alone. In order to be an integral and successful part of a campaign, the tone of voice and presentation style should be cross-promoted with other vehicles in the media mix.

Many of these stand-alone vehicles can do little more than remind and entertain. Their inability to tell a story, educate, and encourage purchase discourages many marketers from including them in their marketing mix.

Nothing about these unique vehicles fits snuggly into a known media mold. Some advertising choices are small, allowing little to be said, but are visually memorable. Others are large and use the canvas to extend the key consumer benefit's visual/verbal message through the use of stunning visuals and creatively written copy. The cost is not dependent on size; several of these specialty vehicles are expensive to reproduce (whether large or small), but most require more creative ingenuity than a big budget.

What these specialty vehicles often do best is to capture attention with memorable, nontraditional messages that receive a lot of word of mouth and virtual attention. After using one of these specialty vehicles, any buzz that a campaign receives is viewed as a pocketable return on investment (ROI) and serves to reinforce the reality of what creative ingenuity can bring to a campaign. The more unusual, the more attention the event can get. Once it grabs the target's attention, they may stop and take a picture with their mobile phone. They may send the picture to friends or family; those on the receiving end might be just as captivated by the image as the sender, so they upload it to their social media site, and so on.

Large marketers with deep pockets have put imaginative nontraditional media vehicles on the advertising map. Companies like Procter & Gamble, Johnson & Johnson, Kellogg's, and IKEA are often fearless in their open-minded embrace of new media and technology, successfully opening the door for smaller brands to confidently dip their marketing toe into this enormous creative pool.

Many of the diverse vehicles referenced in Chapter 5 on first examination appear to have limited or little potential, but if you pair the right vehicles up with the attributes of a particular brand, the possible options are astounding. Let's take a parking meter, for example. This awkward surface presents a great opportunity to remind parking customers about a restaurant, a brand of soda or tea, retail clothing shops, drug stores, banks, car dealerships, hair salons, office or auto part stores, and so on. You don't need to tell the target much about being thirsty, only remind them how your brand can solve their problem.

Strategically, most of these unique vehicles are excellent at promoting a brand's image but cannot effectively deliver the key consumer benefit or build or maintain a relationship with the target. Their strengths are built around their ability to engage, remind, and build or maintain awareness rather than a relationship.

Determining whether these vehicles are right for a product or service and the role they fulfill in any marketing strategy depends on the answers to the following questions: 1) Who is the target audience? 2) What are the objectives? 3) Where is the brand in its life cycle stage? 4) What are the strategies? 5) Can the visual/verbal message be adapted to these unique vehicles? and 6) What vehicles currently make up the media mix? The need for a solid understanding of the message to be delivered, how it will be delivered, and for how long, helps to determine how each of these points can be emphasized and supported.

Brands should consider the use of these unique vehicles early on in a campaign's development rather than throwing them in at the last minute. Accommodating the visual/verbal message to their unique shapes, locations, and sizes requires some forethought, but can prove to be a successful way to deliver a stronger more integrated message. For example, an insurance company might consider using parking garage gates, walls, and parking stubs. They may also want to consider construction barricades, cranes, and scaffolding. Don't forget about those parking meters, or car or bus wraps, street graffiti, trash cans, or even orange construction cones. Alone, these vehicles cannot deliver a strategically strong visual/verbal message. However, when paired with a mix of more traditional vehicles such as television or magazines, the visual/verbal message is reinforced, making it easier for the target to recognize and relate to the less detailed messages seen on these varied specialty vehicles.

Media choices that are based on a campaign's creative direction have a better chance of effectively selling the key consumer benefit in a unique visual/verbal way. Last minute additions to the promotional mix make it more difficult to seamlessly weave the points of a key consumer benefit and the visual/verbal message into a vehicle with limited space.

Nontraditional Vehicles Take Their Innovative Message to an Attentive Target

Incorporating these unique vehicles into a campaign requires a hard look at the selected target audience to be reached, the objectives to be accomplished, the key consumer benefit to be promoted, and the features and benefits that differentiate the brand from its competitors. As is true when using nontraditional surfaces, unique vehicles cannot target a specific audience, launch or reinvent a brand, or build an image comparable to traditional mass media vehicles. However, they are creative, unusual, often charismatic, and individualistic. The unique use and image of the vehicle, because of its rarity, can be tied to a brand in a positive and memorable way. Their job is to awe, surprise, entertain, and capture and hold the target's fleeting attention for more than the requisite three to five seconds.

Many of these specialty vehicles are typically placed in a prominent location in order for the target to easily see or interact with them. Many types can be placed directly in the target's hand, where the message can be carried or the vehicle used for an indeterminate length of time, ensuring that these types of vehicles will most certainly get more attention than any thirty-second television spot or color magazine spread.

A large majority of specialty vehicles are mass produced (e.g., coffee cups and sleeves, or shopping bags), while others like green graffiti may be seen in only a few select locations. Creatively, most of these diverse surfaces are loosely tied to other messages within the campaign by nothing more than color, typeface, logo and slogan or tagline, or the use of a spokesperson or character representative.

After study, it is not unusual or surprising to learn that consumers often frown on and complain about advertising that is 1) not relevant to their needs and wants, 2) deemed offensive, and 3) considered a blight on the landscape, or society in general. However, they rarely complain about any message or surface they see used in a creative way. To their target audience, it indicates something unique and innovative about their brands, when marketers embrace these creative surfaces.

Identifying a Medium's Strengths and Weaknesses Reinforces and Highlights the Visual/Verbal Message

Before deciding where or if a more specialized form of nontraditional media fits in a campaign, it is important that both marketers and the advertising teams understand how it can positively enhance or negatively affect a campaign's message. Let's take a quick look at both its capabilities and limitations.

Specialized Nontraditional Media Strengths

1. **Cost.** Many vehicles are inexpensive to purchase.

2. **Creative.** The unique uses for these diverse surfaces are memorable and often innovative.

3. **Diverse.** The multitude of surfaces allows for brands to choose a vehicle that matches the brand's use or image.

4. **Buzz building.** The more unique they are, the farther the message is carried and the more excitement is generated.

Specialized Nontraditional Media Weaknesses

1. **Limited message.** Many surfaces allow for little more than a logo and slogan or tagline.

2. **Reach.** Many vehicles are viewable in only a handful of locations.

3. **Mass media.** Because these vehicles are placed in public locations, it is difficult to target a specific audience.

4. **Return on investment.** Unless the vehicle encourages buzz or asks the target to do something, it is difficult to assess the reach of the message within the target audience or determine the target's response, if any.

Inventive and Creative Examples of Specialty Forms of Nontraditional Media

What makes these creative vehicles a better choice than more proven, traditionally based vehicles? The creative use, of course. Let's take a look at some of the more creative and expressive examples.

Finding new ways to promote a known brand can reposition it to stand out. Some products are so well-known that consumers often ignore their message; but give the brand a new use or purpose, and you can create interest where it once did not exist. Downy is a good example. The Procter & Gamble brand decided to promote itself as a sleep aid. Why? Because consumers kept telling them they were looking forward to sleeping on newly washed sheets. To find out more, Procter & Gamble funded a sleep study by an outside research firm that found that a large number of participants stated that clean sheets that smell good helped them sleep better. To promote their findings, P&G decided to talk with fans and interact with them online by partnering with Macy's and using a live window display featuring comedian Mike Birbiglia. Birbiglia is known for making fun of the fact that he is a sleepwalker.

One of the newest forms of specialty media is scent marketing. Many retailers today are turning down the music and turning up the ambient scents to encourage consumers to linger just a little longer and perhaps buy just a little bit more.

In a 2011 Reuters article, "Scent makers sweeten the smell of commerce," the author Jane Sutton describes

A New Balance store in Beijing [that introduced consumers] to a 'total sensory experience' designed to convey heritage and craftsmanship. [They] used a nostalgic wood and leather scent, decorated the wooden-floored store with vintage ads and compiled a soundtrack of 1950s bebop music. (Sutton, 2011, p. 1)

Thanks to good music, and the sweet smell of leather, research showed shoppers stayed longer and bought more. However, regardless of how good the smells, a brand has to be careful when employing aromatherapy because even the best of smells can offend. Sutton goes on to tell us,

The London Underground coated the platforms at some of its tube stations with encapsulated fragrance, described as a rosy jasmine with a hint of herbs, during a test aimed at making the subway more pleasant in 2001. It was quickly halted when some commuters complained that it made them feel sick. (Sutton, 2011, p.2)

Feared allergic reactions also put an end to a promotion for milk in San Francisco when a scent strip with the aroma of chocolate chip cookies was placed in transit shelters.

Goodwill Industries also jumped on the scent bandwagon by spicing up the aroma in their stores with a blend of orange and honeysuckle.

A grocery store chain in North Carolina attached the smell of sizzling steaks to one of their outdoor boards to promote their newest brand of beef.

Another form of specialty media is using facial recognition techniques to design specialized advertising messages directed toward any person standing in front of a digital display, kiosk, or vending machine. The technology can determine your sex and age by measuring the size of your nose, the space between your eyes, and length of your jaw bone; it then compares those features to similar features typical of males and females within varied age groups to determine approximate age. Then the message is customized to that specific target.

In an August 21, 2011 *Los Angeles Times* article, authors Shan Li and David Sarno, give us a few examples of this new technology:

The Venetian resort, hotel and casino in Las Vegas, has started using it on digital displays to tailor suggestions for restaurants, clubs and entertainment to passersby. (Li & Sarno, 2011, para. 4)

A group of U.S. bar owners in Chicago started using facial recognition, in conjunction with mounted cameras, to keep tabs on the male/female ratio and age mixes of their crowds. Patrons planning a night out can use mobile apps to get a real-time check of a venue's vibe. (para. 6)

Product placement is going digital. Viewers can now use their iPad to electronically purchase what the characters in their favorite shows are wearing. Glamour is teaming up with Gap.com and the reality series *Glamour Girls* to endorse a promotion that allows viewers to purchase the clothing worn by their favorite characters. The series features 10 to 12 minutes of content that can only be viewed on an iPad, making it that much easier to pause and purchase.

General Mills is resurrecting the surprise prize back into their cereal boxes. But this time, the prizes are not forgettable but favored editions of select DC comic books.

There is no advertising except for a small mention about the books being "brought to you by General Mills." Unlike its earlier sponsorship of comic book heroes, the story does not end on the pages of the book; fans can continue reading on a special microsite set up to keep the storyline going and the interest building.

If you have just a little to say, be sure to use a big canvas. As did Southwest Airlines before it, Spirit Airlines will sell space on the exteriors of their planes. If the campaign dictates more copy—how about the flight attendants' aprons, or a napkin, a tray table, an overhead bin or even a seat back. To date, there is no news on whether advertisers will occupy space in the lavatories, but for now, the space is visually and verbally silent.

Advertising placed on or in conjunction with another brand can be tricky. Although these surfaces reach a captive audience, remember that the advertiser can be negatively affected by rude service, long delays, safety issues, or excessive fees associated, not with their brand, but with the airline.

Do you hate to get out of your car to pump gas during allergy season? Halls Cough Drops wants you to know that they've got you covered with ads appearing on video screens atop the gas pumps touting their cough drops, along with a sponsored message on the day's pollen count.

McDonald's decided to use a scavenger hunt to launch its new Caramel Mocha espresso drink. The rules are simple, find the three giant McCafé coffee cups that McDonald's has hidden throughout varying cities. Clues to the cups' locations will be placed on Twitter. A year's worth of free McCafé beverages will be the prize for the first person to find each cup. Free small McCafé drinks will be rewarded to the next 100 people in each participating city to find a cup.

If you don't feel like walking all over the store, J.C. Penney's "FindMore" fixture has a 52-inch touch screen that is capable of showing their entire inventory. Once an item is found, users can e-mail the material to themselves or scan a barcode to find out more product details. The database also allows the customer to get advice on any accompanying accessories to their desired purchase, such as what type of chair and pillows go with the selected sofa.

IPG (Interpublic Group) is turning its storefront windows into a giant touch screen. No more plastic mannequins or animated felt characters, this technology allows consumers to interact with the screen in order to select outfits for an avatar or human manifestation on the screen. Nearby kiosks allow shoppers to interact with a virtual sales associate to receive assistance on multiple topics—for example, how a certain type of digital camera works.

Have you ever interacted with a gift card for longer than it takes to hand it over to the cashier? Probably not, and because of that many new gift cards now allow the giver to record a message; others light up or can be turned into finger puppets; some just smell good; and still others can be sent via text message or Facebook post. Some of Home Depot's gift cards suggest possible products when held up to a computer's webcam. If you want to make someone's stomach growl, one Walmart card has a scratch and sniff option. American Eagle can send their cards as a text message, Amazon.com can send theirs as a Facebook post, and a company called Wildcard can send its gift cards to someone's mobile phone.

Advertising agencies that plan to use logo graffiti need to be certain to ask city officials first and include the costs for all required clean up. This form of nontraditional media uses sidewalks and public areas to place logos and other advertising materials. Although inexpensive and attention getting, cities are getting tired of using taxpayer money to clean up these public thoroughfares. The city of Los Angeles imposed a $45,000 fine on a local agency representing the Zynga Game Network's social game, Mafia Wars, for gluing play money onto city sidewalks. Still other cities are arresting independent contractors for vandalism.

A large majority of specialty vehicles are mass produced (e.g., coffee cups and sleeves, or shopping bags), while others like *green graffiti* may be seen in only a few select locations. Green graffiti is all about cleaning a surface such as a street or sidewalk by placing a stencil down and using a power washer to clean away the dirt and grime, leaving a nice clean image or message behind.

Domino's Pizza was one of the first to use green graffiti as a promotional device, introducing a form of scavenger hunt that asked participants to find one of the sidewalk ads and e-mail a picture of themselves beside the message to Domino's. The first 250 people who submitted a correct e-mail won a $15 gift card.

Shredded Wheat cereal used a different type of green graffiti when it swathed its logo into the British wheat field that supplied the grain used to make its cereal. Additionally, a sports channel in London sent employees out to stamp their logo into snowdrifts after a particularly large snowstorm, and Volkswagen found a way to draw attention to its brand by creating a life-size Volkswagen made entirely out of sand.

Kangaroo Express restaurants developed an interactive campaign built around college basketball's March Madness. To take advantage of the rivalry between three local universities participating in the tournament, Kangaroo is targeting students from each university with a coffee and branded cup promotion. Fans can come into the store to fill up a cup featuring their school's colors and logo with their favorite brand of coffee. Every university cup sold awards that school one point.

On behalf of Kangaroo Express, the winning school will have $20,000 donated to a charity of their choice. Each of the runners-up receives $5,000 for their favorite charities. Participants can track results on a special website set up for the promotion. Additional media outlets include TV, radio, in-store posters and displays, online banner ads, and campus events, as well as a presence on Facebook and Twitter. All advertising carries the campaign's tagline: "Drink up, fans. The battle is on."

Advertising often reflects current events. Take the swine flu outbreak; companies that sell soap, hand sanitizers, and flu preventions are placing their products as front and center solutions to a widespread problem of public concern. Creative teams also jumped on the flu prevention wagon when a New York advertising agency launched a line of designer facemasks it plans to sell via its website, for a $100 donation to charity. The unusual masks come in six different designs: one with a mustache and bright red lips, another featuring a crossed out pig snout, with the words "It's Not Me, It's You." Who is the intended target? The market audience are those people afraid of spreading germs and others who are just believers in self-expression.

Social networking games are a great advertising specialty medium because 1) they are engaging, 2) they reach a large Facebook audience, 3) they are popular, 4) advertisers can promote real products in a virtual world, 5) brands can become part of the game, and 6) brands can give something back to players who interact with them.

Farmers Insurance successfully incorporated each of the above steps, when they placed a blimp sporting the Farmers' logo in the popular Facebook game, FarmVille. Players who choose to have it fly over their farms had their crops protected for ten days. McDonald's is also putting its advertising clout behind FarmVille.

Old Navy became an interactive part of the social game, CrowdStar. Female players could purchase Old Navy virtual clothing for themselves or give it to their friends. Advertising in the virtual store reflected real-world discounts.

Honda is using Car Town, the new Facebook game that centers around the collecting of virtual cars, to promote its new CR-Z. Honda's advertising in Car Town not only includes embedded billboards that feature the new vehicle but a virtual showroom that plays Honda commercials.

Microsoft, as a way to introduce Bing, their new search engine site, gave away free "Farm Cash" to FarmVille players who joined up to become a fan of the site. Many gamers are not pleased with the idea of advertising in games and often consider it deceptive; still other players do accept ads in computer games, as long as they don't get in the way of the fun.

Redken created a game they call the Busy Scissor, a hair styling game for Nintendo and Wii. This role-playing game lets players pretend that they own a salon and cater to a beautiful and rich clientele. Players win points by shampooing, coloring, and cutting their client's hair, thus ensuring that they have a good hair day. To promote the game, Redken placed it in their salons so that clients waiting to get their hair done could play the game. As an added bonus, Redken is also raffling off a Wii and copies of the game.

To demonstrate their service coverage of the globe, FedEx launched their "FedEx Delivers to a Changing World" campaign with a specific phase that uses augmented reality. All readers have to do to demonstrate the FedEx tagline is to place the magazine ad in front of their webcams to see a 3-D globe emerge from a FedEx box.

A clever trashcan ad that reminds passersby that smoking is bad for you converts a trashcan lid by adding a small circular opening. This is important because the top of the can is painted as an eyeball. The opening is the lens surrounded by a beautiful blue iris, surrounded by the sclera or the white of the eye. The copy on the lid reads: "Smoking causes blindness," followed by the logo.

Show It Big by Featuring the Product Oversized

Thinking of picking up a yellow highlighter? FedEx Kinko's Office and Print Center wants you to remember that they sell highlighters by placing a huge (taller than a man) 3-D highlighter on the sidewalk. The yellow marker is strategically placed at the end of the yellow no parking line typically drawn on city curbs. The idea, did the city paint that line or was it created by the highlighter?

Want to show solar action, use a billboard, a car, and a ball. The visual for this inventive ad showed a soccer player in action; to his right is a circle outline signifying where the ball should have been. The big soccer ball, with Nike swoosh, shows up below where it has unfortunately squished the car parked there. Now that is an engaging play.

The Wrigley Company, to graphically illustrate the icy freshness of its Orbitz Ice Mints, placed an enormous bust of a man in the snow at a ski resort. The bust was appropriately attired in ski cap and coat. A cold icy breath of smoke blew out of his mouth to show the mint's breath-freshening capabilities. Attached to his left sleeve was a big roll of the mints.

In order to demonstrate that the number of people killed in car accidents is less than those who die due to smoking-related causes, extremely realistic props were needed to drive the point home. To draw attention to National Non-Smoking Week and the British Columbia Lung Association, advertisers used a car seemingly crushed by the seven-foot cigarette sitting on its roof to make their point. Leaning against the car is a large placard that explained the mortality statistics.

Terminix wanted to demonstrate that termites eat 24-hours a day. To illustrate that point, they created a super-sized red package and placed wood pieces the size of 2x4's inside that resembled french fries, in order to trigger the viewer to think about eating and about bugs eating.

Another inventive and unconditional use of specialty media is the example of an office products store that placed an open 3-D bottle of whiteout (as large as a person) on a city street, near a crosswalk, to remind the error-prone public of its use. The top with the brush was removed and lying beside the bottle. The ad creates the illusion that the white crosswalk lines have been created with the correction fluid.

Cinema advertising is big, creative, targetable, and a great way to reach a captive audience. Shown as consumers are entering the theater and before the coming attractions, cinema advertising is basically a TV commercial that is displayed oversized and in full digital sound. This still popular form of entertainment is extremely targetable, especially to the 18- to 34-year-old demographic. It is a great way to beat consumer disinterest since they are generally in a positive mood in the theater and cannot tune out the advertisement. Because of this, it is important any ad selected for this venue is as creative and unique as possible and relevant to that target demographic. To that point, in Germany, BMW found a way to use cinema ads to burn its logo onto the inside of their target's eyes with flash projection. Viewers are asked to close their eyes after they see a bright flash, not unlike a camera flash. Immediately emerging behind their lids is the BMW logo created by the bright flash.

To begin the action, a local celebrity talks about himself while images of his professional racing accomplishments are projected on the screen. Once the flash occurs, the speaker tells viewers to "Just close your eyes. Look deep into yourself. Maybe it's your dream, too. It's in you. Close your eyes and you will see it." He talks directly to the audience when he orders them to "Close them. Now" (Hall, 2010, p. 1).

In the Not So Distant Future
Innovation Is the Stuff of Science Fiction

Marketers are looking into a myriad of specialty advertising options that are possible in the not so distant future. Imagine advanced technology attached to the consumer's home television set able to measure and determine a woman's jean size or man's suit size, allowing the immediate placement of an order—that is almost as exciting as having a suit tailor-made.

Additionally, digital technology is coming to a mall or shopping center near you: visualize department store mirrors with interactive selections, kiosks that feature virtual customer service reps, and shopping carts with digital scanners that offer personalized discounts.

Other time-saving technology advances on the horizon are mirrors that allow shoppers to scan an article of clothing and then project it onto their body before trying it on. By tapping the mirror, the super shopper can view different colors and find matching accessories, as well as send the image to her Facebook page.

This customer service and time-saving technological future is a direct result of the fragmentation of traditional media. To reach their customer in a more personalized way, retailers are supercharging their in-store marketing efforts in the hopes of connecting with the customer in real time—when they are in the store shopping.

Size Doesn't Affect the Success of All Forms of Nontraditional Media

The future of all forms of nontraditional media is bright. Like guerrilla marketing, nontraditional media is a bargain for small business owners who must compete against larger, more successful brands. As we show in the previous examples, its palette is so diverse that retailers who know their target and their brand can effectively tailor a message for a unique vehicle in a multitude of creative ways.

Smaller businesses do not necessarily have to blanket an entire city with their message (think larger brands) in order to reach their target. In that case, newspapers or out-of-home may be less effective than a flyer, green graffiti, or an ambient scent.

Larger marketers will employ nontraditional media as a support vehicle to their primary media buys. While their use of nontraditional vehicles may be more spectacular and oftentimes more costly, it's important to remember that a creative idea properly placed in the right vehicle often can produce benefits far beyond the initial investment.

Big brands know that to stand out in the cluttered advertising arena and to be remembered, they have to supplement their traditional media messages with those that grab attention in a memorable way. Not all messages need to educate; there are other outlets such as traditional vehicles, direct marketing, the Internet and social media outlets that can educate the target about the product or service. The goal with all forms of nontraditional media is to get the target talking and inspired about the creativity associated with a particular product or service.

Most successful brands, large and small, have a loyal niche of consumers who follow the brand. These groups do not react to traditional forms of advertising with a generic message. These are the groups who not only want their choice in brands to continue to wow them with excellent product performance but also to mirror their own image and style. This is the buyer who responds to a creative pitch, or causes a loyal competitive user to switch brands because the message and brand reflects their own unique perspective of themselves.

Especially for small businesses, nontraditional options make it economically possible to stay in the public eye during slow economic times. Research has repeatedly proven that businesses electing to continue advertising during economic downturns reap the benefits when the economy improves. This continued advertising presence keeps the brand top-of-mind, making it the first choice the target turns to when purchasing, thereby giving it a definite competitive advantage. When the economy improves, brands that cut back on their advertising have to work doubly hard to regain the public's confidence. Oftentimes, these brands must spend more on advertising efforts and many never regain their lost equity.

Chapter 11 Exercises

1. Working in the same or new groups, use the brief that was developed for the national brand from Chapter 2 and present the final developed campaign. Illustrate how the visual/verbal message was used in each medium and how the key consumer benefit is projected throughout.

2. Based on what was laid out in the marketing plan, present how the group chose the visual/verbal voice of the campaign and how it is different from the advertising of the competition. Be prepared to defend your choices.

3. What visual/verbal direction was used to accomplish the directives laid out in both the marketing plan and creative brief? How will you tie the visual/verbal and promotional message together to create a cohesive look across all selected vehicles? Tie creative decisions back to the creative brief and marketing plan.

4. In the presentation discuss why certain vehicles were deleted and others retained. Additionally, cover why this final media mix is the best choice for the brand. Each team must defend their position based on information found in both documents.

5. Once the advertising team presents their final ideas, the marketing team should critique their direction based on whether or not they feel the direction will accomplish the business directives set forth in the marketing plan. Be able to back up your decisions.

6. Present all findings to the class or to the marketing team.

7. Follow the same steps for the small, local business selected in Chapter 2.

Memory Box

Green Graffiti

Innovative Nontraditional Media

Glossary

Advergaming: Advertising placed inside of video games that are purchased or provided for free, and played on a computer, television, or mobile device.

Advertising: Uses a promotional set of vehicles that the sponsoring brand employs to persuade, inform, entertain, and remind in order to build a lasting relationship with the intended target. It almost exclusively uses paid forms of nontraditional and mass media vehicles to clearly and creatively identify the sponsor of an advertised message.

Airborne Advertising: Also known as aerial advertising or skywriting, this low cost promotional vehicle uses exhaust from a plane to create white puffy letters. These mega-sized messages are difficult to ignore as there is no page to turn or remote to click. Other aerial advertising surfaces include hot air balloons.

Applications (Apps): Buttons that direct the mobile user to a specific Internet site.

Ambient Marketing: See Guerrilla Marketing.

Augmented Reality: Superimposes real-world images over digital images, text, and graphics to create a 3-D holographic image. It is rarely used to sell anything, playing a largely promotional role in the media mix. Its main job is to engage and extend the time the target spends with the brand.

Behavioristics: Behavioristic segmentation is basically a combination of all target data that help to determine the reasons why a person buys and how they purchase.

Big Idea: See unique selling proposition.

Blogs: An online discussion or information site publishing personal commentaries, diaries, and conversations between the seller of a product or service and multiple consumers.

Building Wraps: An advertisement printed on vinyl used as an enormous outdoor board that typically wraps around a building on two or more sides, and which often uses the building's windows in the design.

Business-to-Business Sales Promotions: Incentives offered to retailers to promote a certain brand over another.

Creative Brief: The first step in the communication process. The creative and media teams, along with any nontraditional media suppliers, use the brief as a springboard to determine what communication activities need to be accomplished. It is the creative brief that outlines how advertising efforts are to achieve the business directives laid out in the marketing plan.

Consumer-Generated Media: See User-Generated Content.

Cooperative Advertising: Usually partners two like brands to promote them together and also to share the cost of advertising.

Covert Marketing: See Stealth Marketing.

Cross Promotion: Entails a type of guerilla marketing where similar products are promoted together, which is a great way to bring attention to two or more brands at the same time.

Crowdsourcing: A way to gather information that uses the general public to inform on a brand, service, or current event.

Database Marketing: Messages that rely on a compilation of specific data to reach the right target audience with the right message are often referred to as database marketing. Uses prospected information that is gathered from search and purchase history, opt-in or e-mail lists, and demographic and psychographic information, to name just a few.

Demographics: Deals with individual target traits such as age, gender, income, marital status, level of education, and number of children in the household, to name just a few.

Digital Billboards: See Digital Out-Of-Home.

Digital Marketing: See Internet Marketing.

Digital Out-of-Home: Also known as digital billboards, these are electronic billboards that are not only creative but often interactive. A simple click of a mouse can quickly change or update images that once required a team of workers to create and build.

Direct Marketing: A promotion and communication strategy that allows you to target a specific market using different media in order to stimulate your customer's behavior in a way that you can measure, track, and analyze all the information involved in the process and store it on a database for future use.

Direct Premium: Premiums can be given away or offered at a discounted price. The premium may be included in the packaging known as a direct premium or offered as free gifts to the first one hundred store visitors. This type of premium is known as a *traffic-builder*.

Direct Response: A type of direct marketing, also known as relationship marketing, it is a great way to develop and maintain a relationship with the target over time. It ignores the middleman or retailer, allowing the manufacturer to interact and sell directly to the targeted audience. It is a great way to individualize mass media tactics, thus making it a great relationship-enhancing tool.

E-mail Marketing: This "opt in" or permission form of advertising is a great relationship building and maintenance tool. Permission means the targeted recipients have given their consent for a certain marketer to send them advertised materials. E-mail campaigns are a powerful and personal form of one-to-one marketing.

Emotional Purchases: Purchases such as jewelry, expensive cars, or digital equipment that do not sustain life, but they enhance it.

Engagement: Results when a brand interacts with the target by capturing their attention or by engaging them in a one-to-one conversation or activity.

Experiential Marketing: See Guerrilla Marketing.

Facebook: An interactive social media website where users can communicate visually through pictures or verbally through posted comments in real-time with friends, family, or a brand or service.

Freestanding Insert: A form of direct response, freestanding inserts are inserted into a newspaper after printing; these often four-color, single or double-sided inserts feature multiple coupons or offers.

Focus Group: A focus group is usually made up of 10 or 12 members of the researched targeted audience who are asked to interact with the brand or its advertised message in a controlled environment.

Geographics: Data that is used to determine where the target lives regionally, with additional breakdowns by state, city, and even zip code.

Grassroots Marketing: Brands built by word-of-mouth advertising.

Green Graffiti: A form of advertising that is all about cleaning a surface such as a street or sidewalk by placing a stencil down and using a power washer to clean away the dirt and grime, leaving a nice clean image or message behind.

Guerrilla Marketing: According to Jay Conrad Levinson, whose book popularized the term, it is "the unconventional way of performing promotional activities on a very low budget."

Inbound Telemarketing: When consumers use a toll-free number to make a purchase.

Infomercial: An informative commercial that can be found on network and cable television, the radio, and on the Internet. Infomercials (usually 60 to 120 minutes long) are a fact-based type of advertising that drills the brand's message home with demonstrations, testimonials, and often a celebrity spokesperson.

In-game Advertising: See Advergaming.

Innovative Nontraditional Media: Those vehicles that do not fit snugly into any media mold but are visually and/or verbally eye catching.

Internet Marketing: Also known as digital marketing, it is the selling of brands or services via the Internet. Types of delivery to name just a few might include search, pay-per-click (ppc), augmented reality, banners, or even e-mail lists to engage the target.

Life Cycle Stage: The three stages a typical brand passes through, including new or introduction, mainstream or mature, and reinvention.

Location-Based Marketing: Location-based services using GPS technology to locate the target and send them promotions near their location.

Marketing: Defined by the American Marketing Association as "the activity, set of institutions, and processes for creating, communication, delivering and exchanging offerings that have value for customers, clients, partners, and society at large."

Marketing Mix: The specific type and number of vehicles that a company uses to control, orchestrate, and accomplish its business objectives. The five Ps of product, price, promotion, place (or distribution) and people and make up what is known as the marketing mix.

Marketing Plan: A company's business plan of action. A hefty sales-related document that varies in scope depending on the size of the company. Its purpose is to detail what the brand wants to accomplish, usually over the next fiscal year.

Media Mix: The individual vehicles a campaign uses to deliver their visual/verbal message, such as magazines, direct mail, or television.

Mobile Augmented Reality: See Augmented Reality.

Mobile Marketing: The selling or promotion of a brand or service through a mobile device that actively engages the target.

Nontraditional Media: Refers to vehicles that are used as an alternative choice to more traditional mass media vehicles directed at a mass audience such as print (newspaper and magazines) and broadcast (radio and television).

Online Video: An inexpensive way to bring television storytelling, product demonstrations, and testimonials to the web.

Outbound Telemarketing: A type of telemarketing where the call originates from a sales center.

Out-of-Home Advertising: Simply defined as anything seen outside of the home. The canvases most often associated with out-of-home include traditional and electronic billboards, wallscapes, and street furniture.

Pay-per-click ads: Simple text ads that are placed on one or more heavily visited websites. The ad's main goal is to attract enough attention to encourage the viewer to click on the ad and be immediately taken to the sponsoring website.

Pop-Up Stores: Also known as pop-ups, these are temporary retail stores that promote a product or service or are used as a way to sell seasonal products such as Christmas decorations or Halloween costumes.

Primary Market: The primary target market is those users/consumers currently using the product or service or those who are likely to use the product in the future.

Primary Media: Primary media vehicles are those mediums most likely to be seen by the target, or those vehicles that the target is exposed to the most often and where the most advertising dollars are dedicated.

Promoted Accounts: Accounts that Twitter puts at the top of the queue and, as such, a way for brands to gain more followers.

Promoted Trends: Puts a sponsored topic at the top of Twitter's "trending topics" box, which reflects the most-discussed topics on Twitter at any given time.

Promoted Tweets: Tweets that are ads. They show up at the top of searches on related topics, and at the top of a user's timeline when the user follows the account.

Promotional Mix: A combination of media vehicles used in a campaign that research demonstrates will both reach the target and accomplish the marketing objectives or goals.

Promotional Pricing: These short-term price reduction promotions are best known as sales.

Psychographics: Data that focuses on the target's lifestyle, attitudes, activities, and interests, and how this information affects the target's views on product repurchase.

Qualitative Research: Also known as inductive or secondary data, this type of research uses existing research and/or small groups of respondents to gather information that will not be analyzed using statistical techniques. This type of research assists in pinpointing any past trends or significant changes, or trends that are currently occurring in the marketplace, and to identify any emerging opportunities or threats to the brand.

Quantitative Research: Deductive research also known as primary research that is original or new data gathered by either the marketing or advertising team. This type of research uses a large sample of respondents in an attempt to find the answer(s) to a specific set of questions.

Quick Response Code: QR codes allow visitors to quickly and wirelessly connect to websites, and view photos or videos from a sponsoring advertiser.

Rational Purchases: Those purchases of products used on a day-to-day basis by the majority of the population such as food, cleaning products, and toiletries.

Referral Premium: A premium that rewards both new and existing customers.

Relationship Marketing: Also known as Direct Marketing, an ongoing association between the target and the brand.

Return on Engagement (ROE): All about developing a message that asks the target to do something (active) rather than just sitting back and listening (passive).

Return On Investment (ROI): A performance measure. Refers to whether the client's benefits outweigh the client's costs on their advertising efforts.

Rooftop Advertising: Rooftop advertising places bigger than life 3-D logos atop tall buildings where they can be seen for miles.

Sales Promotion: A sales tool that increases interest in a product or service in order to increase a brand's value and achieve a set of marketing objectives. Defined as media and non-media marketing pressure applied for a predetermined, limited period of time in order to stimulate trial, increase consumer demand, or improve product quality.

Search Engine Marketing (SEM): Where a brand pays a search engine company, such as Google or Yahoo to place their websites high in key word searches in order to increase the chances that the searcher will click on their site.

Search Engine Optimization (SEO): Ensures the website includes links to other relevant sites to increase target interest and knowledge.

Secondary Market: A secondary target audience encompasses those users/consumers most likely to purchase the product on behalf of the primary audience or those who influence the purchases of the primary audiences.

Secondary Media: Secondary media vehicles are used to support or expound on the messages conveyed in the primary vehicles.

SMS: Short Message Service. See Text Messaging.

Social Media: The visual/verbal sharing of thoughts and ideas with others having the same or similar interests that have been placed on the Internet by non-media professionals. See User-Generated Content and Consumer-Generated Media.

Stealth Marketing: Also known as undercover or ambush marketing, it is often misleading since the targeted consumer does not immediately realize that they are the recipient of a marketing message.

Street Marketing: Refers to specialized marketing techniques used in public places to promote a product or service in a personalized, yet often unconventional way.

Street Team: A team composed of a group of individuals who move among pedestrians to promote a product or service. It is an inexpensive way to get the brand into the target's hand and to personally deliver a message.

Supplemental Advertising: See Freestanding Insert.

Target Audience: Those persons who consumer research has determined are most likely to purchase the product or use the service.

Text Messaging: Also known as Short Message Service, it is the largest and most common form of mobile delivery.

Traditional Media: Vehicles directed at a mass audience such as print (newspaper and magazines) and broadcast (radio and television).

Traffic-builder: See Direct Premium.

Transit Advertising: Any brand-sponsored message appearing in or on public transportation (buses, taxis), on benches, in shelters, waiting areas, and terminals.

Tweets: Immediate updates, this is a great way to add a viral component and public relations boost to any campaign.

Twitter: The Internet's version of KISS—keep it simple stupid—allows consumers to interact with a brand, service, company, or other consumers in little bite-sized discussions.

Unique Selling Proposition: Is usually the key consumer benefit or the one feature/benefit combination that is either unique to the brand or can be positioned as unique through creative advertising efforts—also known as a Big Idea.

User-Generated Content (UGC): Also known as consumer-generated media (CGM), UGC is the visual/verbal sharing of thoughts and ideas with others having the same or similar interests that have been placed on the Internet by non-media professionals. See Social Media.

Viral E-Mails: E-mails that are unusual and creative enough that consumers and family, friends, or colleagues will want to pass them along, inundating other mailboxes with the messages.

Viral Marketing: Also known as word-of-mouth advertising, it is a message that is shared with others via the Internet or in person.

Viral Video: A video that is promoted through word of mouth.

Virtual Product Demonstrations: Demonstrations that give consumers an interactive chance to experience the brand and its many features before they buy.

Wallscape: A banner that is a huge out-of-home advertising vehicle that can be painted directly on vinyl, or onto the outside of a building, or hung off a structure.

Webinar: Used to inform, educate, and inspire participation. Before creating a webinar, determine what information your target audience needs to have in order to encourage the action(s) you want them to take.

Widgets: According to the Interactive Advertising Bureau (IAB), widgets are "portable applications that allow both users and sites to have a hand in the content." A web application that can be downloaded and placed into a web page, personal blog, or profile page that can be shared live with viewers, such as a local weather report.

Wikis: A collection of information posted on a website about a specific topic. Many are open to all willing to add content while others may require a membership to add information, which is usually made up of topic-qualified individuals.

Word of Mouth: See Viral Marketing.

YouTube: A video-sharing website.

Bibliography

Allen, G., & Zaba, G. (2000). *Internet resources for integrated marketing communication*. Orlando, FL: Harcourt.

Altstiel, T., & Grow, J. (2006). *Advertising strategy: Creative tactics from the outside/in*. Thousand Oaks, CA: Sage.

Altstiel, T., & Grow, J. (2010). *Advertising creative*. Thousand Oaks, CA: Sage.

American Marketing Association (AMA). (2007, Oct.). *Marketing power*. Retrieved from http://www.marketingpower.com/AboutAMA/Pages/Definitionofmarketing.

Avery, J. (2000). *Advertising campaign planning*. Chicago, IL: Copy Workshop.

Bachman, K. (2011, Jan. 31). DMA: We will enforce industry's web privacy guidelines. *Ad Week*. Retrieved from http://www.adweek.com/fdcp.

Baker, D. (2010, Oct. 4). The new social marketing paradigm. *MediaPost.com*. Retrieved from http://www.mediapost.com/publications/?a=Articles.

Bangs, D. H. (1998). *The market planning guide* (5th ed.). Chicago, IL: Upstart.

Beard, M., & McCrindle, M. (2010). *Seriously cool—Marketing and communicating with diverse generations*. New South Wales, AU. Retrieved from http://www.mccrindle.com.au/marketing-communicating-with-diverse-generations.

Bendinger, B. (1993). *The copy workshop workbook*. Chicago, IL: Copy Workshop.

Bercovici, J. (2011, Mar. 14). America's most loved spokescharacters. *Forbes*. Retrieved from www.forbes.com/2011/03/11/old-spice-snoopy-m-and-m-most-loved-spokescharacters.html.

Berman, M. (2007). *Street-smart advertising: How to win the battle of the buzz*. Lanham, MD: Rowman & Littlefield.

Bernbach, W. (1989). *Bill Bernbach said . . .* New York, NY: DDB Needham Worldwide Books.

Bernstein, R. (2010, Jan. 20). Integrate social media with traditional advertising for higher returns. *Social Media Today*. Retrieved from http://socialmediatoday.com/SMC/167993.

Beyer, G. (2010, Sept. 12). A career in marketing/advertising. *Wall Street Journal*. Retrieved from http://online.wsj.com/article/SB10001424052748703453804575480221659764174.html.

Birgfeld, R. (2010, Sept. 20). Social with a KISS: Keep it short, stupid [web log post]. *SmartBlog.com*. Retrieved from http://smartblogs.com/socialmedia/2010/09/20.

Blake, G., & Bly, R. W. (1997). *The elements of copywriting*. New York, NY: Simon & Schuster.

Blakeman, R. (2004). *The bare bones of advertising print design*. Boulder, CO: Rowman & Littlefield.

Blakeman, R. (2007). *Integrated marketing communication: Creative strategy, from idea to implementation*. Boulder, CO: Rowman & Littlefield.

Blakeman, R. (2009). *The bare bones introduction to integrated marketing communication*. Lanham, MD: Rowman & Littlefield.

Blakeman, R. (2011a). *Strategic uses of alternative media: Just the essentials*. Armonk, NY: M. E Sharp.

Blakeman, R. (2011b). *Advertising campaign design: Just the essentials*. Armonk, NY: M. E. Sharp.

Blanchard, R. (1999). Parting essay. *Brand/cool marketing: Resources, brand quotes*. Retrieved from http://www.brandcool.com/node/21.

Book, A. C., & Schick, D. C. (1997). *Fundamentals of copy and layout* (3rd ed.). Lincolnwood, IL: NTC Business Books.

Bratt, E. (2011, Feb. 6). Social media: Adding video to your digital marketing plan. *Sign On San Diego*. Retrieved from http://signonsandiego.printthis.clickability.com.

Brogan, C. (2010, Nov. 1). Alternatives to straight advertising. *Open Forum .com*. Retrieved from http://www.openforum.com/idea-hub/topics/marketing/article.

Bulik, B. S. (2010, Nov. 1). You are what you watch, market data suggest. *Advertising Age*. Retrieved from http://adage.com/print?article.

Burnett, J., & Moriarty, S. (1998). *Introduction to marketing communication*. Upper Saddle River, NJ: Prentice Hall.

Burnett, L. (1995). *100 LEO's*. Lincolnwood, IL: NTC Business Books.

Burton, P. W. (1999). *Advertising copywriting* (7th ed.). Lincolnwood, IL: NTC Business Books.

Busche, L. (2011, May 11). Domino's CMO to share 'pizza turnaround' story at NRA marketing meeting. *National Restaurant Association*. Retrieved from http://www.resturant.org/nra_news_blog/2011.

Carr, A. (2010, Oct. 11). Twitter crushing Facebook's click-through rate: Report. *Fast Company.com*. Retrieved from http://www.fastcompany.com/1694174/twitter-crushing-facebooks-click-through-rate-report.

Chiat, J., Altstiel, T., & Grow, J. (2006). *Advertising strategy: Creative tactics from the outside/in*. Thousand Oaks, CA: Sage.

Clow, K. A., & Baack, D. (2002). *Integrated advertising, promotion and marketing communications*. Upper Saddle River, NJ: Prentice Hall.

Conn, M. (2010, Oct. 11). Healthkey: Doctors experimenting with social media. *The Baltimore Sun*. Retrieved from http://www.baltimoresun.com/health/bs-hs-groupon-and-health.

Constantakis-Valdez, P. (2009, Aug. 15). Interactive television. *The Museum of Broadcast Television*. Retrieved from http://www.museum.tv/eotvsection.php?entrycode=interactivet.

Cortes, D. (2011, Mar. 29). Direct info. marketing—The complete vision concept (Part 1). Retrieved from http://www.ezinearticles.com/?Direct-Info-Marketing.

Coyer, K., Dowmunt, T., & Fountain, A. (2008). *The alternative media handbook.* New York, NY: Routledge.

Crutchfield, D. (2010, Sept. 22). Celebrity endorsements still push product. *Advertising Age.* Retrieved from http://adage.com/print?article.

Dalzell, C. (2009). Building relationships and trust online with e-mail. *The Marketing Site.* Retrieved from http://www.themarketingsite.com.

Della Femina, J. (1970). *From the wonderful folks who gave you Pearl Harbor.* New York, NY: Simon & Schuster.

Duncan, T. (2002). *IMC: Using advertising and promotion to build brands.* Boston, MA: McGraw-Hill.

Elliot, S. (2008, Jun. 18). Traditional media not dead yet for marketing, study says. *New York Times.* Retrieved from http://www.ediadecoder.blogs.nytimes.com/2008/06/18.

Elliot, S. (2010a). 'Ghost' brands come alive with new ads. *The New York Times.* Retrieved from http://www.nytime.com/2010/10/11/business/media.

Elliot, S. (2010b). Pass the hairspray, fight Aids. *Media Decoder.* Retrieved from http://mediadecoder.blogs.nytimes.com/2010/11/30/.

Elliot, S. (2011a). Dr, Dr, give me some clues. *New York Times.* Retrieved from http://www.nytimes.com/2011/02/07/business/media.

Elliot, S. (2011b). Mosaic marketing takes a fresh look at changing society. *New York Times.* Retrieved from http://www.nytimes.com/2011/07/18/business/media.

Elliot, S. (2011c). TNT, in tie-in with Hyatt, will hold 'Armchair Detective' weekends. *New York Times Media Decoder.* Retrieved from http://wwwmediadecoder.blogs.nytimes.com/2011/11/13.

eNotes.com. (2012). *Sales promotion* [Online educational resource]. Retrieved from http://www.enotes.com/small-business-encyclopedia/sales-promotion.

Evans, J. R., & Berman, B. (1990). *Marketing* (4th ed.). New York, NY: Macmillan.

Ferraro, K. (2010). Crowdsourcing your brand? Read these 5 best practices. Retrieved from http://blog.ogilvypr.com/2010/10/crowdsourcing-your-brand.

Friedman, W. (2010, Aug. 2). Fox codes uses ads to pitch shows. *Media Daily News.com.* Retrieved from http://www.mediapost.com/publications/fa=Articles.printFriendly.

Giannini, G. T. (2010). *Marketing public relations.* Upper Saddle River, NJ: Pearson.

Gladwell, M. (2002). *The tipping point.* New York, NY: Back Bay Books.

Gobry, P.-E. (2011, Sept. 23). What they are and how they work. Retrieved from http://articles.businessinsider.com/2011–09–23/research.

Greenburg, K. (2010, Sept. 9). Honda campaign shows how opposites attract. *Marketing Daily.* Retrieved from http://mediapost.com/publications/?fa=Articles.

Grynbaum, M. M. (2010, Dec. 12). Taxi TV screens gain ad business in New York. *New York Times.com.* Retrieved from http://www.nytimes.com/2010/12/13/nyregion/13taxitv.html.

Guth, D. W., & Marsh, C. (2003). *Public relations: A values-driven approach* (2nd ed.). Boston, MA: Allyn and Bacon.

Hall, E. (2010, Dec. 21). BMW Germany makes logo appear inside cinema audience eyelids. *Advertising Age.com.* Retrieved from http://adage.com/print?article.

Hafer, K. W., & White., G. E. (1977). *Advertising writing.* St. Paul, MN: West Publishing.

Hampp, A. (2009, Mar. 18). Opportunities for selling more radio ads still out there. *Ad Age*. Retrieved from http://adage.com/article/mediaworks/opportunities-selling-radio-ads/135324/.

Heine, C. (2011, Apr. 26). Pepto says big shift from TV to digital increased sales. *ClickZ*. Retrieved from http://www.clickz.com/print_article/clickz/news.

Hendley, Nat. (2004, Apr. 22). How to drive traffic to your store. *Profit Magazine*. Retrieved from http://www.clearchanneloutdoor.com/assets/downloads/white-paper/ooh-and-retail-wp.pdf.

Hester, E. L. (1996). *Successful marketing research*. New York, NY: Wiley.

Horovitz, B. (2011, Jan. 24). Why Papa John's, Intel, others said no to Super Bowl ads. *USA Today*. Retrieved from http://www.usatoday.com/money/advertising/2011–01–24/supern024_ST_N.htm.

Jaffe, J. (2005). *Life after the 30-second spot: Energize your brand with a bold mix of alternatives to traditional advertising*. New York, NY: Wiley.

Jakacki, B. C. (2001). *IMC: An integrated marketing communications exercise*. Cincinnati, OH: Southwestern College.

Jantch, J. (2010). 7 steps to creating a sure-fire marketing system. *Open Forum*. Retrieved from http://www.openforum.com/idea-hub/topics/marketing.

Jay, R. (1998). *Marketing on a budget*. Boston, MA: International Thomson Business Press.

Jewler, A. J., & Drewniany, B. L. (2005). *Creative strategy in advertising*. Belmont, CA: Thomson Wadsworth.

Jones, C., & Ryan, D. (2010). When digital marketing actually works. *TechnologyReview.com*. Retrieved from http://www.technologyreview.com.

Jones, S. K. (1998). *Creative strategy in direct marketing* (2nd ed.). Chicago, IL: NTC Business Books.

Kerley, P. (2011, Feb. 17). What brands can learn from Taco Bell's social media lawsuit defense. *Mashable.com*. Retrieved from http://mashable.com/2011/02/17/taco-bell-social-media-defense.

Kessler, D. A. (2009). *The end of overeating* (1st ed.). Emmaus, PA: Rodale Books.

Kiley, D., & Klara, R. (2010). Guerrilla marketing 2010. *Brandweek.com*. http://www.adweek.com/news/advertising-branding/guerrilla-marketing-2010-116438.

Kinnard, S. (2001). *Marketing with e-mail* (3rd ed.). Gulf Breeze, FL: Maximum Press.

Klassen, M. (2010, Sept. 9). Magalogs: A vital piece of the marketing puzzle. *Everything Small Business Journal*. Retrieved from http://esbjournal.com/2010/09/magalogs-a-vital-piece-of-the-marketing-puzzle.

Kraus, S., & Shullman, B. (2011, Aug. 1). Among affluent Americans, print media is tops. *Advertising Age*. Retrieved from http://www.adage.com/print/229002.

Kridler, K. (2004, Jul. 2). Finding alternative sites to TV for advertising messages. *Findarticles.com*. Retrieved from http://articles.com/p/articles/mi_qn4183/is_20040702/ai_n10062673.

Krugman, D. M., Reid, L. N., Dunn, S. W., & Barban, A. M. (1994). *Advertising: Its role in modern marketing* (8th ed.). Fort Worth, TX: Dryden.

Kuchinskas, S. (2010, Nov. 5). How to use social media to build your brand. *Open Forum*. Retrieved from http://www.openforum.com/idea-hub/topics/markting/article.

Lake, L. (2012). Advertising research. *About.com Marketing*. Retrieved from http://marketing.about.com/od/marketingglossary/g/ mrktresearchdef.htm.

Lee, M. W. (2010, Dec. 29). Why the fashion industry is betting big on branded online content. *Mashable Business*. Retrieved from http://mashable.com/2010/12/29/branded-online-content-fashion.

Leggatt, H. (2008, Mar. 27). Use of alternative media to rise. *Biz Report*. Retrieved from http://www.bizreport.com/2008/03/use_of_alternative_media_to_rise.

Levinson, J. C. (2001). *Guerrilla creativity.* New York, NY: Houghton Mifflin.

Levinson, J. C. (2007). *Guerrilla marketing* (4th ed.). New York, NY: Houghton Mifflin.

Li, S., & Sarno, D. (2011, Aug. 21). Advertisers start using facial recognition to tailor pitches. *Los Angeles Times*. Retrieved from http://www.latimes.com/business/la-fi-facial-recognition-20110821.

Lux, E. (2010, Oct. 6). Brand value. *Wall Street Journal.com*. Retrieved from http://online.wsj.com/article.

Malickson, D. L., & Nason, J. W. (1977). *Advertising: How to write the kind that works.* New York, NY: Scribner.

McClellan, S. (2011, Aug. 8). CMOs using less agencies, more collaboration. *MediaDailyNews.com*. Retrieved from http://www.mediapost.com/publications.

McDonald, W. J. (1998). *Direct marketing: An integrated approach.* Boston, MA: Irwin/McGraw-Hill.

McLuhan, M. (1964/1994). *Understanding media: The extensions of man.* Cambridge, MA: MIT Press.

Meece, M. (2011). Ground-level tasting of the best food in the sky. *New York Times*. Retrieved from http://www.nytimes.com/2011/05/05/business/05FOOD.html.

Mitchell, A. (1999, Jan./Apr.). Out of the Shadows. *Journal of Marketing Management, 15*(1–3), 25–42. Retrieved from www.brandcoolmarketing.com.

Mobile Marketing Association. (2009). Retrieved from http://www.mmaglobal.com/news/mma-definition-mobile-marketing.

Monahan, T. (2002). *The do it yourself lobotomy.* New York, NY: Wiley.

Moscardelli, D. M. (1999). *Advertising on the Internet.* Upper Saddle River, NJ: Prentice Hall.

Neff, J. (2010, Sept. 27). Cracking viral code: Look at your ads. Now look at Old Spice. *Advertising Age*. Retrieved from http://adage.com/print.

Neff, J. (2011, Mar. 23). CBS: Viewers' age and sex shouldn't matter to marketers. *Advertising Age*. Retrieved from http://adage.com/print.

Newman, A. A. (2011). Bloggers don't follow the script, to ConAgra's chagrin. *New York Times*. Retrieved from http://www.nytimes.com/2011/09/07/business/media/when-bloggers.

Ogden, J. R. (1998). *Developing a creative and innovative integrated marketing communication plan: A working model.* Upper Saddle River, NJ: Prentice Hall.

Ogilvy, D. (1971). *Confessions of an advertising man*. New York, NY: Ballantine Books.

Ogilvy, D. (1985). *Ogilvy on advertising*. New York, NY: Vintage Books.

O'Guinn, T. C., Allen, C. T., & Semenik, R. J. (2003). *Advertising and integrated brand promotion* (3rd ed.). Mason, OH: Thomson/South-Western.

Olson, E. (2010a). Bonding with fans who can't get enough. *New York Times*. Retrieved from http://www.nytimes.com/2010/09/21/business/media/21adco.

Olson, E. (2010b). Virtual test drive offers vroom, vroom. *New York Times.com*. Retrieved from http://mediadecoder.blogs.nytimes.com/2010/10/07/virtualtest.

Olson, E. (2010c). Bar codes add detail on items in TV ads. *New York Times*. Retrieved from http://www.nytimes.com/2010/10/26/business/media/26adco.

Olson, E. (2010d). Testing a bar code technology for smartphones. *New York Times*. Retrieved from http://www.nytimes.com/2010/10/26/business/media/26adco.

O'Toole J. (1985). *The trouble with advertising*. New York, NY: Times Books.

Parek, R. (2011, Feb. 14). Why the client-agency bond just isn't what it used to be. *Advertising Age*. Retrieved from http://adage.com/print?/article.

Parente, D., Vanden Bergh, B., Barban, A., & Marra, J. *Advertising campaign strategy: A guide to marketing communication plans*. Orlando, FL: Dryden.

Parpis, E. (2010, Sept. 30). Facebook's Sheryl Sandberg on the small, daily touches that pay off the big ad campaigns. *Real Time Advertising Week*. Retrieved from http://realtimeadvertisingweek.com/2010/09.

Percy, L. (1997). *Strategies for implementing integrated marketing communication*. Chicago, IL: NTC Business Books.

Peterson, R. T. (1989). *Principles of marketing*. Orlando, FL: Harcourt Brace Jovanovich.

Quenqua, D. (2010, Nov. 23). 5,000 people drive real-life Mitsubishi over the web. *ClickZ.com*. Retrieved from http://www.clickz.com/print_article/clickz/news.

Ray, R. (2010, Dec. 17). Smartphone mobile app vs. mobile website: Which one wins? *Open Forum.com*. Retrieved from http://www.openforum.com/idea-hub/topics/technology/article.

Reeves, R. (1981). *Reality in advertising*. New York, NY: Alfred A Knopf.

Reidl, A. (2009). Guerrilla marketing principles. *Guerrilamarketingonline*. Retrieved from http://www.guerrillaonline.com/cs/Guerrilla-Marketing-Principles-54.htm.

Rhone, N. (2011, May 18). Local pop-up shops gain popularity. *Atlanta Journal-Constitution*. Retrieved from http://www.ajc.com/lifestyle/local-pop-up-shops-949967.

Ries, A. (2010, Aug. 3). Why two names are better than one. *Advertising Age.com*. Retrieved from http://www.adage.com/columns/article?article_id.

Ries, A., & Trout, J. (2000). *Positioning: The battle for your mind*. New York, NY: McGraw-Hill.

Rifkin, A. (2010, Oct. 2). How Facebook can become bigger in five years than Google is today. *TechCrunch.com*. Retrieved from http://techcrunch.com/2010/10/02/facebook-bigger-goggle.

Rightnow Technologies. (1997). Retrieved from http://www.rightnow.com.

Ross, M. (2010). *Branding basics for small businesses: How to create an irresistible brand on any budget.* Bedford, IN: NorLights Press.

Rothenberg, J. (2010, Oct. 27). Is social media driving the economy? *The Atlantic.* Retrieved from http://www.theatlantic.com/technology/archive/2010/10.

Rothenberg, R. (1994). *Where the suckers moon: An advertising story.* New York, NY: Alfred A. Knopf.

Sass E. (2011, Apr. 13). Newspaper ads still guide shopping. *Media Daily News.* Retrieved from http://www.mediapost.com/publications/article/148632/.

Schultz, D. E. (1996). *Essentials of advertising strategy* (3rd ed.). Lincolnwood, IL: NTC Business Books.

Searby, L. (2011, Aug. 18). Cadbury raises augmented reality bar with interactive game. *ConfectionaryNews.com.* Retrieved from http://www.confectionerynews.com/contact/view/print/394091.

Sernovitz, A. (2010, Nov. 10). Andy's answers: The 3 reasons people talk about you. *Smart Brief.* Retrieved from http://smartblogs.com/socialmedia/2010/11/10.

Shaw, G. B. (1903). *Maxims for Revolutionists.* Retrieved from *Notable Quotes. com.* http://www.notable-quotes.com/s/shaw_george_bernard.html.

Shen, M. (2010, Dec. 24). Ad about you. *New York Post.* Retrieved from http://www.nypost.com/f/print/entertainment/tv/ad.

Sherman, A. (2010, Sept. 15). You can stop the social media hype. *GigaOM. com.* Retrieved from http://gigaom.com/collaboration/you-can-stop-the-social-media-hype.

Sheth, N. (2010, Aug. 6). Newest cell phone ads crave entire screen. *Wall Street Journal.com.* Retrieved from http://online.wsj.com/article.

Shields, M. (2011, Jan. 5). Yahoo zeros in on Google's turf with 'connected TV' play. *Adweek.* Retrieved from http://www.adweek.com/news/advertising-branding/yahoo-zeroes-googles-turf-connected-tv-play-125317.

Shimp, T. A. (2000). *Advertising promotion: Supplemental aspects of integrated marketing communications* (5th ed.). Orlando, FL: Dryden.

Sirgy, J. M. (1998). *Integrated marketing communication: A systems approach.* Upper Saddle River, NJ: Prentice Hall.

Smith, S. (2011, Sept. 9). NBC, Bloomingdale's launch reality 'Part' app. *Online Media Daily.* Retrieved from http://www.mediapost.com/publications?fa=articles.printFriendly.

Stanchak, J. (2010). 8 tools for upgrading your Twitter experience. *SmartBlogs. com.* Retrieved from http://smartblogs.com/socialmedia/2010/10/10/8-tools-for-upgrading-your-Twitter-experience.

Steel, E., & Fowler, G. A. (2010, Oct. 8). Facebook in privacy breach. *Wall Street Journal.com.* Retrieved from http://online.wsj.com/article.

Steinberg, B. (2009, Feb. 26). 'Chris Isaak Hour' makes debut with new ad format. *Ad Age.* Retrieved from http://adage.com/article/mediaworks/chris-isaak-hour-makes-debut-advertising-format/134904/.

Stelter, B. (2010, Dec. 20). The myth of fast forwarding past the ads. *New York Times.* Retrieved from http://www.nytimes.com/2010/12/21/business/media/21adco.html.

Sutton, J. (2011, Dec. 19). Scent makers sweeten the smell of commerce. *Reuters*. Retrieved from http://www.reuters.com/assets/print?aid=USTRE7BI1PF20111219.

Swallow, E. (2010, Nov. 16). How to define the role of your social media team. *Mashable.com*. Retrieved from http://mashable.com/2010/11/16/social-media -team-role/.

Thaler, L. K., & Koval, R. (2003). *Bang! Getting your message heard in a noisy world*. New York, NY: Doubleday.

Thomaselli, R. (2011, Oct. 26). Hey advertisers: New York has a bridge to sell you. *Ad Age*. Retrieved from http://adage.com/article/news/hey-advertisers-york-a -bridge-sell/230643/.

Throckmorton, J. (1997). *Winning direct response advertising* (2nd ed.). Lincolnwood, IL: NTC Business Books.

Thurm, S., & Iwatani Kane, Y. (2010, Dec. 18). Your apps are watching you. *Wall Street Journal.com*. Retrieved from http://online.wsj.com/article.

Townsend, M. (2010, Nov. 11). The staying power of pop-up stores. *Bloomberg Businessweek.com*. Retrieved from http://www.businessweek.com/magazine/ content/10_47/b4204026293305.htm.

Trap, J. (2010, Dec. 4). Domino's delivers on its turnaround plan. *Detroit News. com*. Retrieved from http://detnews.com/article/2010/12/04/BIZ.

TV commercial is meant for dogs. (2011, Oct. 4). *Washington Post*. Retrieved from http://www.washingtonpost.com/lifestyle/kidspost/tv-commercial-is-just -for-dogs-/2011/10/04/.

Twain, M. (1889). *A Connecticult Yankee in King Arthur's Court*. Retrieved from http://www.brainyquote.com/quotes/authors/m/mark_twain_6html.

van Bel, E. J. (2004). Want loyalty? Buy a dog! *The Marketing Site*. Retrieved from http:// www.themarketingsite.com, 2004.

Van Grove, J. (2010, Jul. 20). Why QR codes are poised to hit the mainstream. *Mashable.com*. Retrieved from http://mashable.com/2010/07/20/qr-code -mainstream.

Vanden Bergh, B., & Katz, H. (1999). *Advertising principles*. Lincolnwood, IL: NTC Business Books.

Vascellaro, J. E., Schechner, S., Smith, E., Trachtenberg, J. A., Adams, R., Wingfield, N., & Steel, E. (2011, Jan. 4). The year ahead for media: Digital or die. *Wall Street Journal.com*. Retrieved from http:// www.wsj.com/article.

Vega, T. (2010a). Plucked from their web writing to promote a Vaseline brand. *New York Times*. Retrieved from http://www.nytimes.com/2010/11/08/ media/09adcom.ht.

Vega, T. (2010b). Marketers discover trucks can deliver more than food. *New York Times.com*. Retrieved from http://www.nytimes.com/2010/11/29/busi-ness/media/29truck.html.

Vega, T. (2011). A campaign to introduce Keds to a new generation. *New York Times*, Retrieved from http://www.nytimes.com/2011/02/23/business/ media/23adco.

Vonk, N., & Kestin, J. (2005). *Pick me: Breaking into advertising and staying there*. New York, NY: Wiley.

Wakabayashi, D., & Osawa, J. (2010, Sept. 2). Billboards that can see you. *Wall Street Journal*. Retrieved from http://online.wsj.com/article.

Walsh, M. (2011, Jan. 31). Razorfish: Facebook, Twitter don't make customers feel valued. *Media Post*. Retrieved from http://mediapost.com/publications.

West, L. (2011, Jan. 28). Top 8 social media truths for 2011. *Open Forum*. Retrieved from http://www.openforum.com/idea-hub/topics/marketing/article.

Wilcox, D. L., Cameron, G. L., Ault, P. H., & Agee, W. K. (2003). *Public relations strategies and tactics* (7th ed.). Boston, MA: Allyn and Bacon.

Wong, E. (2010, Oct. 22). Why more brands are dangling incentives on Facebook. *Brandweek*. Retrieved from http://www.brandweek.com.

York, E. B. (2009, Apr. 8). Kraft will deliver frozen pies to tweetups to generate word-of-mouth. *Ad Age*. Retrieved from http://adage.com/article/digital/digiorno-turns-twitter-flatbread-pizza-launch/135876/.

Zmuda, N. (2010, Nov. 15). Check-in apps' next stop: Your supermarket aisles. *Advertising Age.com*. Retrieved from http://adage.com/print?article_id.

Index

About the Author

Robyn Blakeman received her M.L.A. at Southern Methodist University and her B.A. at the University of Nebraska. She is an associate professor at the University of Tennessee, Knoxville, where she teaches Advertising & Public Relations Design and Advertising Creative Strategy.

Professor Blakeman began teaching advertising and graphic design in 1987, first with the Art Institute of Dallas and then as an assistant professor of advertising at Southern Methodist University, teaching both graphic and computer design. As an assistant professor of advertising at West Virginia University, Professor Blakeman developed the creative track in layout and design and was responsible for designing and developing the first online Integrated Marketing Communication Graduate program in the country.

Professor Blakeman is the author of six other books:

The Bare Bones of Advertising Print Design,

Integrated Marketing Communication: Creative Strategy From Idea to Implementation,

The Bare Bones Introduction to Integrated Marketing Communication,

The Brains Behind Great Ad Campaigns,

Advertising Campaign Design: Just the Essentials, and

Strategic Uses of Alternative Media: Just the Essentials.

◉SAGE research**methods**

The essential online tool for researchers from the world's leading methods publisher

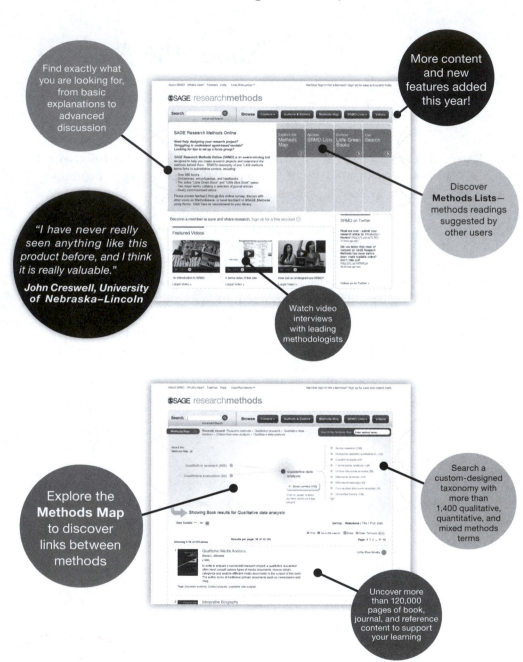

Find exactly what you are looking for, from basic explanations to advanced discussion

More content and new features added this year!

Discover **Methods Lists**—methods readings suggested by other users

"I have never really seen anything like this product before, and I think it is really valuable."

John Creswell, University of Nebraska–Lincoln

Watch video interviews with leading methodologists

Explore the **Methods Map** to discover links between methods

Search a custom-designed taxonomy with more than 1,400 qualitative, quantitative, and mixed methods terms

Uncover more than 120,000 pages of book, journal, and reference content to support your learning

Find out more at
www.sageresearchmethods.com